THE CELTIC VISION

BY

JOHN MEIRION MORRIS

With the co-operation of Gwyn Thomas

Design Ceri Jones

In memory

of DYLAN

The Celtic Vision

John Meirion Morris

y Lolfa

Acknowledgments

I want to thank so many people. First and foremost, Professor Gwyn Thomas, who was my tutor when I first wrote on this subject, many years ago. I wish to thank him for looking closely at this book, making it so much more readable and concise, and suggesting different terminology. I am grateful to The Cathryn and Lady Grace James Trust for their £1,000 contribution towards the research; also to Mr Eryl Rothwell Hughes for being so ready to let us borrow photographs from his Celtic collection.

I am grateful to Y Lolfa for their readiness to publish this book, and especially to Mared for her care and for collecting many of the images from museums across Europe. I am grateful to Ceri, the designer, for his patience and readiness to accept changes to the design of the book.

Lastly, I'd like to thank Gwawr and the children for their patience and readiness to accept my single-minded determination to persue this research through hard times, and to give me all their support.

John Meirion Morris

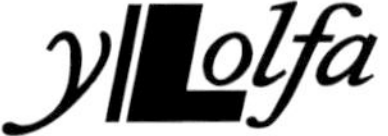

Supported by an 'Arts for All' Lottery grant from the Arts Council of Wales

ISBN: 0 86243 635 4

Published and printed in Wales by
Y Lolfa Cyf., Talybont, Ceredigion SY24 5AP
e-mail ylolfa@ylolfa.com
website www.ylolfa.com
phone +44 (0)1970 832 304
fax 832 782
isdn 832 813

Contents

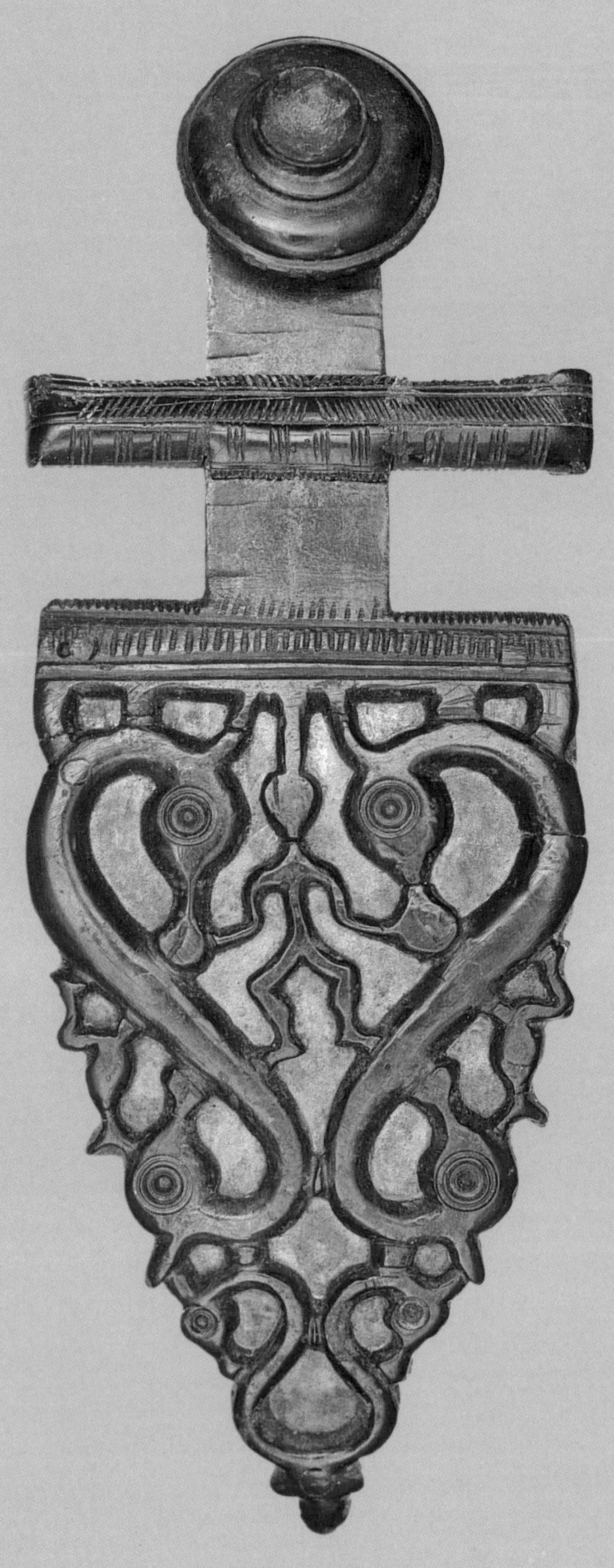

Introduction

In an International Celtic Conference several years ago I met one who was an acknowledged expert on Celtic art. I asked him whether he had sought the opinion of any artist on the art of the Celts. He said that he had not, and that was that. I could not help feeling that this was a pity, for the opinion of a practising artist on the work of the old Celtic artists could be interesting and could well be enlightening.

Some years after this encounter my friend, John Meirion Morris expressed an interest in doing research on the art of the Celts: I was well pleased. Not only was John an artist of distinction and originality, but he had also spent time in Africa and was interested in the art of that continent. Here was a man who could look at the art of the Celts with a distinctive imagination. This book is a version of John's research thesis.

The press wanted a more concise and a more tractable form of John's work for publishing. The sum of my collaboration was to produce the form published here. The book contains John's ideas, his terms and, more often than not, some form of his words. It has been my privilege to be of help in bringing about the publication of this exciting book.

Gwyn Thomas

The head is an image created in the
imagination and mind of the artist, it is an
INTERNAL image

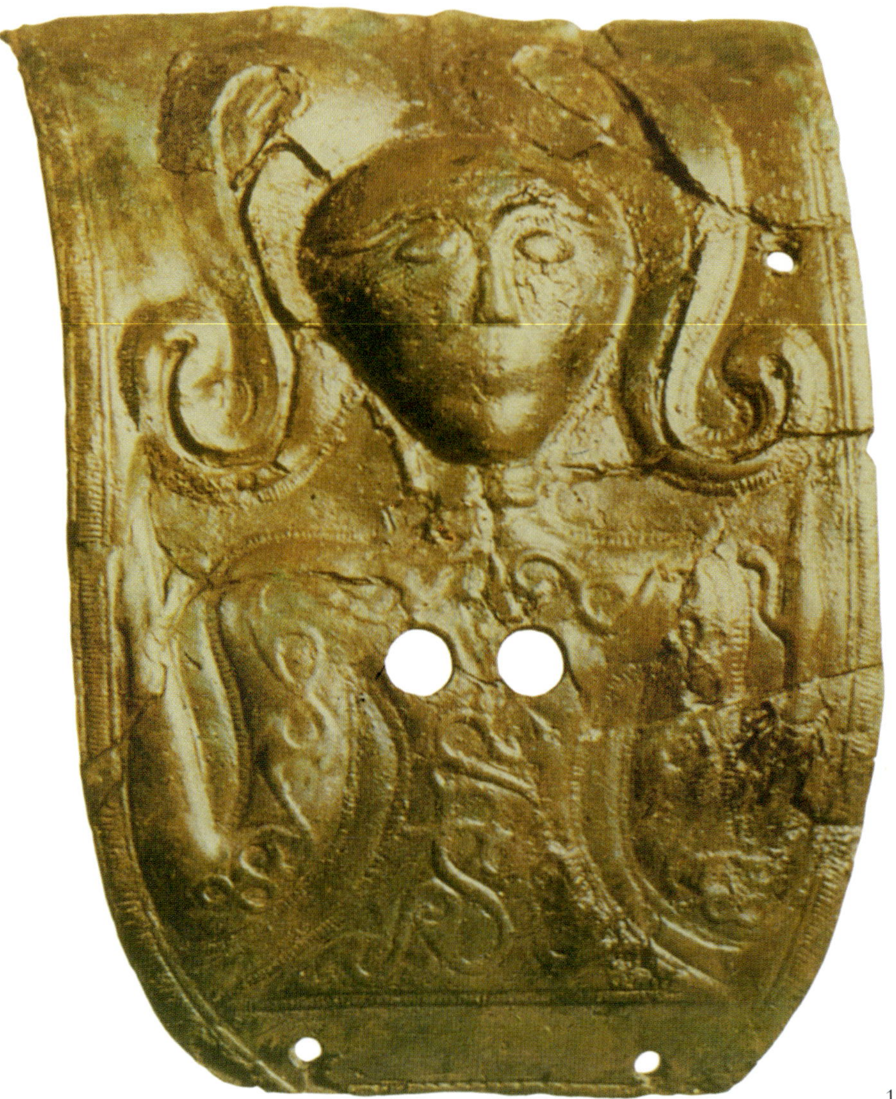

1

The most important thing to realize is that it is not an art
that attempts to create a likeness of objects found in our
world. Consider the head on the bronze mount from
Waldalgesheim, c. 250 BC, figure 1, for example

Foreword

The purpose of this book is to discuss the Celtic way of seeing and thinking, according to the evidence available in their art, especially in the period called La Tène, that is, roughly between 500 BC and 100 AD. This art is the only original Celtic source that we have from that period.

La Tène is not the only period of Celtic art. There is the Hallstatt period, between *c.* 1,200 BC and 500 BC, as well as the Celto-Roman and Celto-Christian periods which followed the La Tène period.

Although the art of La Tène is an original source of evidence, it needs to be interpreted. As a sculptor I felt that the academic world, and especially archaeologists, had not begun to appreciate this art. I was extremely suspicious of archaeologists' typical descriptions of this art: geometric, non-representational, floral, decorative, ambiguous and so on. In my opinion, these are superficial descriptions; they are categorical, and are not descriptions which attempt to interpret the art.

As I studied the art of La Tène some things became very evident to me. The most important thing to realize is that it is not an art that attempts to create a likeness of objects found in our world. Consider the head on the bronze mount from Waldalgesheim, *c.* 250 BC, **1**, for example.

It is not a representation of the likeness of anyone's head: it is an evocative symbol. It has a suggestion of a head, but there is in it a hint of a phallus as well. The hair suggests horns or leaves. No-one would see a head like this out in the world about us, so this is not an EXTERNAL seeing. The head is an image created in the imagination and mind of the artist, it is an INTERNAL image. The images of the art of La Tène are inner images of this kind. This is where I began to understand this art.

I shall attempt to show that the art of La Tène has a religious significance. Once we mention religion, we begin to think of a god or gods. The archaeologist, Dr Miranda Green, and others claim that there are such things as Celtic gods. Although we have the names of beings who are supposed to be Celtic gods, I am not strongly convinced of their existence – at least not according to the evidence of the art of La Tène.

As Dr Green acknowledges, most of our information about Celtic 'gods' derives from the iconography and inscriptions of the Roman period, but she adds:

... although the Druid and sacrificial ceremonies are discussed at length by such commentators as Strabo and Caesar, there is little mention of the gods themselves.[1]

She goes on to acknowledge that no consistent tradition of representing divinity amongst Celts of the Iron Age existed:

In general, Iron Age Celts did not possess the tradition of consistent physical representation of the divinities.[2]

In the Celto-Roman period, when the influence of Rome on the Celts is evident, representations of Celtic 'gods' became numerous, as Dr Green writes:

... the presence of divine images vastly increases under the influence of Rome when the stimulus of mimetic representation applied to previously tactic, aniconic divine concepts brings the Celtic gods into sharp focus for the first time.[3]

It may well be that images of the Celto-Roman period reflect something of the spiritual awareness of the Celts, but giving the forms of beings to the gods, I contend, is something that we would expect to see in Roman art. We would not expect the imitation ('mimetic representation') of the forms of external beings in Celtic art. It operates in another way; it is 'aniconic', it has no need of images that imitate beings. Celtic art symbolizes different kinds of forces; the artist would experience a particular sort of force and express it symbolically. In my opinion the following comment by Dr Green is misleading:

But the fully developed nature of these [Celtic] divinities early in the Roman period, combined with archaeological evidence, demonstrates that many of these beings must have been present as concepts in the earlier 'free' Celtic phase.[4]

We see that 'concepts' become 'beings'. That is, what we have here is a new way of seeing, an EXTERNAL, naturalistic vision, instead of the old Inner, symbolic vision. In short, we have Roman and not Celtic art.

Here is another comment by Dr Green:

Unsupported by written sources from the Celts themselves, who were virtually illiterate, iconography is both ambiguous and potentially misleading.[5]

It is claimed that the 'iconography' of the Celts is too ambiguous to tell us anything definite about them. Yet Dr Green maintains that some features in the symbols of Celtic art are sufficiently special to indicate a religious mode of thought:

None the less, certain features of Celtic symbolism are sufficiently distinctive to suggest recurrent patterns of religious thought-processes.[6]

'Religious thought-processes' are not synonymous with 'gods'. I contend that indigenous Celtic art tells us nothing about gods. This relates to my contention that Celtic art does not portray any 'beings'.

On the whole, it is archaeologists that have discussed Celtic art and commented on it. There is a great deal of truth in what the famous archaeologist Stuart Piggott once said:

The archaeologist's view of the past is inevitably a technological and materialistic one, simply because it is based on ancient technology, and not because this viewpoint has any particular intrinsic validity.[7]

Of course, the work of archaeologists can be extremely valuable, as is the work of the distinguished Paul Jacobsthal, but it is not the work of the archaeologist to discuss the significance of art. Looking for the significance of works of art belongs to the field of aesthetics, not archaeology. In this book, the word 'aesthetics' is used for the attempt to analyze the form and content of the art of the Celts from an artistic perspective, in order to show the significance of their works.

It is important to realize that there is a world of difference between what may be called the 'personal' art of today, art which – above all – gives expression to the vision of some individual or other, and the early art of Europe and Asia, where art was closely associated with religion. Religion in art is an extremely important consideration. There is also a fundamental difference between ways of seeing, a difference that has already been mentioned, that is, EXTERNAL and INTERNAL (or Inner) vision.

There is a world of difference between what may be called the 'personal' art of today, art which – above all – gives expression to the vision of some individual or other, and the early art of Europe and Asia, where art was closely associated with religion

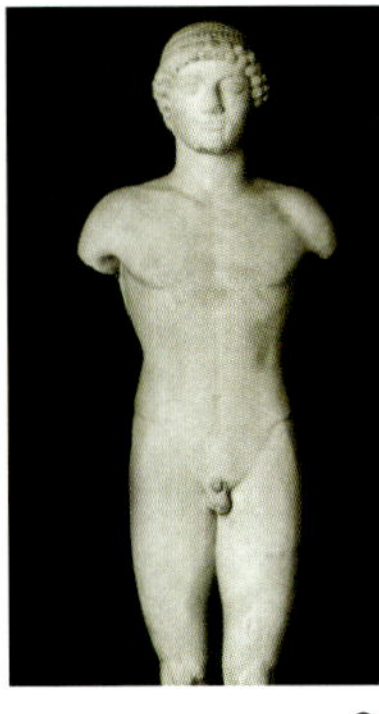

2

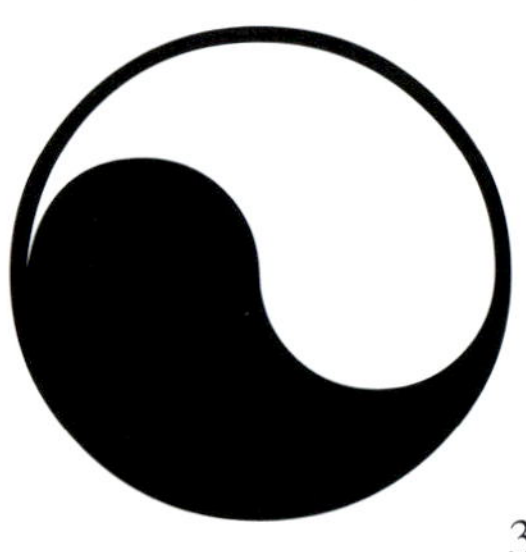

3

Let us consider Classical art, the art of early Greece and Rome, for example. Consider the image of the Greek god Apollo, **2**.

The figure resembles a man; it is based on the external appearance of a man. Now consider the art of Asia, the Ying-Yang of the Chinese, for example, **3**.

This is not an imitation; it is not meant to create a likeness of anything in the world outside. Works like this are the result of meditation or inner emotion; they are symbols. They represent the eternal and restless forces of light and darkness, for example, and are not imitations of objects.

The art of the Celts is more like the art of Asia than Classical art. This is the key to an examination of it.

A study and analysis of the forms, patterns, and images of Celtic art will, in my opinion, reveal its secret and its significance. Note that I have not given much attention to the colours or the nature of the materials used in the art of La Tène – whether they have been made of various metals, coral, enamel and so on. It was not possible for me to view many of the original works of art, which are housed in museums across the whole of Europe, and I could not rely on photographs of them.

Instead, in the first instance, I examined Celtic works of art from all parts of Europe, a whole spectrum of works, from Romania to Ireland. I also studied the works of art of various tribes. It is remarkable how consistent the significant components of the art were.

After the examination came the analysis. I grouped together examples of La Tène art that are similar in form, content and feeling. This is the best way to see the significance of each component. I realized that many components have a similarity and a consistency of form, that they were symbols and frameworks of Spiritual Transformation – the cyclical experience of rebirth – and religious consciousness. (The meaning of all these matters will be made clear in the book.) All this is helpful in revealing the special significance of the whole. I attempted to understand works by comparing them. The symbols were always studied in their contexts.

My study has persuaded me that there is more to this sophisticated art than decorative patterns and ambiguous shapes, as commentators say. My study has also convinced me that the bases of Celtic art are religious.

Notes on page 114

The Inner Vision:
A Spiritual Vision

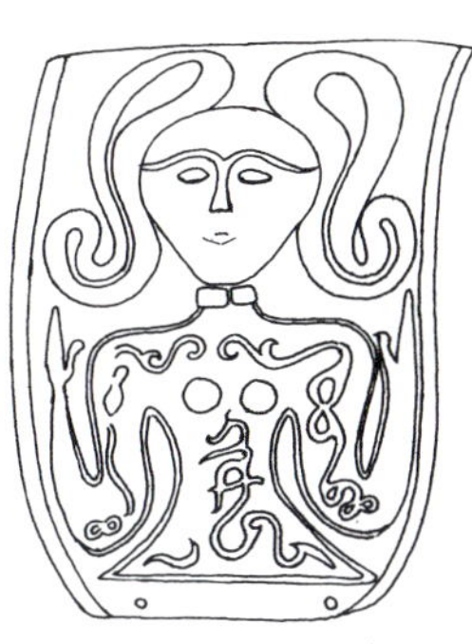

1

It has already been shown that what is being conveyed in the head in figure **1** is an inner experience, rather than a likeness to any object in the external world. Furthermore, I maintain that this head shows an awareness of a sacred and spiritual presence. The meditative eyes and the gesture of the arms create a ritual, religious feeling. Let us explore this spiritual component in more detail.

We shall examine three other heads. We begin with **4**.

Altogether, the head creates a feeling of the Other World, of the spirit and of ascent

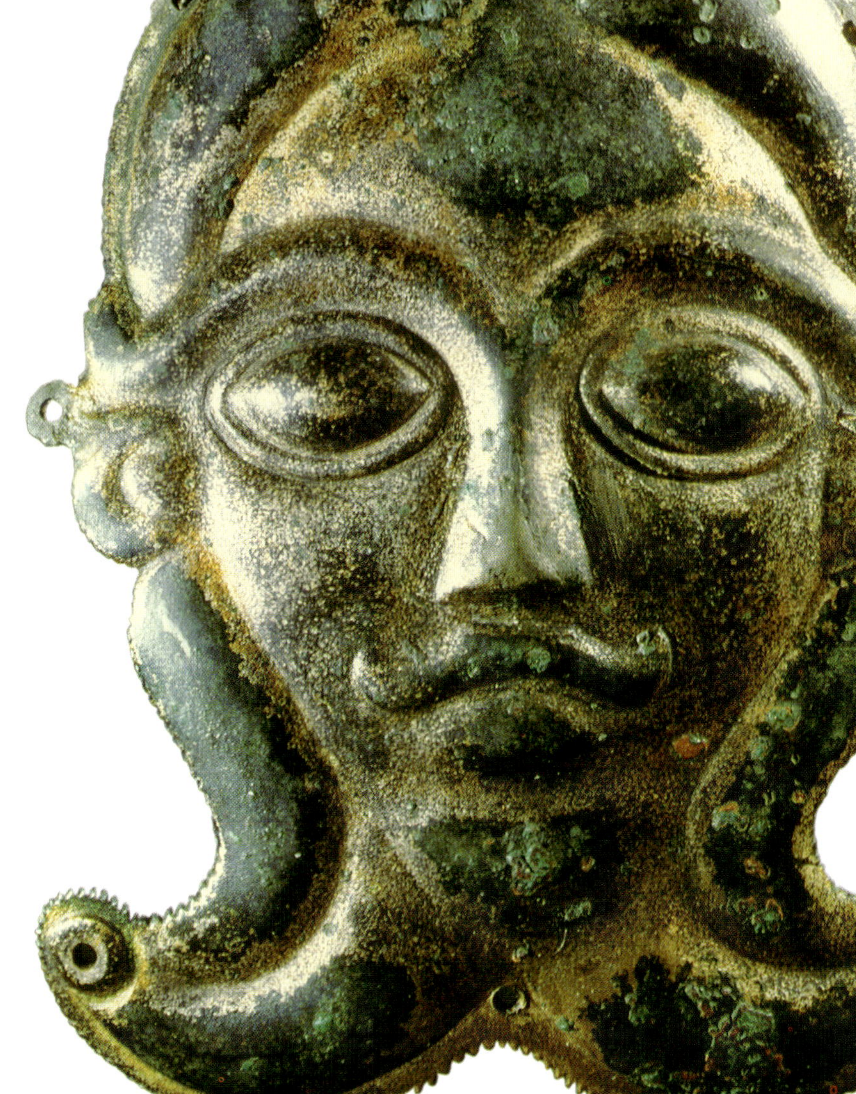

4

Look at the centre of the head, especially the eyes. The eyes are hypnotic. I would call them 'magical' because they make us aware of a dimension beyond the material. We can call this dimension 'otherworldly'. Secondly, we see that the head is also a leafy plant: there are leaves on each side of the forehead and the face, and the bottom suggests a leafy root that turns outwards. This creates a feeling that the head represents a natural process (coming to leaf), as well as suggesting that we are also a part of this natural process. Thirdly, the aspect of the face creates a frontal, vertical stillness. The shape of the head, like a balloon, creates an impression of ascent. Altogether, the head creates a feeling of the Other World, of the spirit and of ascent.

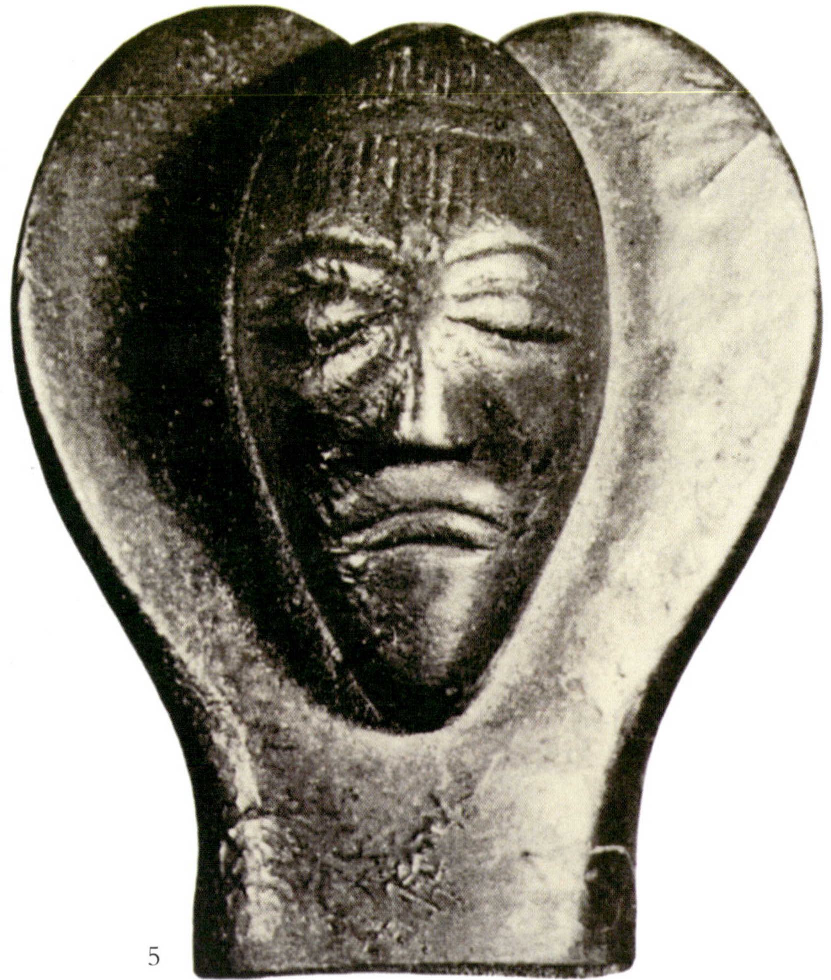

5

This head conveys two things simultaneously; on the one hand, meditation, and on the other, a power of ascent

In the head shown in **5**, the eyes are meditative and the lips droop. This head is again shaped like a balloon, and the forms on each side of it create a strong impression of ascent. This is not a plain head either: it is like a bud opening, or the force of semen rising through a phallus. This head conveys two things simultaneously; on the one hand, meditation, and on the other, a power of ascent.

It creates an impression of a phallus, and of leaves like ascending balloons

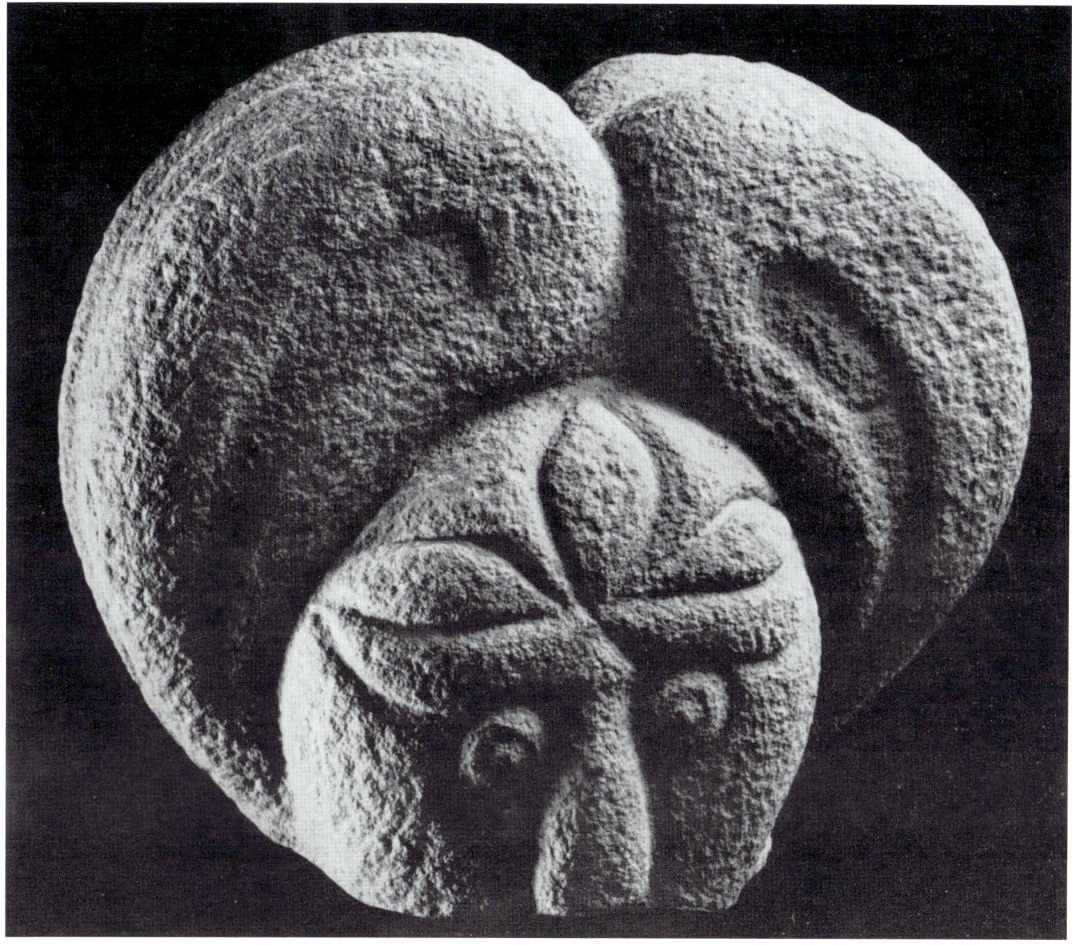

6

The stone head in **6** gives an impression of lightness.

Once again, this is not a plain head. It creates an impression of a phallus, and of leaves like ascending balloons.

In these three heads there is a feeling or an experience of forces; they do not present any things or objects. This is one of the main features of the art of La Tène. The heads discussed so far convey an INNER experience of an uplifting force, the force that can be seen in the growth of plants in the natural world. They also give a feeling of meditation. These two sensations are permanent, eternal, and are not ephemeral impressions of things. These heads suggest that throughout the world there is a stillness of meditation in the midst of the upward surge of growth in the natural world. (We shall see, later on, that this art also conveys the power of death and rebirth as well.)

Figure **7** is an explanatory diagram which shows the forces at work in the fundamental image of the heads.

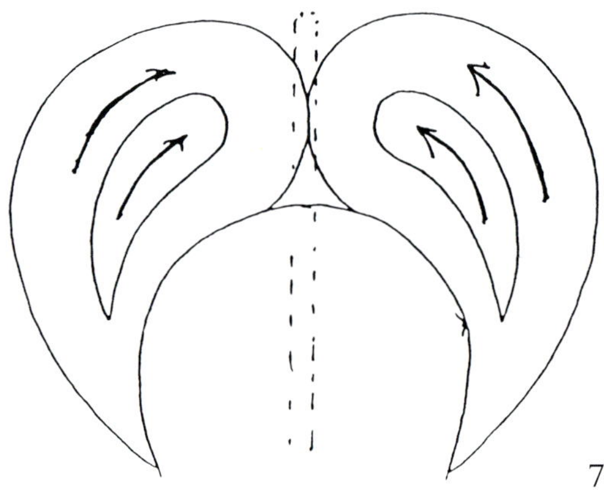

7

In the centre we can see a tranquil meditation which is, in my opinion, a spiritual meditation. Note that the centre conveys neither sadness nor joy, fear nor hatred, nor love, nor any agitation. Here we have a neutral quietude. For me, it is an impersonal and absolute spiritual quietude.

As noted above, a spiritual feeling is created by the eyes. As well as being meditative, the eyes of these figures can be hypnotic, in some way magical. Consider the following examples of eyes as shown in **8** and **9**.

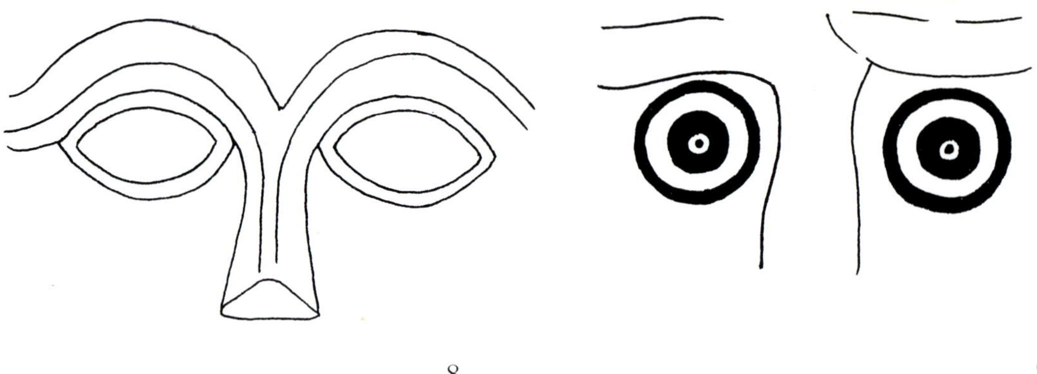

8

9

One reason for the magical appearance of the eyes is the use of one circle within another, or one shape within another, to create an intoxicating optical effect. The hypnotic effect may be even stronger in **9** than in **8**. This intoxication releases us from the grasp of material things. Once again I would say that a spiritual experience is conveyed here.

Another feature of the heads that contributes strongly to their total effect is the balance in their shapes, a symmetry which gives a very strong impression of a pattern. The right side corresponds exactly to the left side. The lines of the leaves, the eyebrows and the moustache are repeated in the two halves of the image and contribute to the light feeling of the whole work. Put this symmetry and the eyes together and we have the features of **10**.

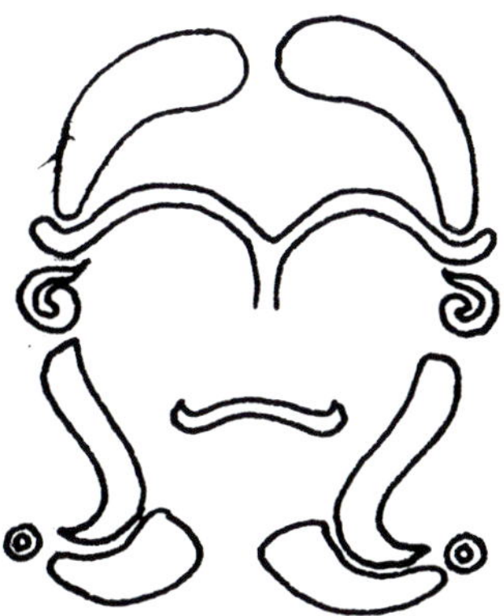

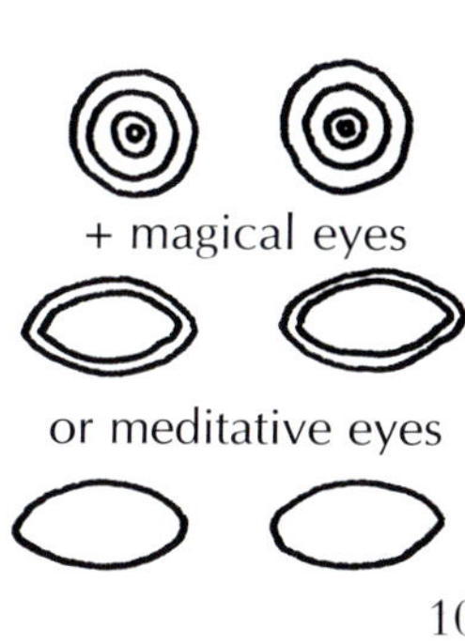

A symmetry
which gives a
very strong
impression of a
pattern

The symmetry of the shapes and the patterns is particularly strong in the most striking heads and creates a powerful impression of something not material. It is something 'spiritual'.

The diagrams which follow (**11**) show the power of symmetry:

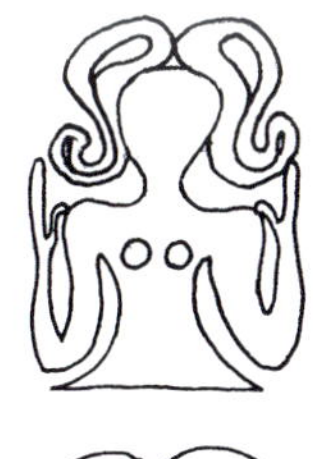

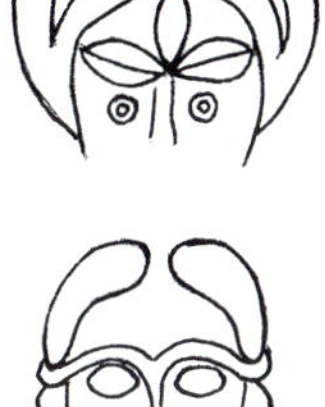

The shape of these three heads are partly due to the esthetic balance of the mind

Through the centre of these works of art we have an impression of a silent, spiritual meditation. On the two sides is conveyed the upward surge of growth

Through the centre of these works of art we have an impression of a silent, spiritual meditation. On the two sides is conveyed the upward surge of growth. The Celtic artists felt all of this before they created it. As we look at them these works of art ought to instil in us a feeling of quiet meditation and a sense of the upward surge of growth. One author summarized this very act of creation that we are discussing in this way:

The great Celtic artist must have had the power of visualising beforehand a completed work in its final state and materials. That ability, as in all forms of art, has to be acquired by experience.[1]

This artistic experience survives amongst nations who are considered to be Celtic (in this instance, Irish) in the Christian era and in Christian works. The bronze gilt plaque, **12**, shows Christ on the cross. It was made *c.* 800 AD. Observe that the image is symmetrical, and that we have here not only a body on a cross, but also a hint of a phallic head. It even has meditative eyes.

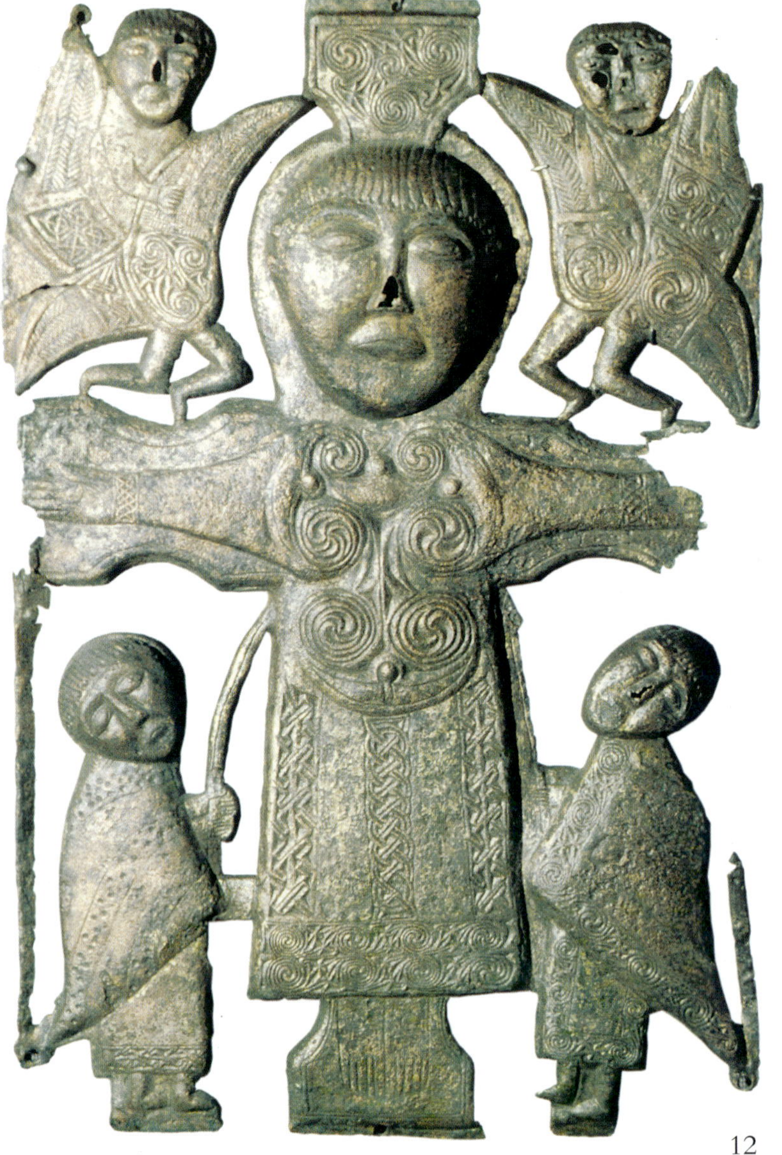

12

Observe that the image is symmetrical, and that we have here not only a body on a cross, but also a hint of a phallic head. It even has meditative eyes

What has been said of the elements found in the Celtic heads of La Tène art may be summed up by considering one head from Austria, **13**.

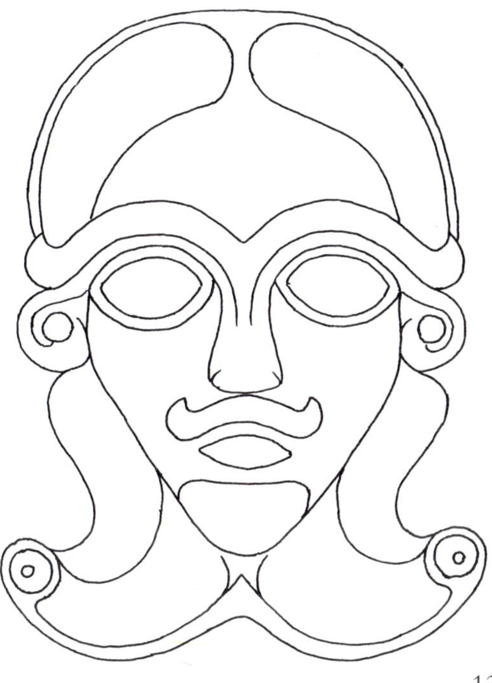

13

In the composition as a whole there is a symmetry that invigorates the pattern. The work is an expression of the inner, Celtic vision

In the centre we have quiet meditation, which presents a kind of magical presence. The look on the face is neutral and impassive. I call this an expression of one of the eternal and absolute powers of the Celts' universe. There are here, as well, light, ascending shapes that convey the force of growth in nature, another of the abiding powers of the world. In the composition as a whole there is a symmetry that invigorates the pattern. The work is an expression of the inner, Celtic vision.

Notes on page 114

The Deep can be
regarded as a
womb and as a
grave. This
Lower Region is
feminine in
character and is
an aspect of the
Earth-mother

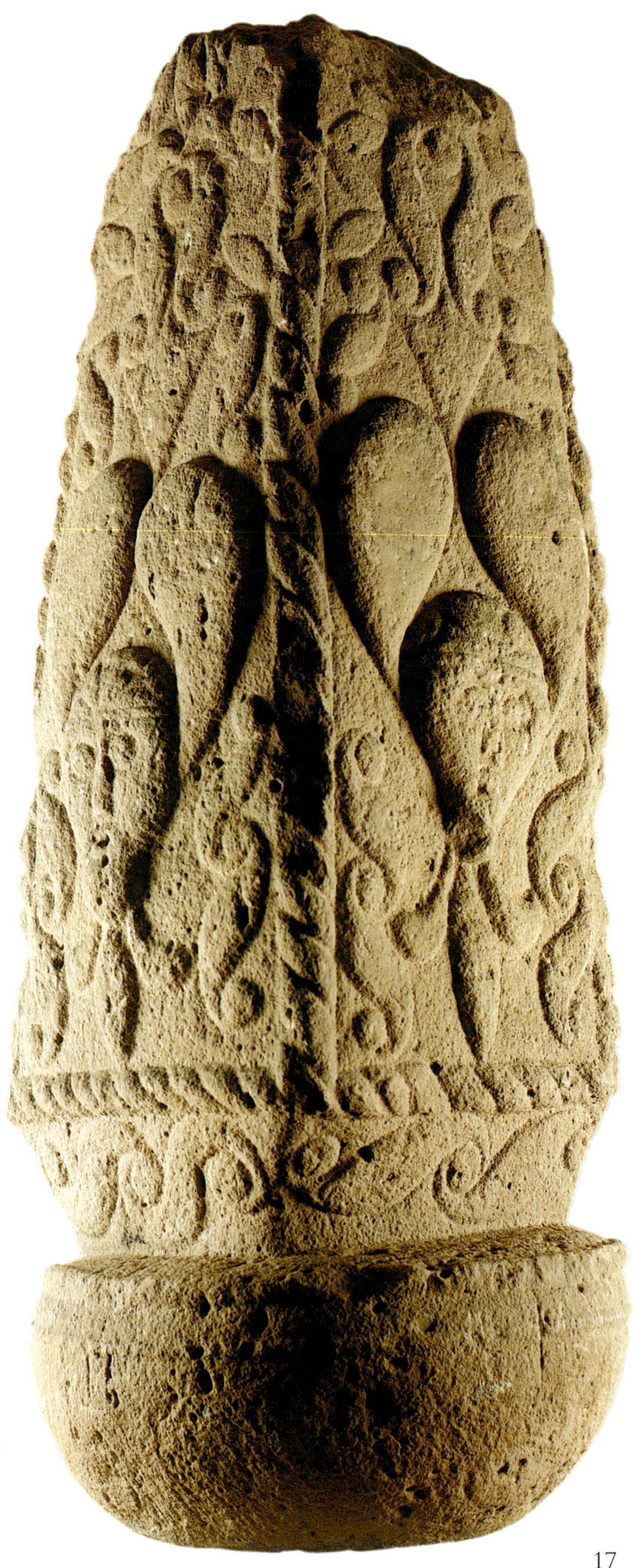

17

2 Art and Nature

In the first chapter we discussed the feeling of ascending growth that is present in the heads examined. In this chapter we shall concentrate on the distinctive connection with the world of nature that is found in works of art of the La Tène period. We shall give particular attention to the Lower Part of the Celtic sculptures discussed, the part below the head. We shall be referring to this region as the Deep. It can be regarded as a womb and as a grave. This Lower Region is feminine in character and is an aspect of the Earth-mother.

Let us consider examples in order to make all of this clearer. In **14** we have a phallic head (therefore characterized as masculine) upon a feminine body (feminine because there are holes on the figure to represent breasts). In **15** (and **18**) we see two heads, one of them upside down and the other pointing upwards.

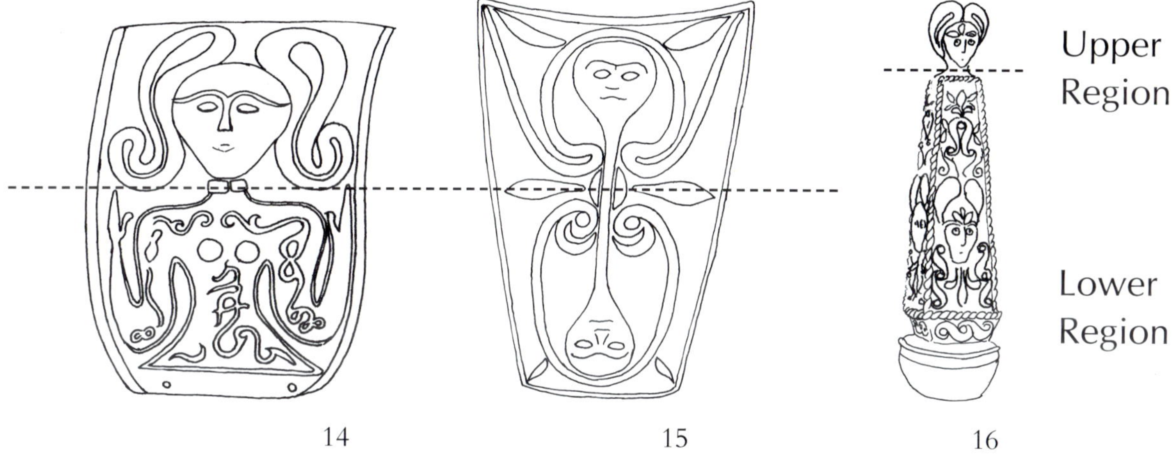

14   15   16

I regard the upside down phallic head, as being in the womb of the Earth-mother. In figure **16** I have introduced a head onto the obelisk (the head which was once on it has been lost). Beneath this head we see other heads as if they were in a shaft, a shaft which I consider to be going down into the ground, but which also allows an ascent out of it. In all of these examples, it seems to me that the heads in the Upper Region are masculine and that several things in the Lower Region are feminine, signifying the Earth-mother.

This is a symbolical way of thinking. The Lower Region of these works can symbolize a womb, a grave or a part of the Earth-mother. The phallic head can be in a womb, a grave or inside the Earth-mother. The concept of a phallic head in a womb or a grave can signify a dualism: it can denote a death, which is also a conceiving, that will lead to a birth, suggesting life is as a cycle of birth, death and rebirth.

Let us look in more detail at the Lower Region. In the Lower Region of **14** we see that the focus is on some kind of agitation, represented by the restless perturbation of the lines. In the Lower Region of **15** (and **18**) there is an emphasis on an exciting experience, conveyed through the phallic head in the womb of the earth. The excitement is expressed through the spiralling at the neck of the womb. The head seems to be heavy, which suggests that the emphasis is on the force of the experience rather than on the phallic head as an object. Similarly, in **16** and **17**, we see an emphasis on the power of the heads, that seem to be moving up and down, and on the force expressed by the spiralling and the symbolic shapes of leaves which seem to be falling to the bottom.

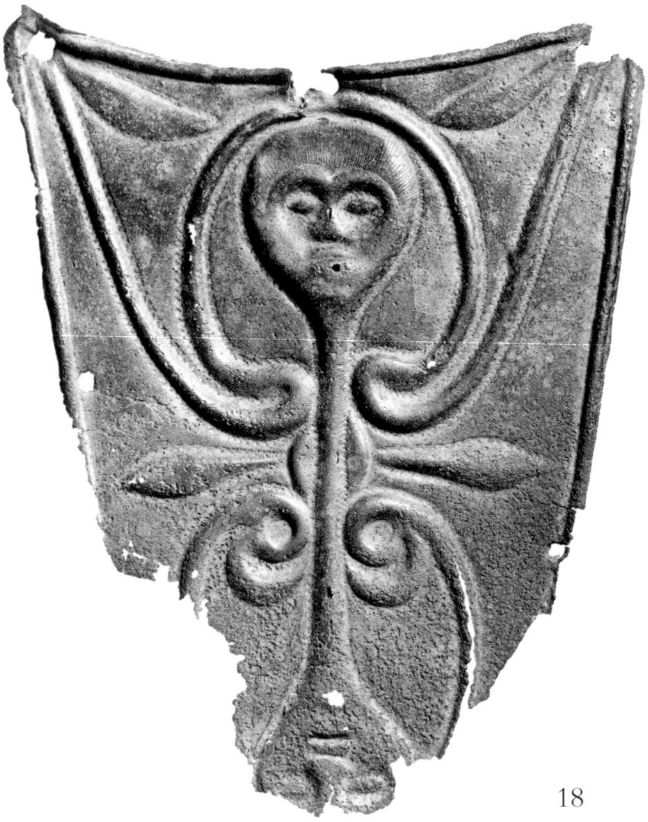

It is significant that there is such agitation in the Deep or Lower Region, an excitement in the symbolic grave or womb. I call this strange excitement, that signifies death and rebirth, Spiritual Transformation.

Although I designate this a Spiritual Transformation, it also connects with the biological transformation that occurs in the natural world, where we have an endless cycle of growth and death, growth and death.

18

Let us examine all of this as it is found in one particular example, the Tal-y-llyn plaque (**15** and **18**). In the Upper Region of the work there is a phallic head with shapes like leaves on either side of it, extending upwards. In the Lower Region, there is again a phallic head with leaves on either side of it, as if they were falling down. The Upper Region signifies the force of life, and the Lower Region the power of death. But a phallus going into a womb also signifies conception and birth. Neither life nor death is the end of either process. Death, the grave, is also a womb that will give birth to life. And, after arising from the Deep to the Upper Region, everything must return to the Deep. This plaque symbolizes the unending cycle of existence.

There is also a symbolic Borderline in the work between the Upper and the Lower Regions. In this case, in the mouth of the shape that is like a womb or vagina. This Borderline is a regular feature of Celtic art. If we simplify the interpretation to some extent, it could be said that it is a division point between the force of life (the Upper Region) and the power of death and rebirth (the Lower Region). But we have to bear in mind that neither of these two forces is final (nor entirely separate, as the grave is also a womb): the two are part of the complete process of existence. Figure **19** provides an explanatory diagram of this process.

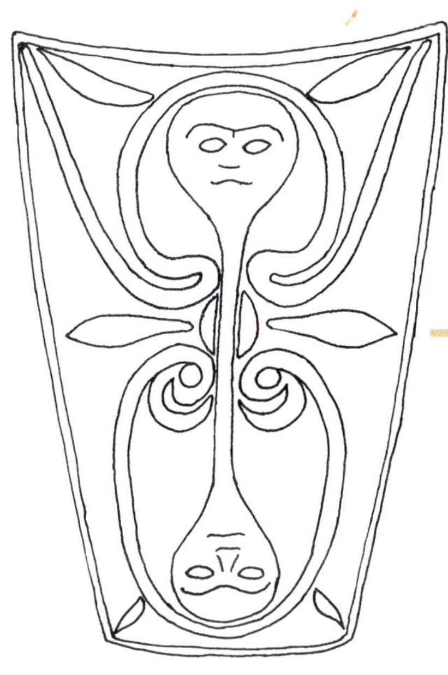

19

It is significant that there is such agitation in the Deep or Lower Region, an excitement in the symbolic grave or womb. I call this strange excitement, that signifies death and rebirth, Spiritual Transformation

I have said that the Borderline is a regular feature of the art of the Celts. Figures **20**, **21** and **22** show the two forces and the Borderline between them, and suggest how commonplace the pattern is. It suggests how conscious the Celts were of the complete process of existence.

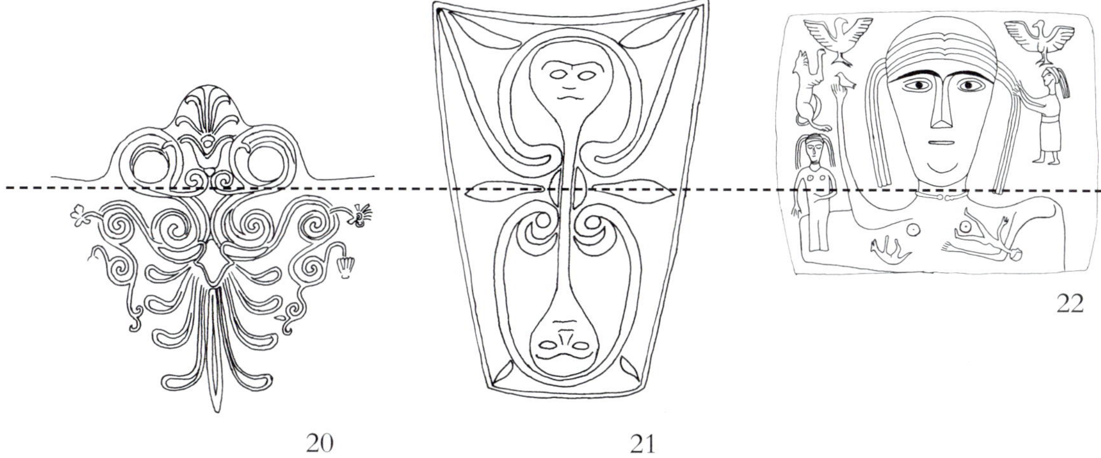

20

21

22

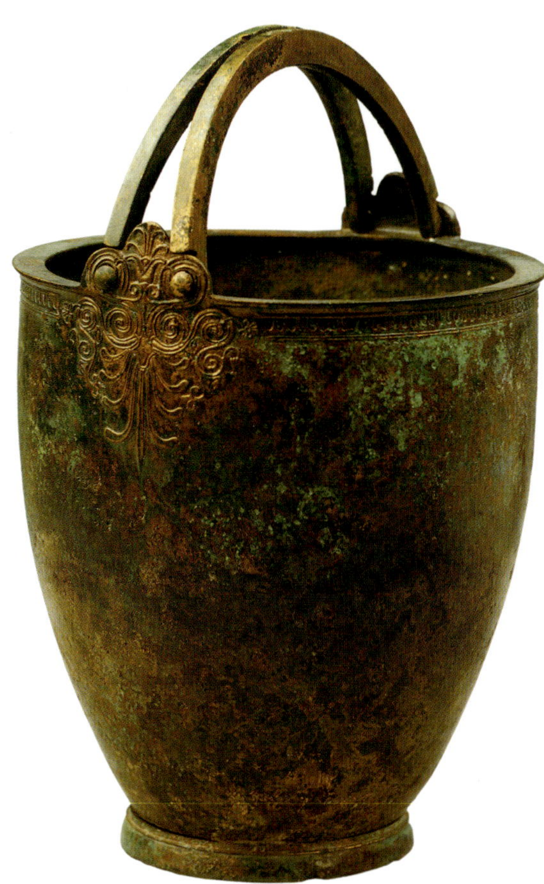

23

Some of the features of these works are worth noting. In the first place, there is the emphasis on the Lower Region, the Deep, the womb that is also a grave. The Borderline is an entry point between the Upper and Lower Regions. In the case of the Great Mother, **22**, the Borderline is on the neck. There is a torque on that Borderline.

In figures **20** and **23** – the bucket – there are two types of agitation, represented by the spiralling. The most powerful agitation is in the Lower Region of the 'tree'. This powerful agitation occurs in the frame or body of the bucket, which has a 'feminine' shape. In the exciting whirl of the lines we have an impression of falling down and arising. In short, we have a feeling of leaves falling in wintertime and burgeoning forth in springtime – a Biological Transformation which is a symbol of Spiritual Transformation.

In figure **21** there is a downward force in the phallic head that moves into the vagina and there is agitation conveyed by the spiralling lines.

In figure **22** (and **24**), one of the panels of the Gundestrup Cauldron, a feeling of falling is conveyed by some of the forms beneath the neck. By following one dog, for example, we can see that it is going downwards, but there is also a dog moving upwards. In this work the method of presentation is more of a narrative than in the two other works under consideration. The little bird on the light, upraised arm of the 'Mother' also suggests new life. In fact, what is delineated here is the story of the process of existence.

To conclude this chapter let us make a list of the forms that move downwards, into the grave-womb, to die and be reborn:

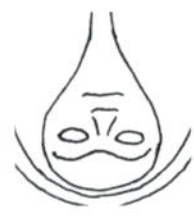 A phallic head, upside down

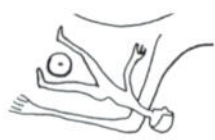 A body that falls downwards

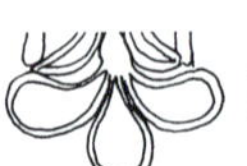 Leaves that are upside down

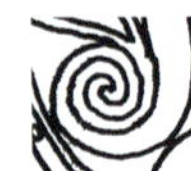 A spiralling line that conveys excitement

 A combination of more than one of these, such as a spiralling line and leaves together

This is the formula that summarizes this chapter: there are elements in the art that convey a Biological Transformation; that transformation is a symbol of a Spiritual Transformation that presents the fundamental and lasting process of existence.

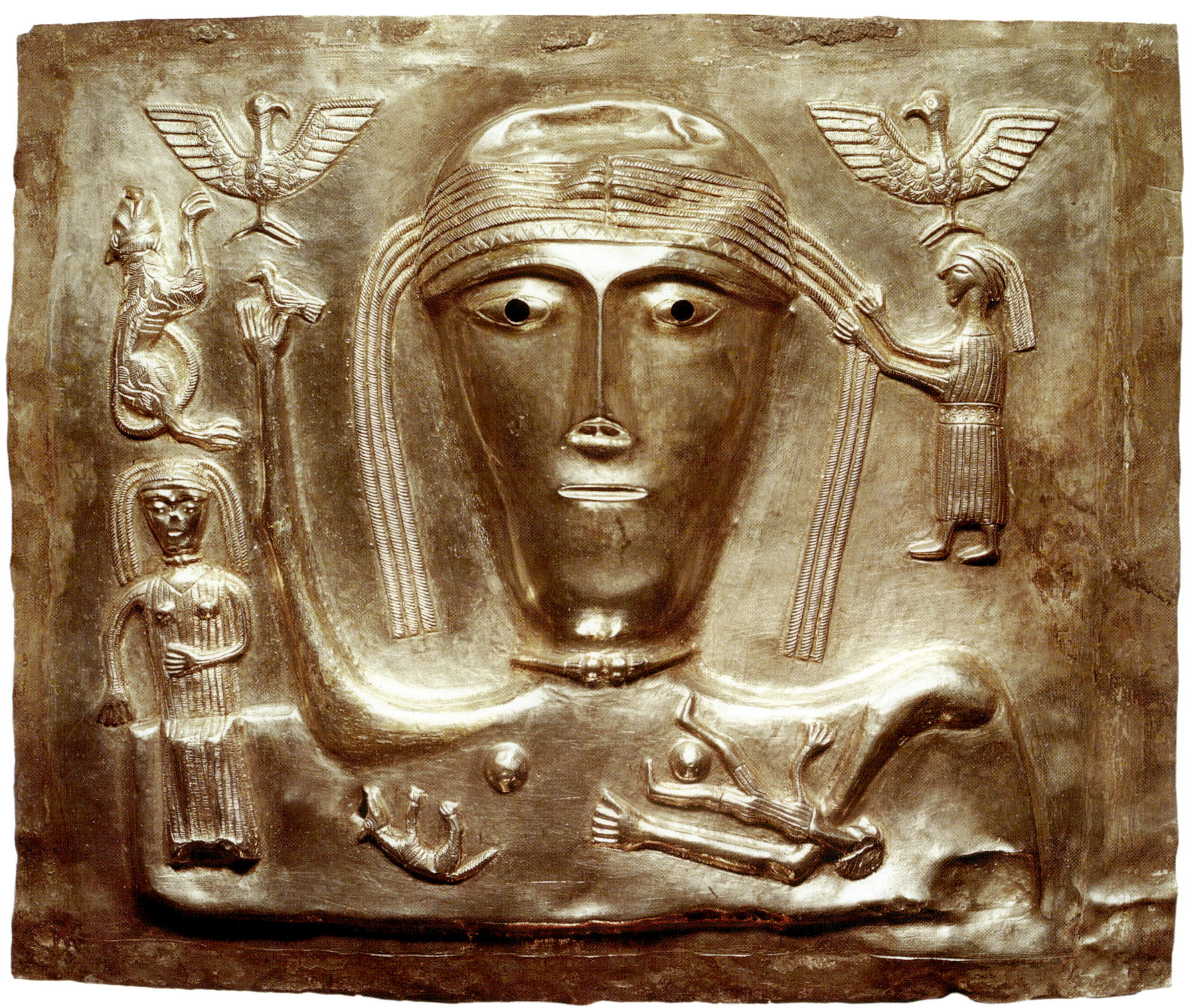

24

By following one dog, for example, we can see
that it is going downwards, but there is also a
dog moving upwards. In this work the method of
presentation is more of a narrative

3 Spiritual Transformation in the Deep

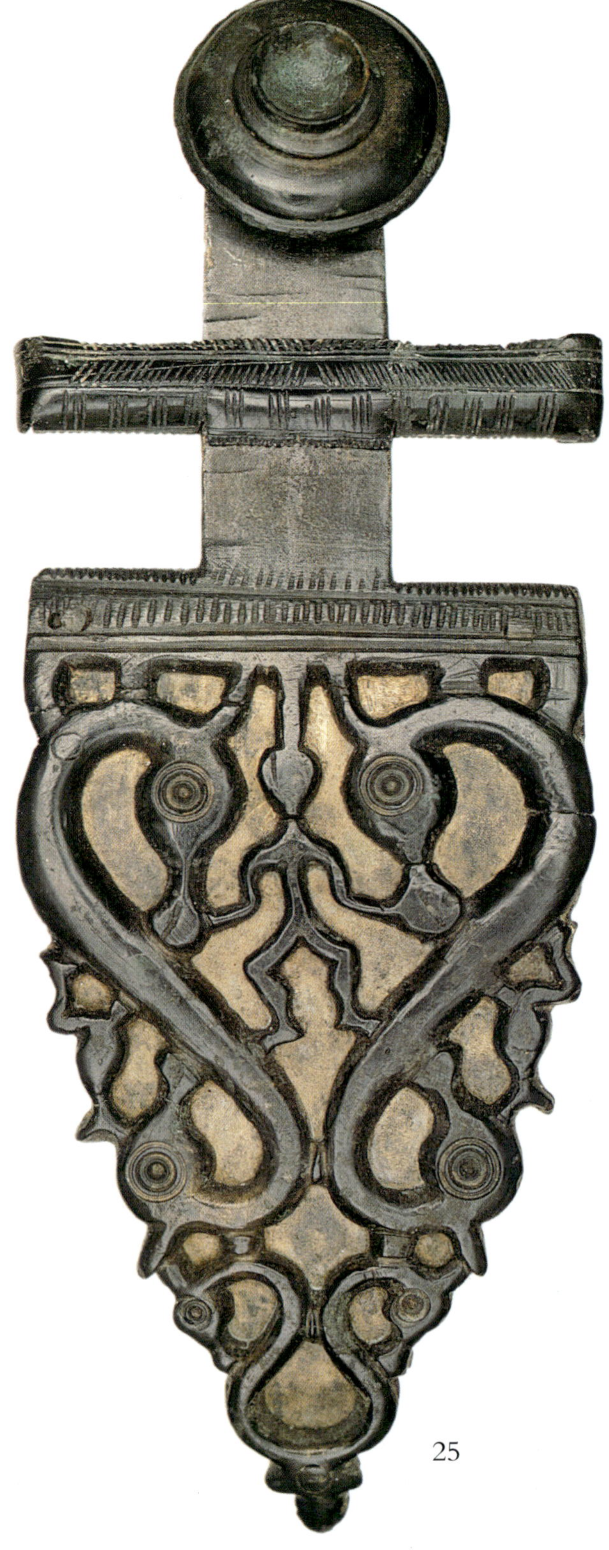

Spiritual Transformation comes from an imaginative experience of living, dying and coming back to life. It is this experience that leads to the feeling of spiritual stillness that is represented by the centre

25

Let us consider the Spiritual Transformation that has already been mentioned in Chapter 2. In the first chapter a reference was made to the mood of the centre of the heads as one of a neutral tranquility, a tranquility that I call spiritual, absolute and impersonal. There is a connection between Spiritual Transformation and this quiet meditation. Spiritual Transformation comes from an imaginative experience of living, dying and coming back to life. It is this experience that leads to the feeling of spiritual stillness that is represented by the centre.

We have already seen examples of Spiritual Transformation. Here are more examples that will be explained by reference to the works reproduced in **26**, **27** and **28**.

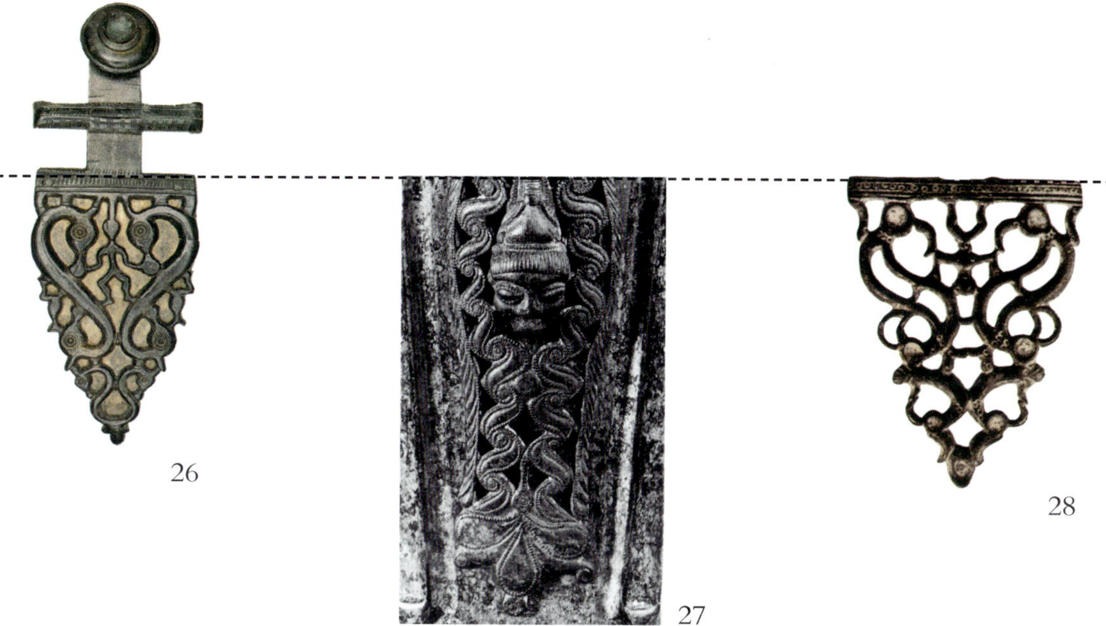

26

27

28

We can see that the handle of the wine flagon (**27**) and one of the belt buckles (**28**) are below the Borderline mentioned in the second chapter. In both buckles there is a figure that appears to be on its way up or down (**26** and **28**). The two of them are in the midst of a turmoil of forms. In both patterns there are S-shaped eyes that entice us into the turmoil of the forms. I call this experience exciting and magical. It is an imaginative experience of dying and rebirth. Note that the eyes are in the symbolic heads of horses in **25** and **26**, and in the symbolic heads of birds in **28** and **29**. These animals suggest that there is a connection with some kind of journey, the soul or the spirit's journey in the imagination. This kind of journey will be discussed in more detail later on.

In **27**, **30** (and **43**), the wine flagon, we see a symbolic head moving up or down in the midst of agitation that is conveyed by lines like leaves and eyes. Three leaves open out at the bottom. Here we have a feeling of falling into a pool or a womb. This is a prelude to an ascent.

If we consider the framework that we have mentioned – namely of a Borderline with an Upper Region, or life, above it, and a Lower Region, the Deep, which is a grave and also a womb, below – then the explanatory diagrams show that we have only one side, the Lower Region, in these works (**27** and **28**). The hook in the Upper Region of **25** is a symbol of a head or phallus, or more precisely, it shows an overhead view of a head or phallus. It is worth noting that this imaginative framework is found on everyday objects, like a belt buckle.

We have also referred to magical eyes and a spiral. These are optical devices to charm us into an experience of terror and to draw us into an experience of a death that leads to rebirth. These devices of enchantment are important and are characteristic features of the art of La Tène.

The consistency of this artistic framework implies that the whole process is like a religious ritual. The art of La Tène is a form of religious expression.

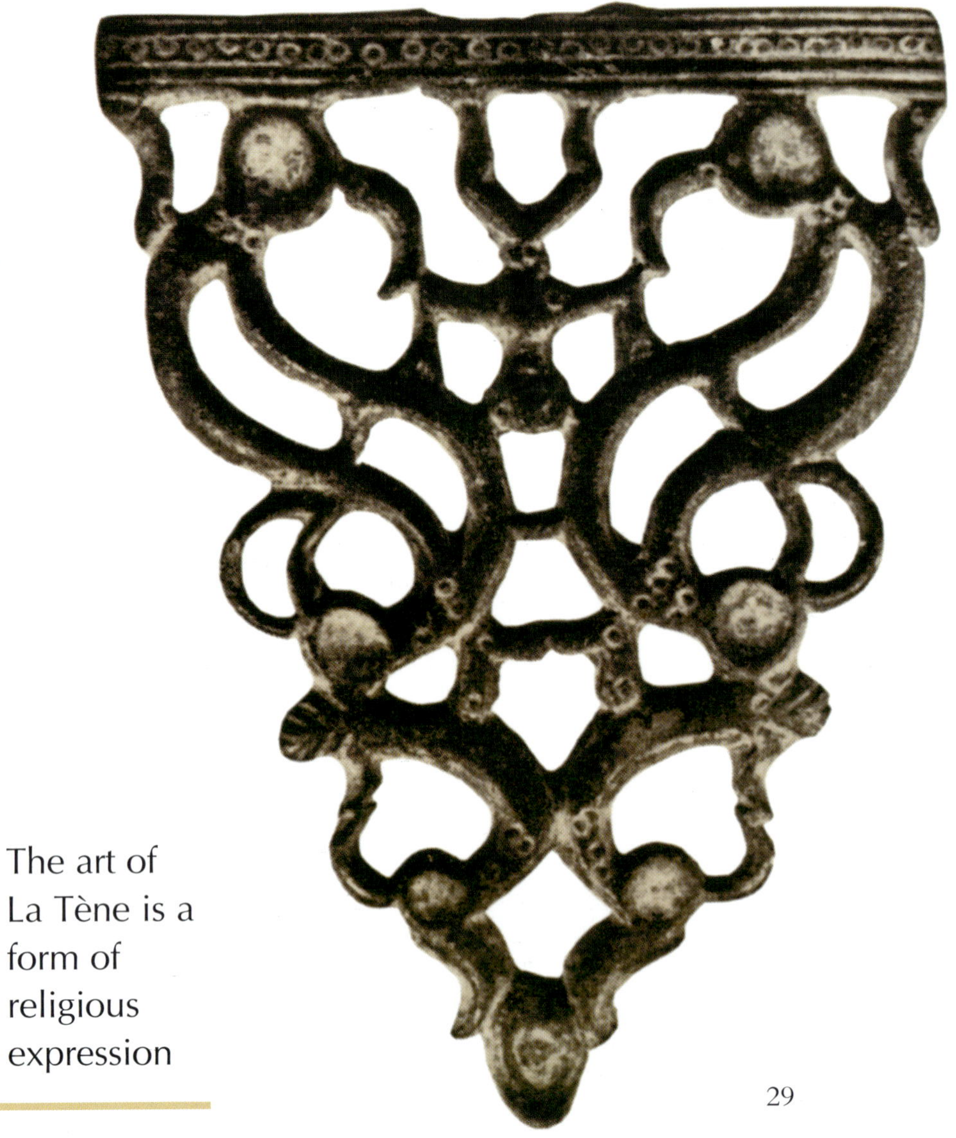

The art of
La Tène is a
form of
religious
expression

29

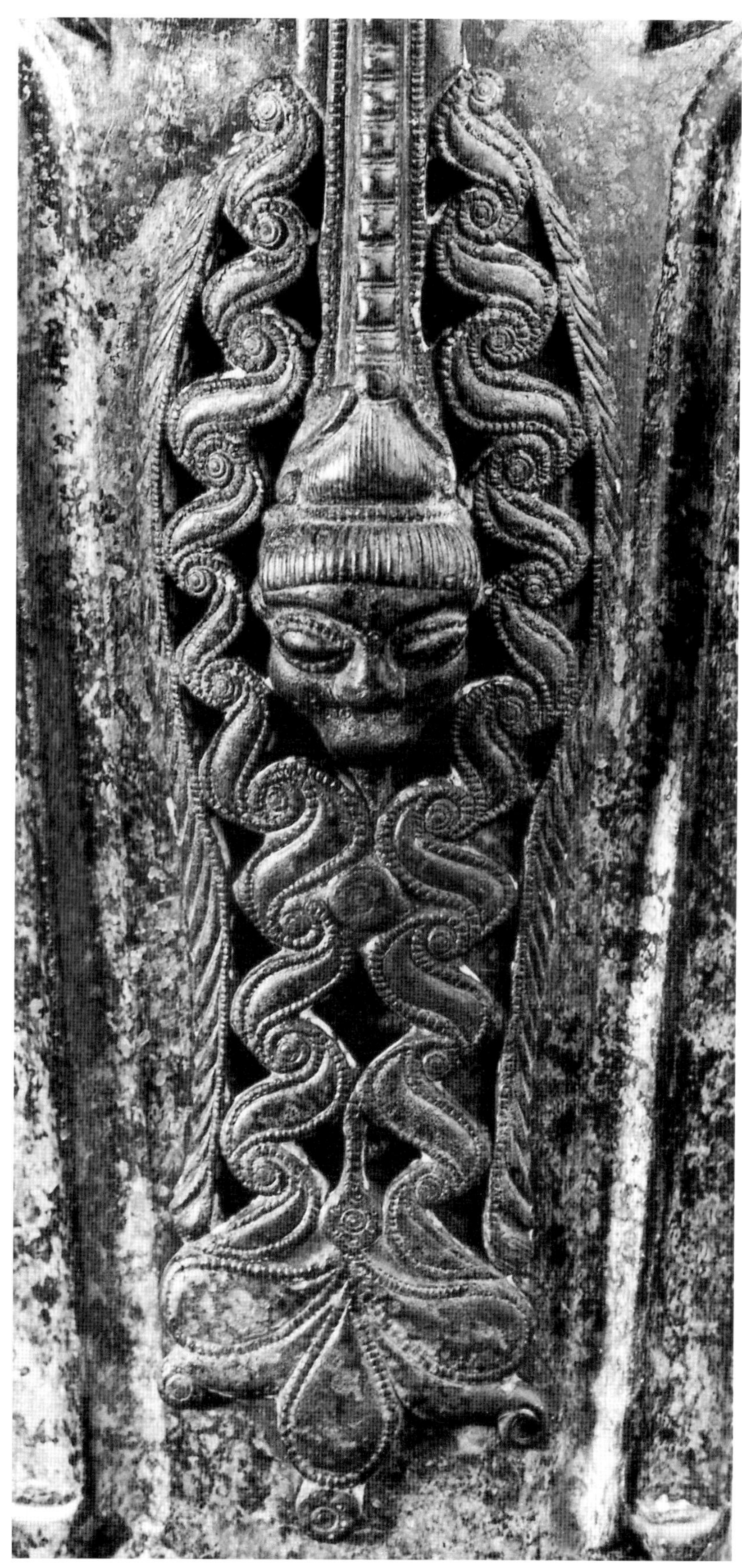

30

We have another example of Spiritual Transformation, but in this case the image seems to be telling a story. It is narrative art

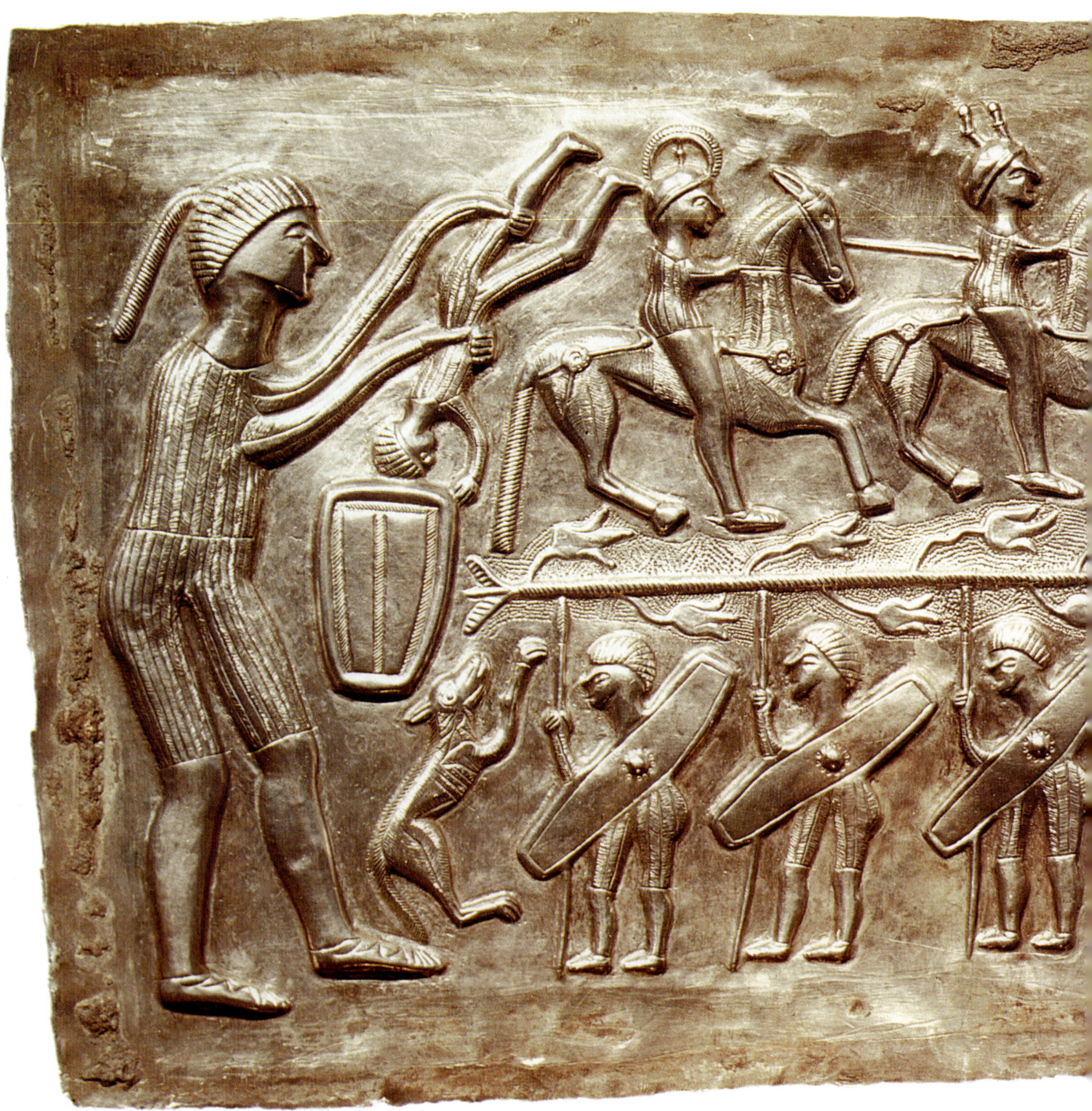

4 The Narrative, Ritual Aspect of the Art

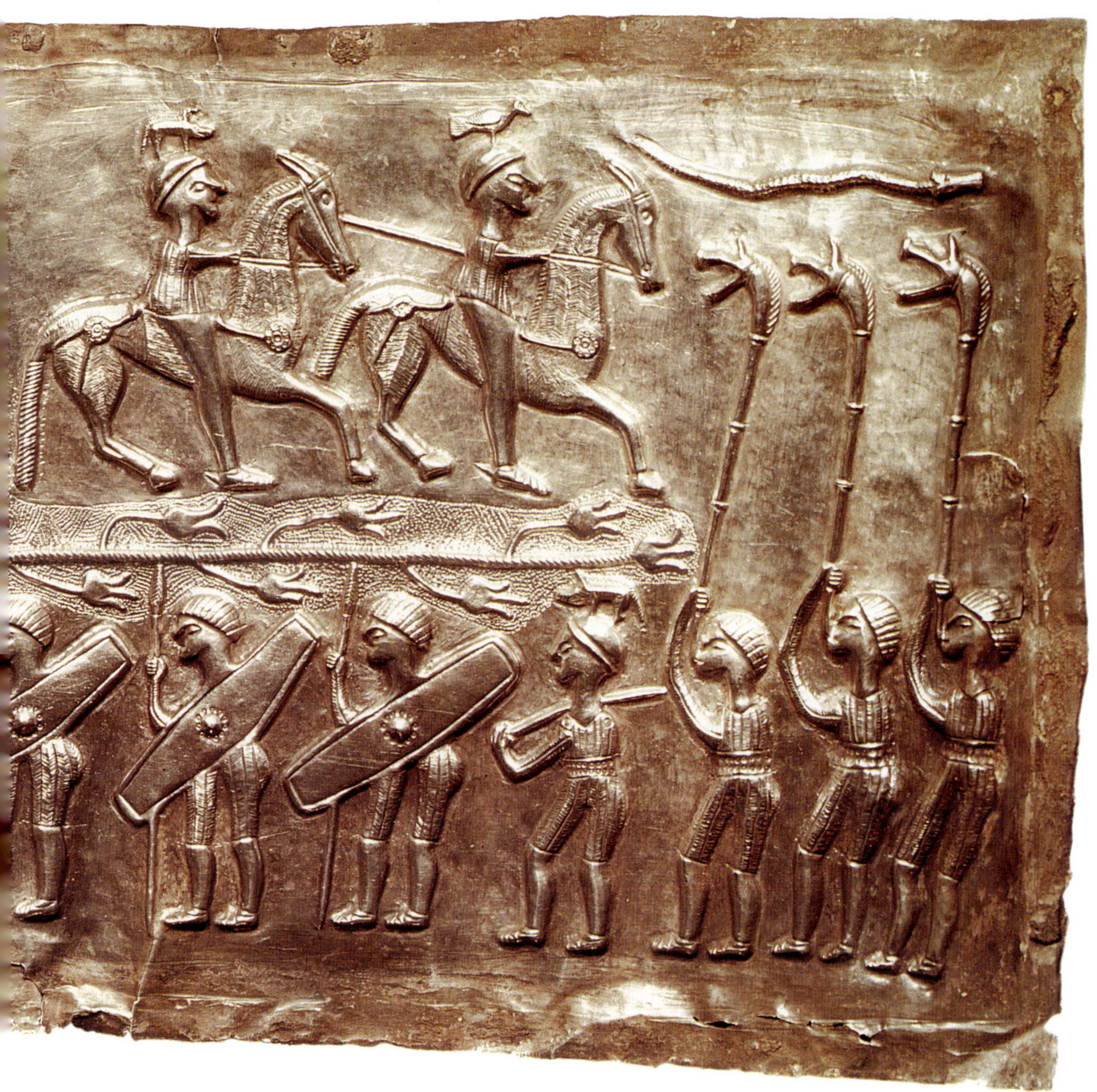

Figure **31** is a reproduction of one the panels of the Gundestrup Cauldron.

It is another example of Spiritual Transformation, but here the whole seems to be telling a story. It is narrative art. We see armed warriors following a dog, to the accompaniment of horns – the 'carnyx'. They follow the dog to the base of a tree. There, they are placed, head downwards, in a cauldron, a Cauldron of Rebirth. This represents the traumatic experience of going into the Deep, of dying and of being born again. Then we see the risen warriors – note the raised aspect of their heads. They are mounted on horses, without weapons, and are following a serpent towards the upper part of the tree, where the Borderline is (see **31**). The eyes of the warriors suggest that they are in a kind of meditation or trance. All this signifies the cyclical journey of existence – birth, death and rebirth – by means of descent and ascent. If we look closely we see that there are significant symbols on the helmets of the warriors, symbols that represent:

a circle or light

animal horns

a boar

a bird

These are signs of the powers of the natural world that lead souls on their journey to the Upper Region. What we have here is a series of experiences, one after the other (that is why they form a narrative), that represents the journey of descent and ascent. It is also a ritual process that represents what occurs in *initiation,* a topic that is discussed more fully later on.

Let us stand the image in **31** upright (**32**) in order to show show more clearly its relationship with the pattern of Transformation in other works.

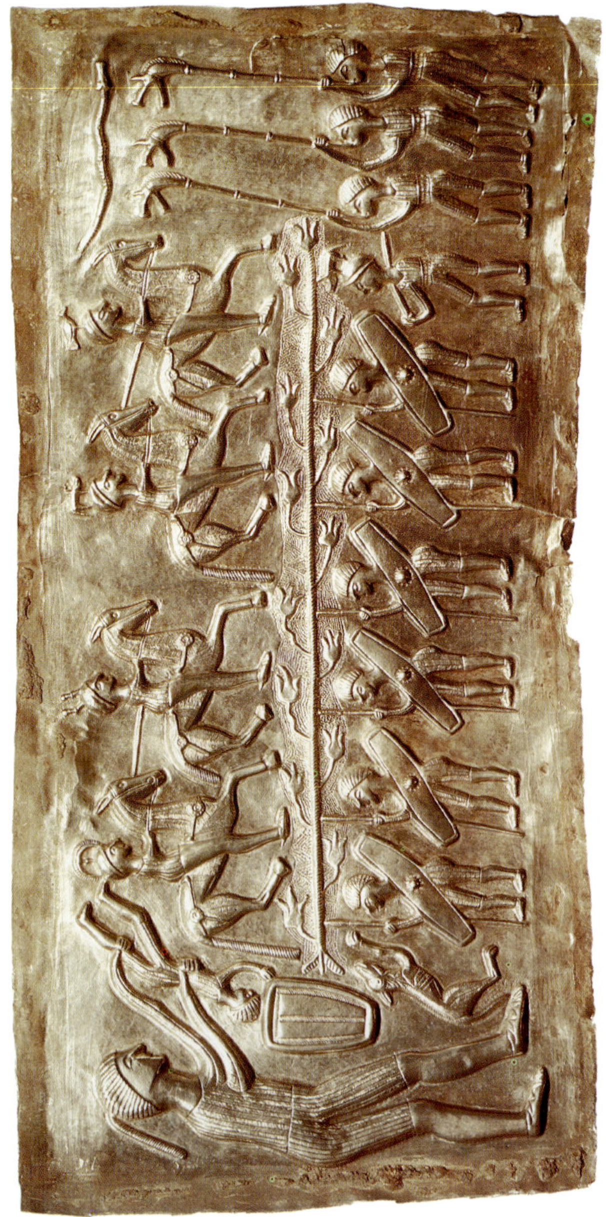

32

Turning the image upright helps us to consider its relationship with deep shafts that the Celts excavated in the earth – see **33**.

The following are some of the comments of Barry Cunliffe on such shafts:

These two shafts from the Vendée area of France date back to the Christian era. They were discovered, along with thirty others, within an area of some four square kilometers. Both shafts contained pottery and animal bones.[1]

The ritual nature of these shafts seems indisputable.[2]

While it is possible that the Celts learned the practice from the Mediterranean world, it is now clear that ritual shafts have an ancient origin in barbarian Europe and, in particular, in Britain. At Wilsford, close to Stonehenge, a shaft some thirty-four meters in depth had been cut into solid chalk in the fourteenth century BC. Although it had functioned as a well, and nothing was found in it, its size and its situation close to Stonehenge strongly suggest a religious use. Perhaps we are seeing here a combination of the superstition associated with a shaft and the belief in the special properties of spring water.[3]

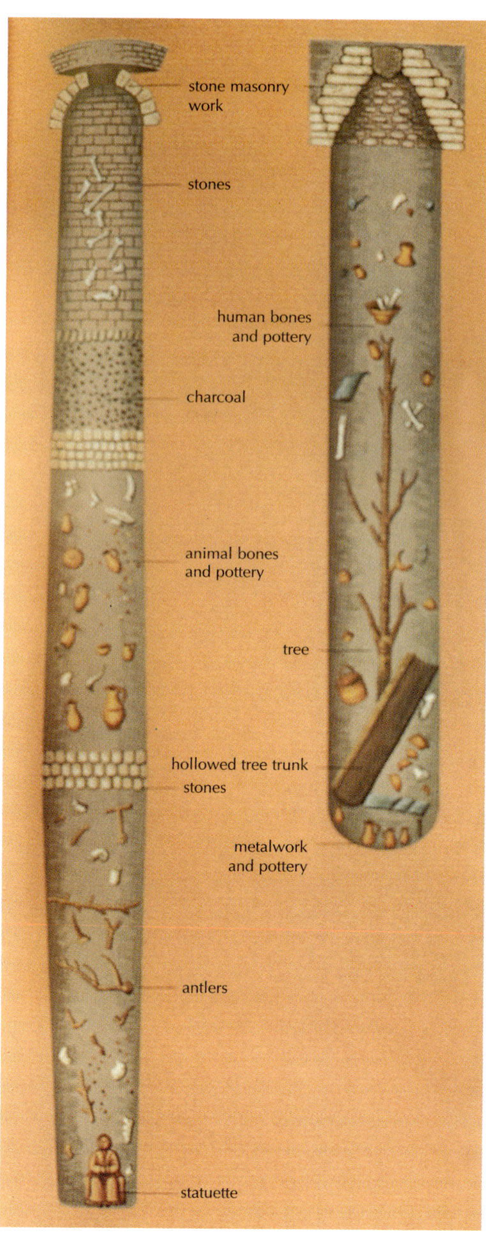

33

If we consider the importance of the Lower Region, the Deep, in the art of the Celts, Cunliffe's comments are extremely interesting. Some of the shafts go down very deep into the earth and the fact that utensils, the debris of the bodies of animals and people, and even trees of a substantial size have been found buried in them, is significant. It is not surprising that Cunliffe suggests that these shafts have religious and ritualistic connotations. The reference to trees in shafts reminds us of the importance of the tree, leaves and leafy phallic heads in so many examples of Spiritual Transformation. It is possible that the Pfalzfeld stone pillar (**17**) and the Heidelberg leafy head (**6**) may have some conceptual relationship with the ritual tree and the shaft.

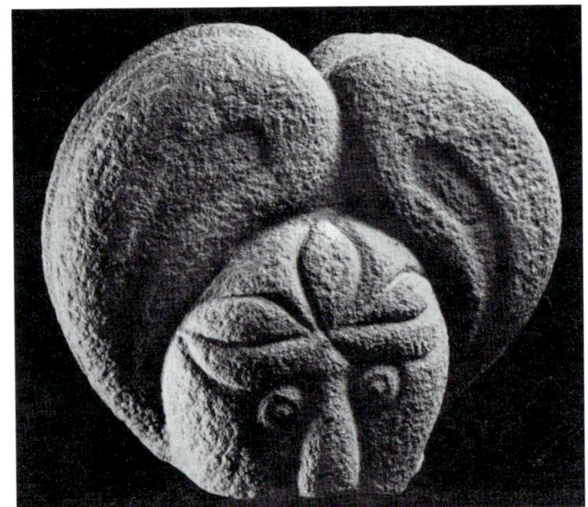

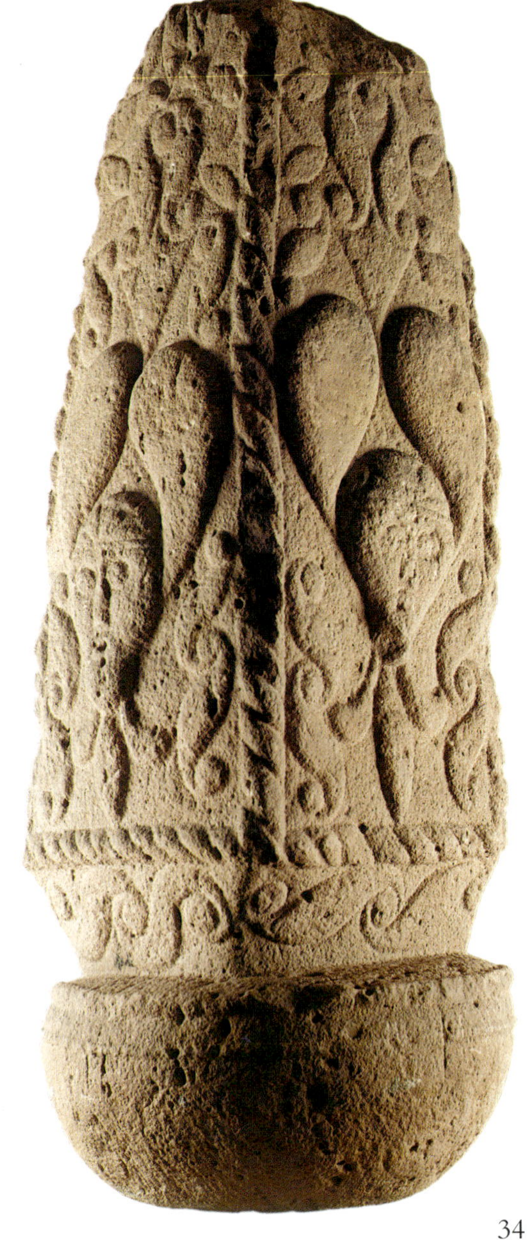

34

I suggest there is a connection between actually casting objects into the deep earth and the descent into the Deep that is conveyed in the art of the Celts. The two activities symbolise Spiritual Transformation

There is ample evidence that the Celts made votive offerings of implements etc. by casting them into subterranean places. Anne Ross and others claim that the Celts cast precious objects, such as decorated ornaments and implements, into shafts, holes in the ground, lakes and wells for religious and ritual purposes:

... the most likely reason for their presence here [lakes] is that they are yet another example of precious objects in water for religious purposes. Apart from making votive offerings in pools and lakes, the Celts put objects of a similar kind into wells and springs and into pits and shafts clearly having a comparable significance in their traditions.[4]

I suggest there is a connection between actually casting objects into the deep earth and the descent into the Deep that is conveyed in the art of the Celts. The two activities symbolise Spiritual Transformation.

It is worth associating all of this with the tradition of storytelling, especially as that tradition was preserved in Ireland – bearing in mind, of course, that early Irish tales were recorded much later than the Celtic period, and in a Christian era. Here are the comments of Alwyn and Brinley Rees on the significance of storytelling in the oral tradition of Ireland:

These stories were told around the fire to while away the long winter evenings. Old people speak of storytellers who could recite a different story every night the whole winter through, but it was unlucky to tell hero tales during day time. Apart from this regular activity of the winter season, storytelling had a recognized place on certain ceremonial occasions: during night vigils at holy wells, after 'stations' and religious services held in private houses, and at wakes and christenings.[5]

This give us some idea of the importance of tales in the life and religion of the Celts.

What tales have been preserved in the panels of the Gundestrup Cauldron? Let us consider one of these panels, **35** (overleaf).

In the centre of the panel is a figure of ritual appearance – note the ritual manner of his sitting, and note the torque about his neck and the torque in his hand. This figure provides an example of tranquil, central meditation: his eyes are the eyes of one in a trance or in deep meditation. The serpent-like shape of the arms, and the fact that he holds a serpent suggest that he feels the forces of the Deep. His horned head and his relationship with the large stag and the little – new-born, perhaps – fawn on his right side suggest that he feels the forces of life. So we have here a version of tranquil meditation and a version of the framework of Spiritual Transformation.

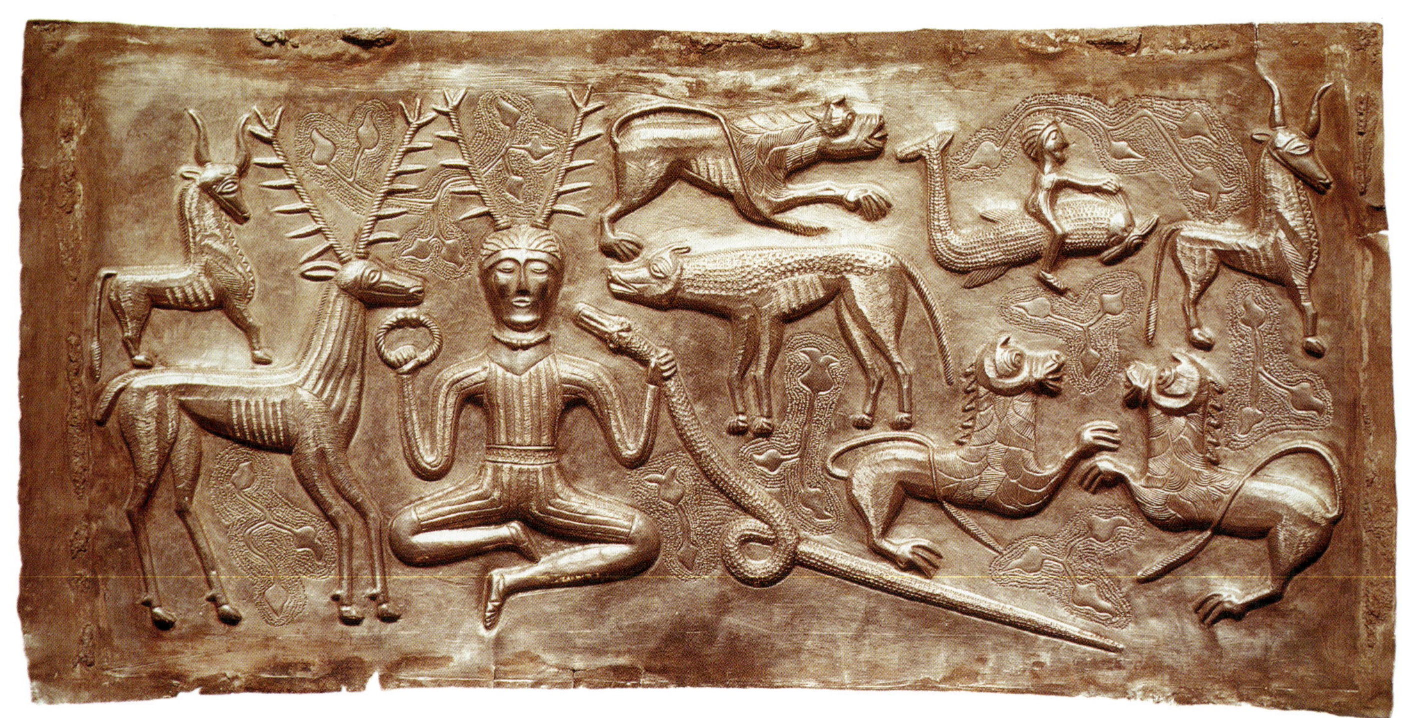

35

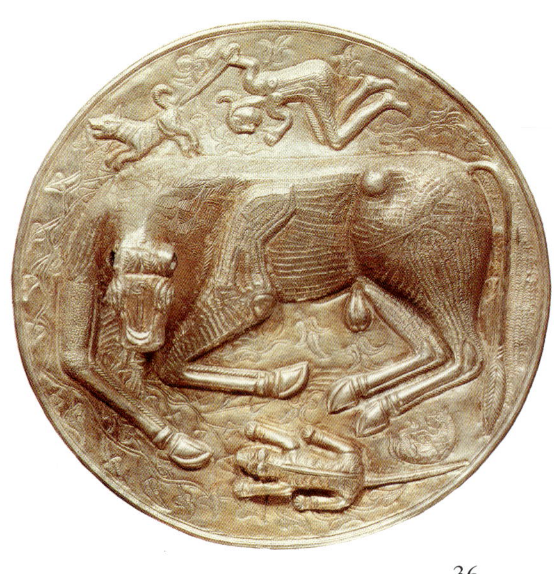

36

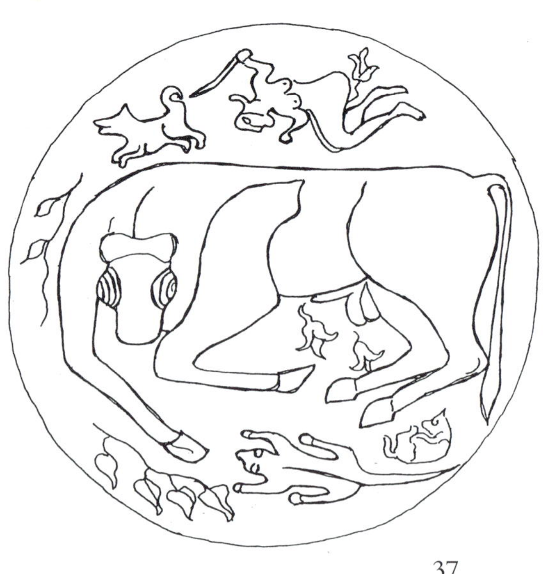

37

36

The impression given by the panels of the Gundestrup Cauldron is that they seem to have been created by an artist or artists who had heard stories being told in religious rituals, or possibly created expressly for rituals

There are still more narrative elements in the panel. Between the horns of the main figure are leaves whose shapes are agitated and magical. On the right of the panel we see two animals one above the other, one with its tail up and the other with its tail down, like a version of Ying-Yang. We observe a child mounted on a fish following a fawn.

My contention is that several of the panels on the Gundestrup Cauldron make up a series of narrative images, which may possibly be related to one another.

Let us consider another part of the Gundestrup Cauldron, namely the round panel which forms the bottom of the cauldron and which is visible as one looks down into it, **36** and **37**.

In this panel several images convey a story connected with sexual activity and birth and death. In the centre we see an enormous bull with an erect penis. Near to it, beneath its rear legs, there is a calf, apparently newly-born. Above the bull is a female with a knife in her hand – hunting a dog, or perhaps about to kill it. Beneath the bull we see a creature with its feet upwards, evocative of death. It is the Lower Region only that is represented on the bottom of the cauldron. The whole panel denotes the power of procreation, and the powers of life and death, the restless agitation of the Deep. Notice that there are leaves here as well, two clusters of three leaves beneath the belly of the bull and one near the female – the significance of the power of triads on the imagination of the Celts will be discussed later on.

In my opinion, we have a story in other panels on the cauldron, as in **38** (overleaf) for example.

In the panel on the left of the cauldron the Mother figure appears to be inviting us to her bosom, and on each side of her we see two figures with their arms held up in a ritual posture.

The impression given by the panels of the Gundestrup Cauldron is that there is, in some of them, intimations of ritual tales. They seem to have been created by an artist or artists who had heard stories being told in religious rituals, or possibly created expressly for rituals. It is likely that listening to such a tale was one method of meditating on the process of Spiritual Transformation.

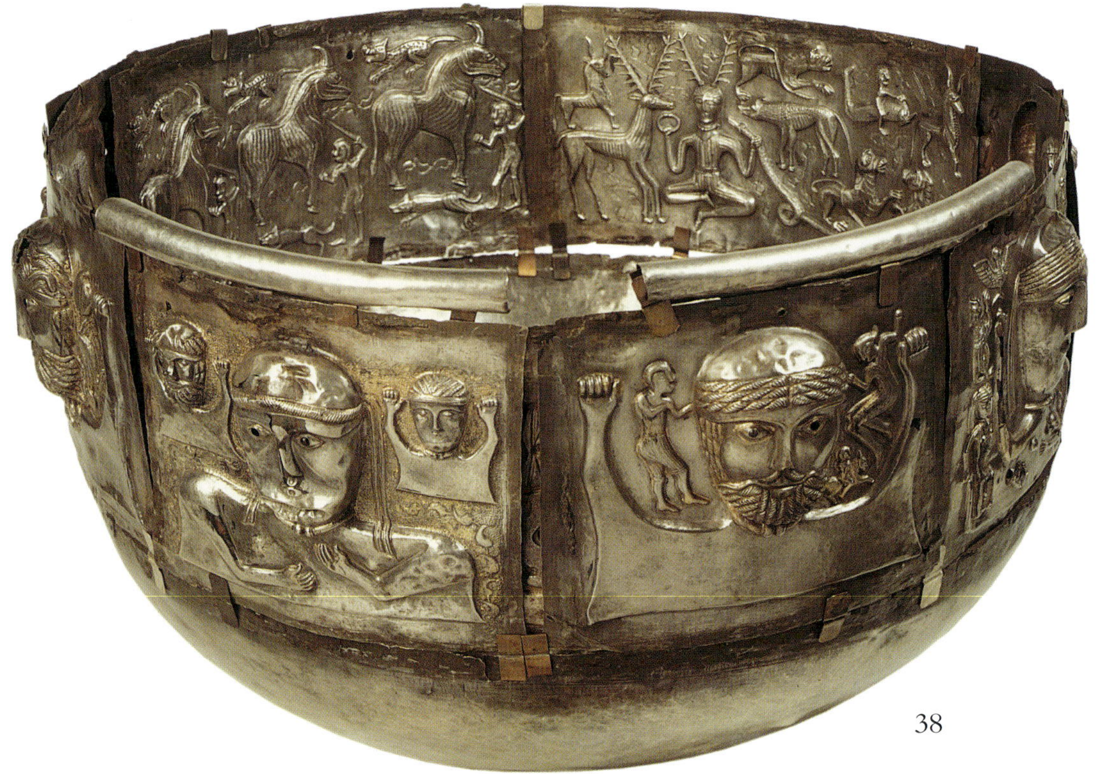

38

If we assume that some of the Celtic artworks show what I have called narrative elements of the main conception of their imagination, namely Spiritual Transformation, then we ought to take heed of Joseph Campbell's definition of the nature of oriental stories:

The supreme aim of Oriental mythology ... is not to establish as substantial any of its divinities or associated rites, but to render by means of these an experience that goes beyond: of identity with the Being of beings which is both immanent and transcendent; yet neither is nor is not. Prayers and chants, images, temples, gods, sages, definitions, and cosmologies are but ferries to a shore of experience beyond the categories of thought, to be abandoned on arrival.[6]

A tale has to impart an experience of the invisible. This is also the most important aim of Celtic art. The consistency with which the experience of Spiritual Transformation is presented in Celtic art, by means of various symbols and forms, shows how important this experience was for them.

It is likely that listening to such a tale was one method of meditating on the process of Spiritual Transformation

The concept of going through a crisis, or, to put it another way, of crossing a Borderline, occurs in many countries. This has already been referred to as *initiation*. Here is Mircea Eliade's definition of this experience:

Prayers and chants, images, temples, gods, sages, definitions, and cosmologies are but ferries to a shore of experience beyond the categories of thought, to be abandoned on arrival

The term initiation in the most general sense denoted a body of rites and oral teachings whose purpose is to produce a decisive alteration in the religious and social status of the person to be initiated. In philosophical terms, initiation is equivalent to a basic change in existential condition; the novice emerges from his ordeal endowed with a totally different being from that which he possessed before his initiation; he has become ANOTHER.[7]

The purpose of Initiation is to change someone.

Eliade says of the characteristic pattern of Initiation in early civilizations:

The majority of initiatory ordeals more or less imply a ritual death followed by resurrection or a new birth. The central moment of every initiation is represented by the ceremony symbolizing the death of the novice and his return to life a new man assuming another mode of being. Initiatory death signifies the end at once of childhood, of ignorance and of the profane condition.[8]

Initiation is an imaginative experience of death and rebirth. This is exactly what we have in the art of La Tène. According to Eliade, ritual death is represented by a variety of symbols:

Initiatory death is indispensable in relation to what it prepares: birth to a higher mode of being ... initiatory death is often symbolized, for example, by darkness, by cosmic night, by the telluric womb, the hut, the belly of a monster. All these images express regression to a preformal state, to a latent mode of being (complementary to the precosmogonic chaos), rather than total annihilation (in the sense in which, for example, a member of the modern societies conceives death). These images and symbols of ritual death are inextricably connected with germination, with embryology; they already indicate a new life in course of preparation.[9]

Eliade's comments show how common, and how essential to people's development, are experiences of symbolic death and symbolic rebirth. The complete symbolic experience re-enacts the darkness of the grave, that transmutes into the darkness of the womb, that gives way to a blossoming and a fertility, symbolising growth.

The purpose of Initiation is to change someone

Notes on page 114

5 Ritual Implements, Ritual Art, Ritual Tales

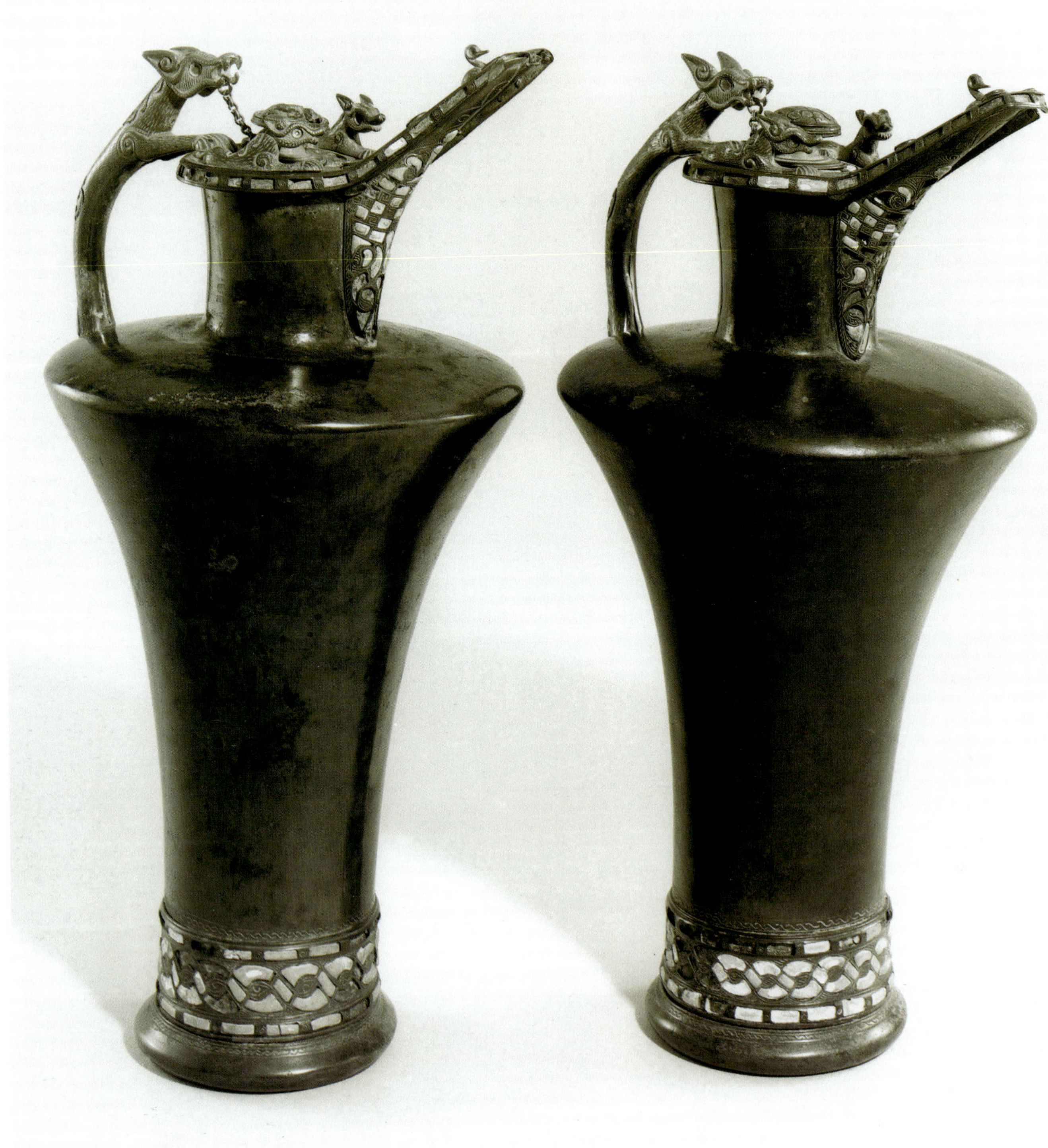

We have already mentioned that images of Spiritual Transformation are to be found on ordinary implements, like belt buckles.

In **39** we can see two wine flagons from Basse-Yutz, France. Note the two threatening dogs on either side of the flagon cover, as if they were guarding something. The third and largest, in the centre, seems to want to frighten us, indeed, its open mouth appears about to swallow us. If we are swallowed, what happens? If we look down to the bottom of its body, we can see an image of a fearful head. The dogs are ritually guarding the Deep, where Spiritual Transformation occurs.

We will recall the dogs on the Gundestrup Cauldron. The dog leads the warriors towards the Cauldron of Rebirth (Chapter 4, figure **31**). And there are the dogs that descend and ascend in figure **23**, Chapter 3. In the First Branch of the Mabinogi, magical dogs 'gleaming white with red ears' are associated with Annwn, the Other World, to which Pwyll, the Prince of Dyfed, went after his encounter with them.

Near the mouth of this wine flagon, its Borderline, a spiral can be seen on the ears of the largest dog and on other parts of its body leading down to the Deep. This enchanting and intoxicating optical device creates in us a sensation of falling down. It may be that imbibing the wine found in the Deep of the flagon was part of a ritual intoxication.

The pattern on the flagon leads down the dog into the Deep. There we experience a feeling of fear and terror, conveyed on the face of the head with its large eyes – not unlike the eyes of an owl at night, **40**. There is also an intoxicating sensation of a release downwards. All this represents the experience of dying.

Is there any representation here of the experience of ascent, of rebirth? There is a suggestion of an ascent up the spout of the flagon. On that spout we see a tranquil symbol of a water bird, like a duck or a small goose, probably newly-born. This bird creates an uplifting connection with the sky by its wings: it also has a connection with water because it is a water bird. This signifies rebirth.

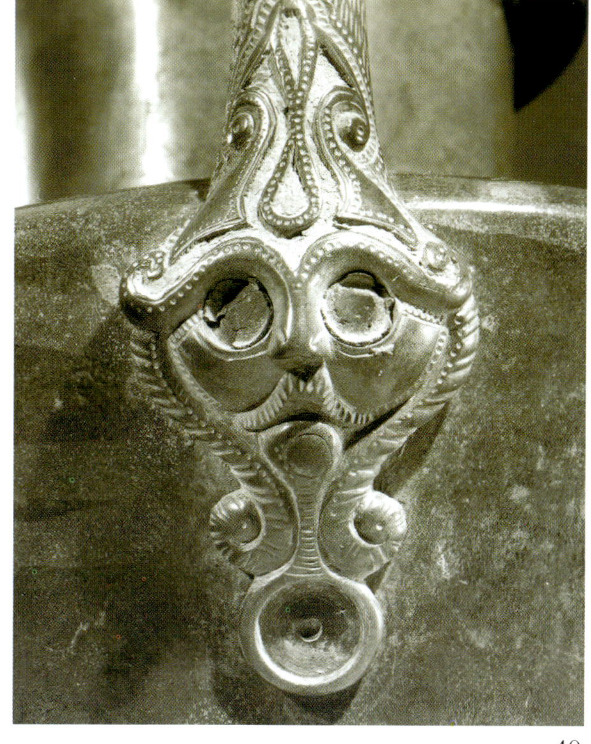

40

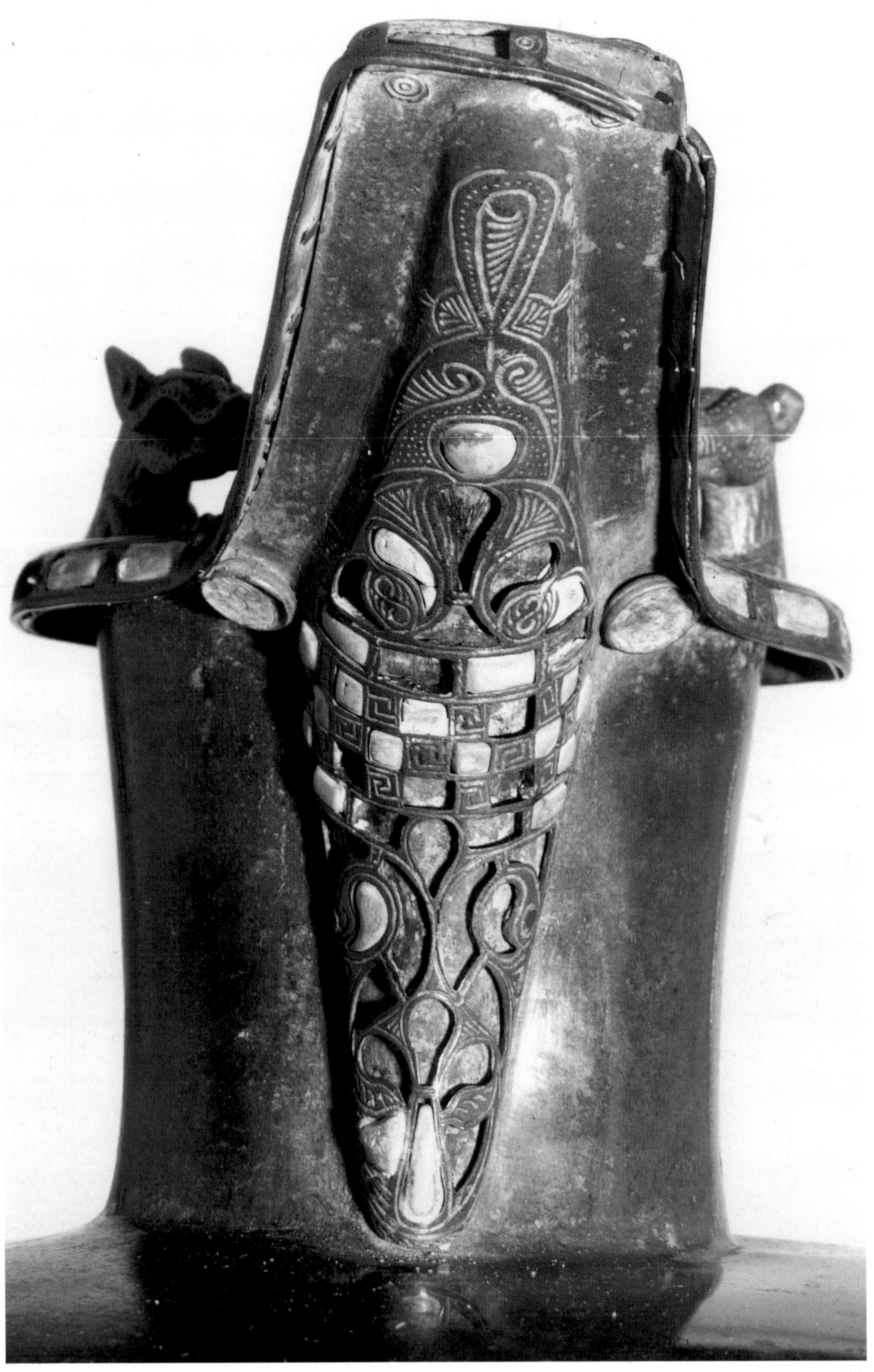

But there is another and a different representation of Transformation on the flagon. In **41** we have a symbolic image of the Mother.

Her big mouth suggests that she, too, has the ability to swallow. Note that her body is pear-shaped: this implies that she is pregnant. But there is also a suggestion of a plant in her figure – signified by the leaves on the upper and lower parts of her body. On the body itself there is a maze of angular and spiral lines, a means of conveying the agitated unease of the Deep. At the bottom of her body there are three light leaves like three balloons suggesting the beginning of an ascent through the maze back to the leafy head and to the spout of the flagon.

Many methods and techniques have been used to convey Spiritual Transformation, to convey the experience of Initiation. A narrative and an artistic method have been used. As for artistic techniques, we see that forms and shapes have been used consciously, as well as a number of optical techniques, such as a spiral, a maze and magical eyes.

Let us consider other flagons. Figures **42–44** show reproductions of a wine flagon from Dürnberg in Austria.

Many methods and techniques have been used to convey Spiritual Transformation, to convey the experience of Initiation

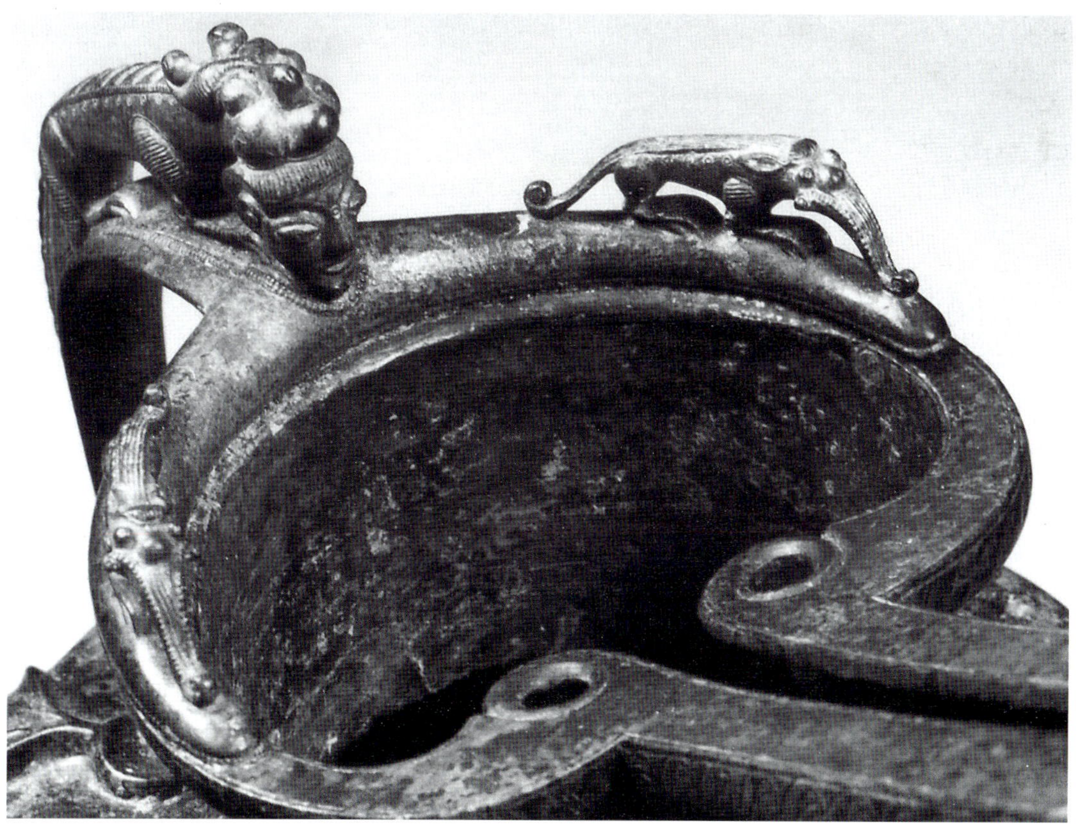

42

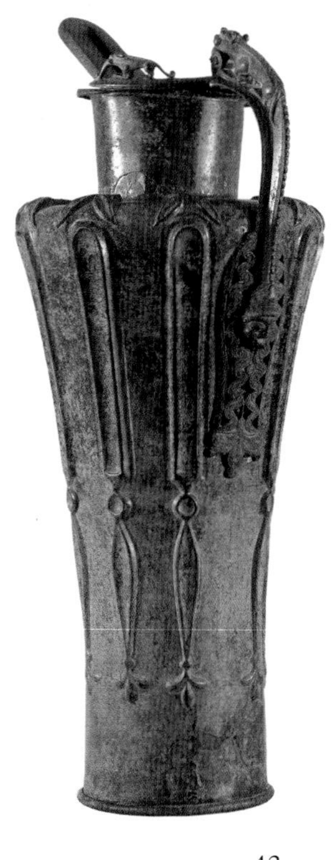

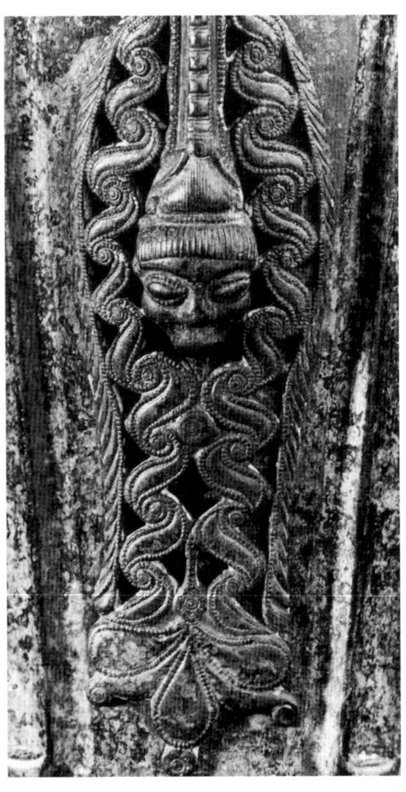

43   44

Swallowing and descent are clearly presented here. Once again, we see three animals in a formal, ritual posture. One large animal with enormous eyes is flanked by two small animals. All of them are on the mouth of the flagon, that is, on the Borderline of the Deep. We find optical techniques here as well – the repetition of a leaf form in the shape of the letter 'S'. This creates a sensation of going up or down in the Deep. The technique creates an intoxicating optical effect – **44** (and **30**).

Figures **45–48** present various aspects of a flagon from Reinheim in Germany.

One of the most striking features of this flagon is the man-horse on its lid. He has a dignified, formal presence, and his face gives an impression of tranquil meditation. The shape of the flagon suggests pregnancy (**46**). On top of the handle there is a leafy, uplifted head (**48**); there are leafy spirals on the head at the base to convey excitement (**44**). The whole conveys Spiritual Transformation. The result of this Transformation is the state of meditation presented by the man-horse.

Experiences like Spiritual Transformation or Initiation are expressed through the artwork on the flagons we have been discussing. These experiences are remarkably similar to what happens in some shamanistic rituals. The shaman is a kind of *gŵr hysbys* (lit. 'one in the know'). Here is Mircea Eliade's essential definition of shamanism:

A first definition of this complex phenomenon, and perhaps the least hazardous, will be: shamanism = technique of ecstasy.[1]

I believe that the main
purpose of the flagons
we have been
discussing is to remind
us of the ritual of
Initiation. It is likely
that tales, especially
those suggested by the
images on the flagons,
were familiar to those
who used them,
especially to the priests
(or shamans) of the
Celts who carried out
the rituals

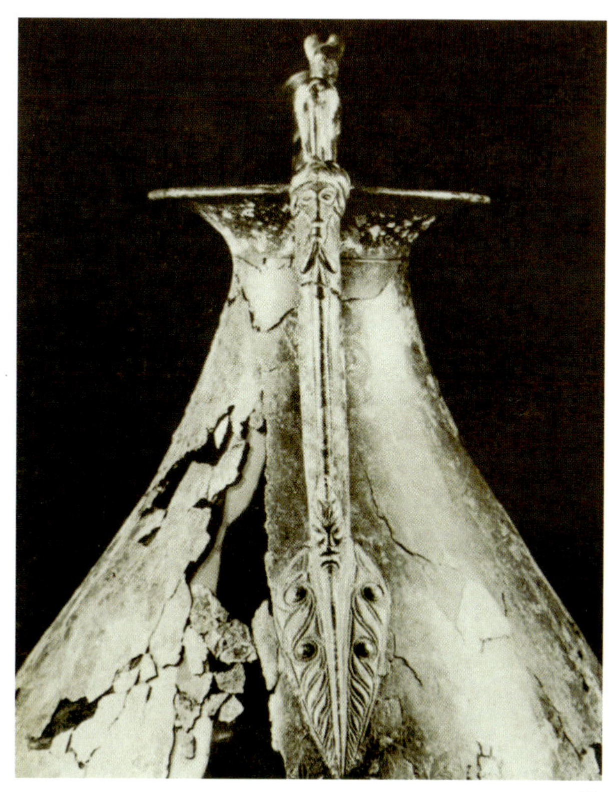

45

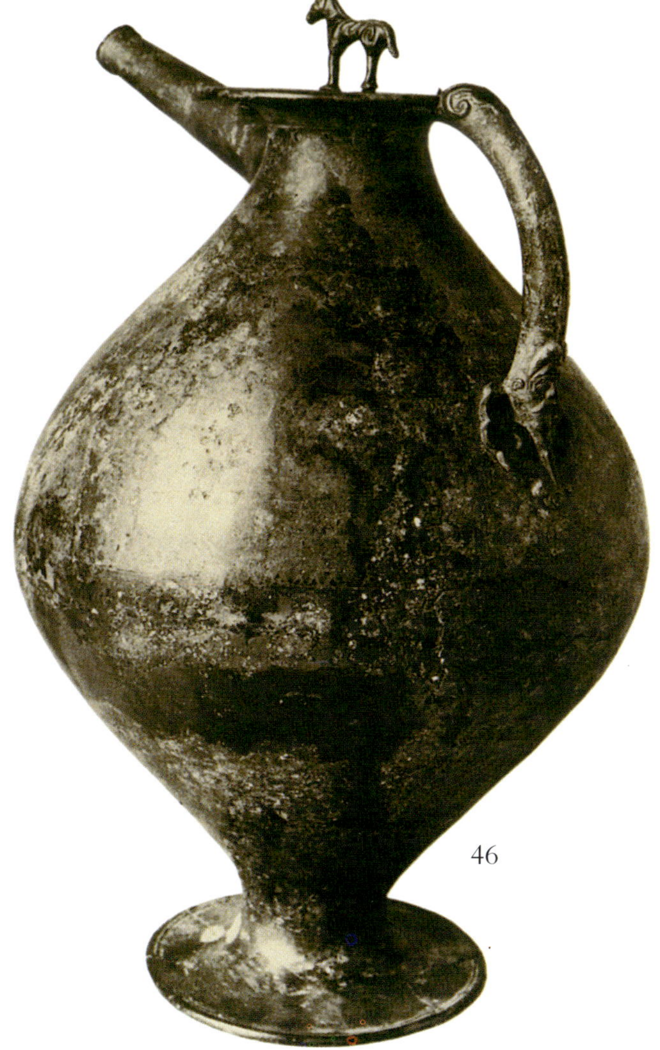

46

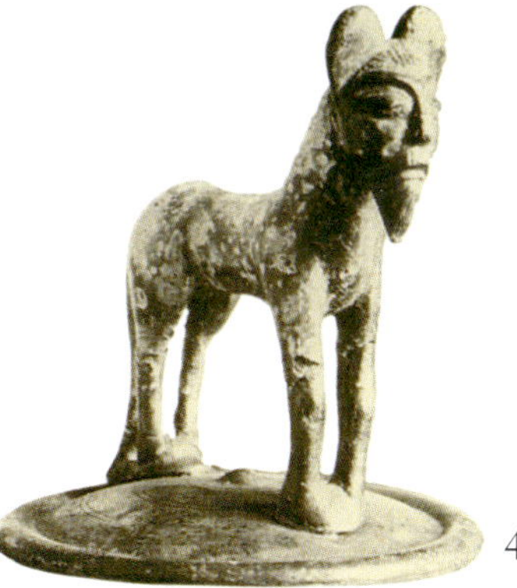

47

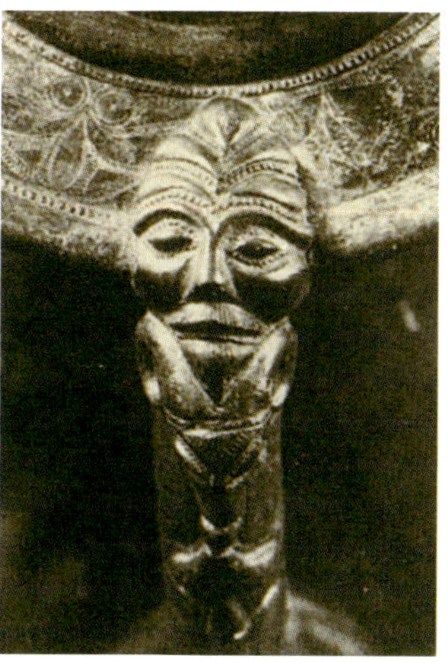

48

We have made several references to meditation or trance whilst discussing Celtic heads; we have mentioned the soul's journey over the Borderline of two worlds; mentioned hypnotic, magical eyes; the agitation caused by spirals, and referred to maze patterns. It is not claimed that all of these are features of shamanism, but it is worth turning again to some of Eliade's comments on shamanism:

... though the shaman is, among other things, a magician, not every magician can properly be termed a shaman. The same distinction must be applied in regard to shamanic healing; every medicine man is a healer, but the shaman employs a method that is his alone. As for the shamanic technique of ecstasy, they do not exhaust all the varieties of ecstatic experience documented in the history of religions and religious ethology. Hence any ecstatic cannot be considered a shaman; the shaman specializes in a trance during which his soul is believed to leave his body and ascend to the sky or descend to the underworld.[2]

Magic and the soul's journey to places above and below are mentioned here, features that are familiar to us already. We realize that such features are part of the ethology or formation of religion.

According to Eliade, Initiation rituals were common, especially in Siberia and Central Asia:

We have several times observed the initiatory essence of the candidate's 'death' followed by his 'resurrection', in whatever form this takes place – ecstatic dream, sickness, unusual events, or ritual proper. Indeed, ceremonies implying passages from one age group to another, or admission into some 'secret society', always presuppose a series of rites that can be summarized in the convenient formula: death and resurrection of the candidate.[3]

An imaginative experience of death, and an experience of rebirth: both are present in the art of La Tène and in shamanism. The experience is present in various religions and Initiation rituals. Is there such a thing as Indo–European shamanism? Here are Eliade's comments:

But is it possible to speak of an Indo-European shamanism in the sense in which we speak of an Altaic or Siberian shamanism? The answer to this question depends partly on the meaning that we give to 'shamanism'. If we understand by it any ecstatic phenomenon and any magical technique whatever, it goes without saying that a number of 'shamanic' features will be found among the Indo-Europeans, just as, to repeat, they will be found among other ethnic or cultural group.[4]

I suggest that the 'tales' in this art are examples
of the ritual method of Initiation

I believe that the main purpose of the flagons we have been discussing is to remind us of the ritual of Initiation. It is likely that tales, especially those suggested by the images on the flagons, were familiar to those who used them, especially to the priests (or shamans) of the Celts who carried out the rituals. I have emphasized that there are narrative or story features in some of the works discussed. On either side of the Tal-y-llyn plaque below (**50**) are two examples of narrative art (**49** and **51**).

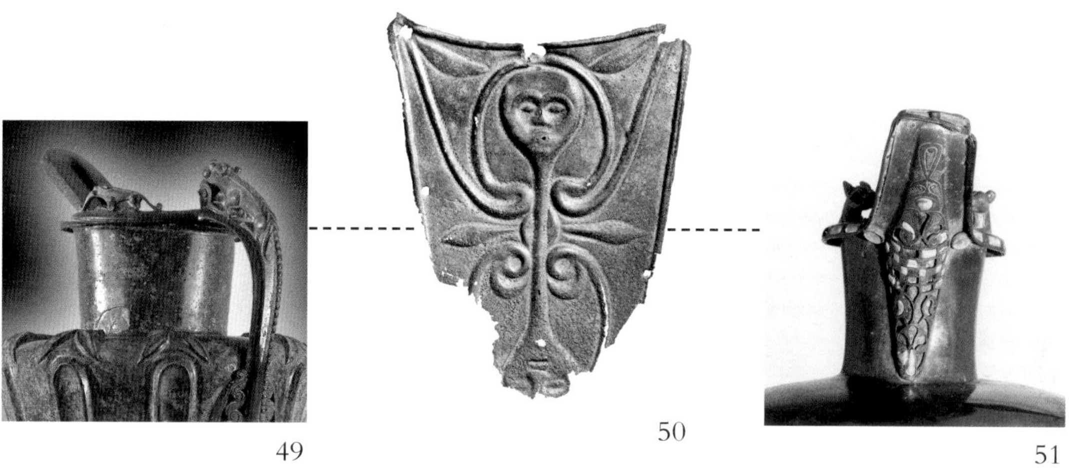

49

50

51

On the Tal-y-llyn plaque we have the basic framework of the Upper Region, the Borderline, and the Deep. In the two other works we have versions of the framework which are closer to narrative. On them we have a confrontation with a monster and a confrontation with the great Mother, conveying the sensation of being swallowed by them, so that we go down into the Deep, before coming up, born again.

I suggest that the 'tales' in this art are examples of the ritual method of Initiation. The purpose of some tales has been explained in this way by the Rees brothers:

... these were originally religious stories which were believed to have a liberating effect upon their hearers. We have inferred that it was appropriate to recount them at birth of human children and have suggested that they had validity as exemplars in the light of which the meaning of ordinary births could be apprehended. But they were not patterns to be emulated in real life. To resolve the paradox the myths must be regarded as symbols of the transcendental meaning of birth, of which birth is seen from the point of the unseen world.[6]

Note the reference to religious tales having a 'liberating effect', and the fact that the tales do not contain patterns to be imitated, but symbols of the transcendental birth. This is exactly what we have in the art that I am discussing.

Let us examine an example of a Welsh tale about Initiation, the Tale of Taliesin. Here is a summary of it. I have put in bold letters some details which are similar to those found in the art of La Tène.

Near Bala Lake a witch called Ceridwen lived with her husband, Tegid. She had a son called Morfran, the ugliest man in the world – he was so ugly that he was given the nickname Afagddu (Hell). In order to compensate for his ugliness Ceridwen decided to make him omniscient. She gathered special herbs and put them in a **CAULDRON** and employed two men, Blind Morda and Little Gwion, to boil the mixture in it. This work would last for a year and a day. At the end of this period all the virtue of the mixture would be contained in **THREE DROPS**. A short time before the end of the period Ceridwen placed her ugly son on the spot where the **THREE DROPS** would fall on him, then she settled down and slept. Little Gwion pushed Morfran from the crucial spot and stood there himself. The **THREE DROPS** shot out of the **CAULDRON** and fell on his finger which he promptly put in his mouth and **SWALLOWED**. By doing this he became omniscient. The **CAULDRON** split and what spilt out was pure poison.

The omniscient Gwion – who knew what had been, what is, and what will be – realized that he was in danger, for Ceridwen would soon wake up, so he fled.

And, indeed, Ceridwen did wake up; she realized what had happened and set off in pursuit of Gwion. He **TRANSFORMED** himself into a hare to get away from her: she **TRANSFORMED** herself into a greyhound bitch. On seeing her draw nearer to him Gwion **TRANSFORMED** himself into a fish: she **TRANSFORMED** herself into an otter bitch. She drew nearer and nearer to him and he **TRANSFORMED** himself into a bird: she **TRANSFORMED** herself into a hawk. She was about to catch him when he dropped into a heap of grain in a barnyard and **TRANSFORMED** himself into a seed of grain: she **TRANSFORMED** herself into a black, red-crested hen and **SWALLOWED** him.

In nine months' time what had been **SWALLOWED** was **REBORN**. The new-born baby was so beautiful that even the livid Ceridwen could not kill him. He was placed in a leather bag and cast into Bala Lake. On the **FIRST OF MAY** Elffin, one of the courtiers of King Maelgwn of Gwynedd, fished out the bag, opened it, saw the beautiful forehead of the **THREE-DAY-OLD** baby inside and said, 'Here's a beautiful forehead,' in Welsh 'Tâl Iesin'.
'LET IT BE TALIESIN,' said the baby, naming himself.

Elffin took baby Taliesin home to the court of his father Gwyddno. He asked the wonder baby, 'Let me know what you can do'. The reply was, '**ALL THE ARTS OF THE WORLD ARE IN FORCE IN MY BELLY, FOR I KNOW WHAT HAS BEEN AND WHAT WILL SOON BE.**'

We shall leave the tale here. It is a story about ritual Initiation. It is Ceridwen, who is a witch (or a female shaman) who carries out the rite. She owns the cauldron. She causes the magic herbs to be prepared. She swallows a form of Gwion to transform him into another being, Taliesin.

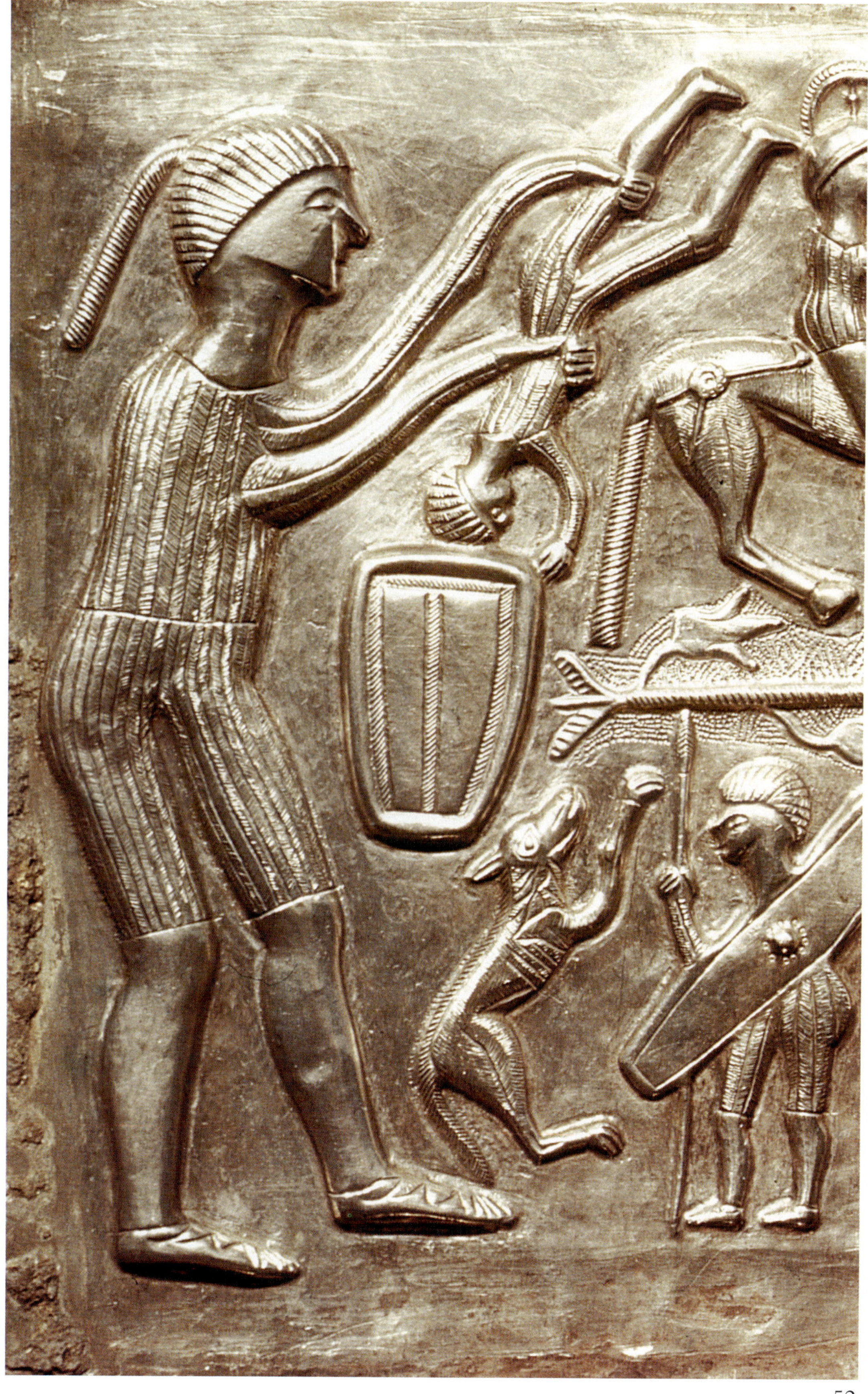

52

Little Gwion faces terrifying experiences. He is almost killed many times, he transforms himself into the shapes of various animals. He goes down into the Deep through being swallowed by Ceridwen, and he comes up again reborn, as Taliesin, who knew what had been, what is, and soon will be. He is one who has attained a state of tranquil, timeless meditation that we find in some of the Celtic heads we have discussed, the head on the Gundestrup Cauldron (figure **23**), for example, or the leafy head of Waldalgesheim (figure **1**).

Other Welsh tales which suggest Initiation and present experiences similar to those conveyed by the art of La Tène could have been discussed. The tale of Pwyll, Prince of Dyfed, the First Branch of the Mabinogi, for example. He reaches a glade, encounters hounds from the Other World, visits that world and returns from there having been transformed. Or the tale of Lleu Llaw Gyffes, of the Fourth Branch of the Mabinogi, who experiences a kind of 'death' and is transformed into an eagle before returning as a successful lord.

In this chapter we have seen an experience of Initiation presented on wine flagons from the La Tène period (as in **52**), it has been suggested that Initiation is presented in tales, and it has also been suggested that this Initiation is not very different from a shamanistic rite.

We shall conclude with another comment from the Rees brothers:

There is evidence from Celtic countries and from India that the poets were also the official historians and the royal genealogists. The poet's praises confirmed and sustained the king in his kingship, while his satire could blast both the king and his kingdom ... Such priestly functions as divination and prophecy also came within the province of these early ... poets who, it may be added, wore cloaks of bright feathers as do shamans of Siberia when, through ritual and trance, they conduct their audiences on journeys to another world. It was initiates with their power and authority who had the custody of the original tales, and they recited them on auspicious occasions, even as the priests of other religions recite their scriptures.[7]

Notes on page 114

6 The Significance of Celtic Torques

So far, we have seen torques around the necks of figures. We have suggested that the torque around the neck represents the Borderline between the Upper Region and the Deep. In this chapter we shall put forward another proposition: the torque is, in itself, a representation of the cycle of Spiritual Transformation, the cycle of Initiation.

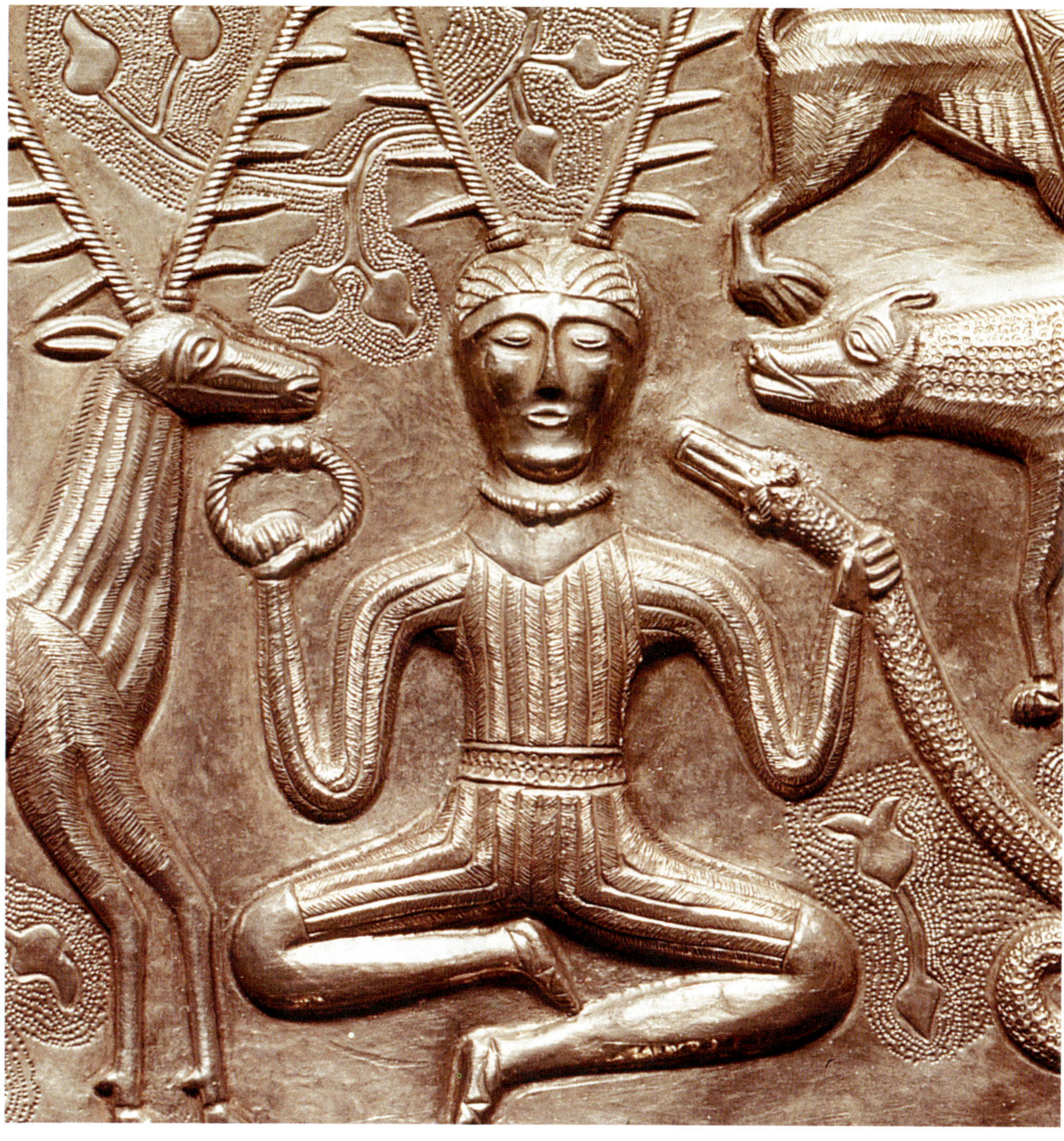

53

The torque is, in itself, a representation of the cycle of Spiritual Transformation, the cycle of Initiation

The two diagrams (**54** and **55**) show what is meant.

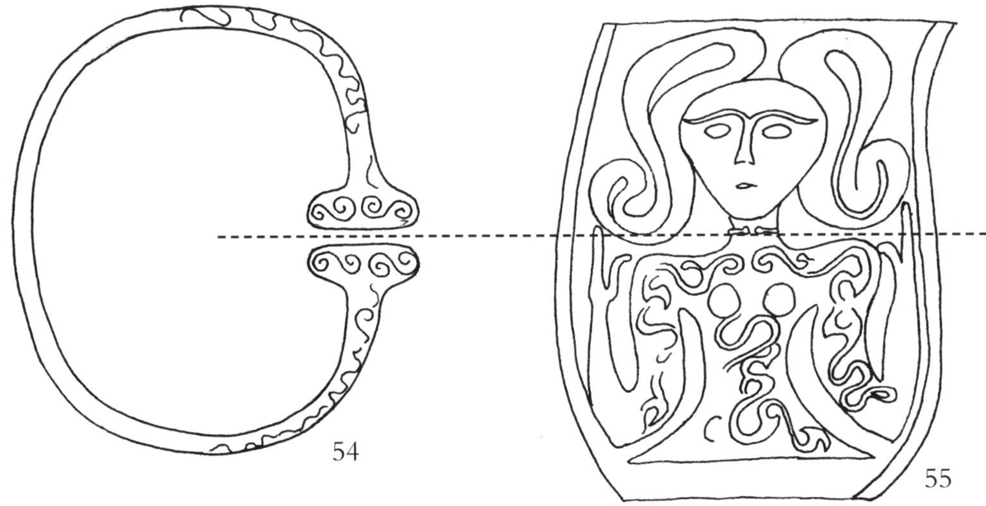

Figure **55** shows the experience of Spiritual Transformation in a way that is, by now, familiar to the reader. Figure **54** represents the experience in the form of a torque.

The torque in **56** is a symbol of the completion of Spiritual Transformation, or the process of Initiation.

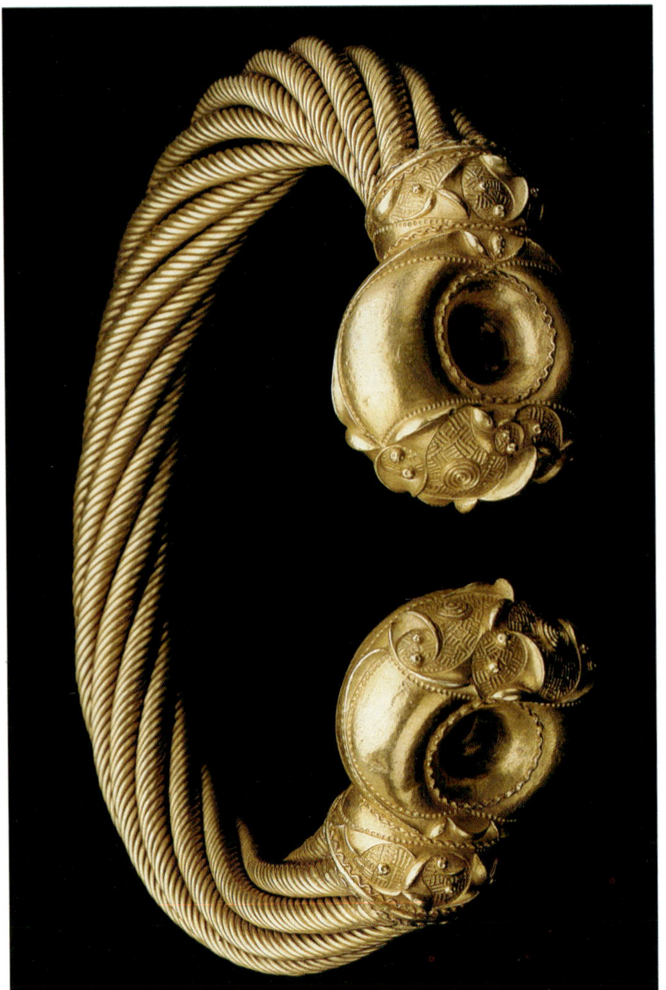

It is worn by those who have been through the process, whether they are priests (or shamans) or poets. Wearing the torque is an honour

It is worn by those who have been through the process, whether they are priests (or shamans) or poets. Wearing the torque is an honour. Note the ritual dignity of the two Mothers, one on a panel from the Gundestrup Cauldron (**57** right), the other on the sculpture from Waldalgesheim (figures **55** and **1**).

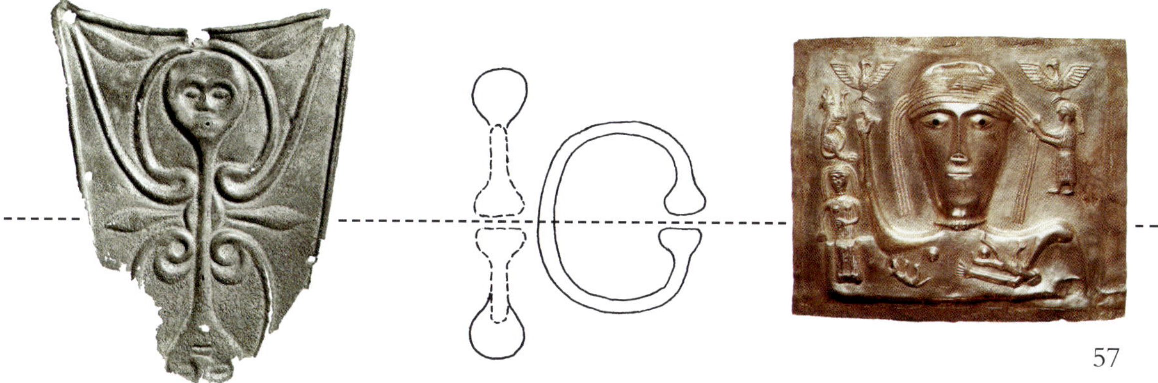

57

They have attained a state of tranquil meditation, having been through the experience of Spiritual Transformation.

Let us consider some examples of torques and bracelets. Figure **58** shows a photograph of a torque and bracelets from Waldalgesheim.

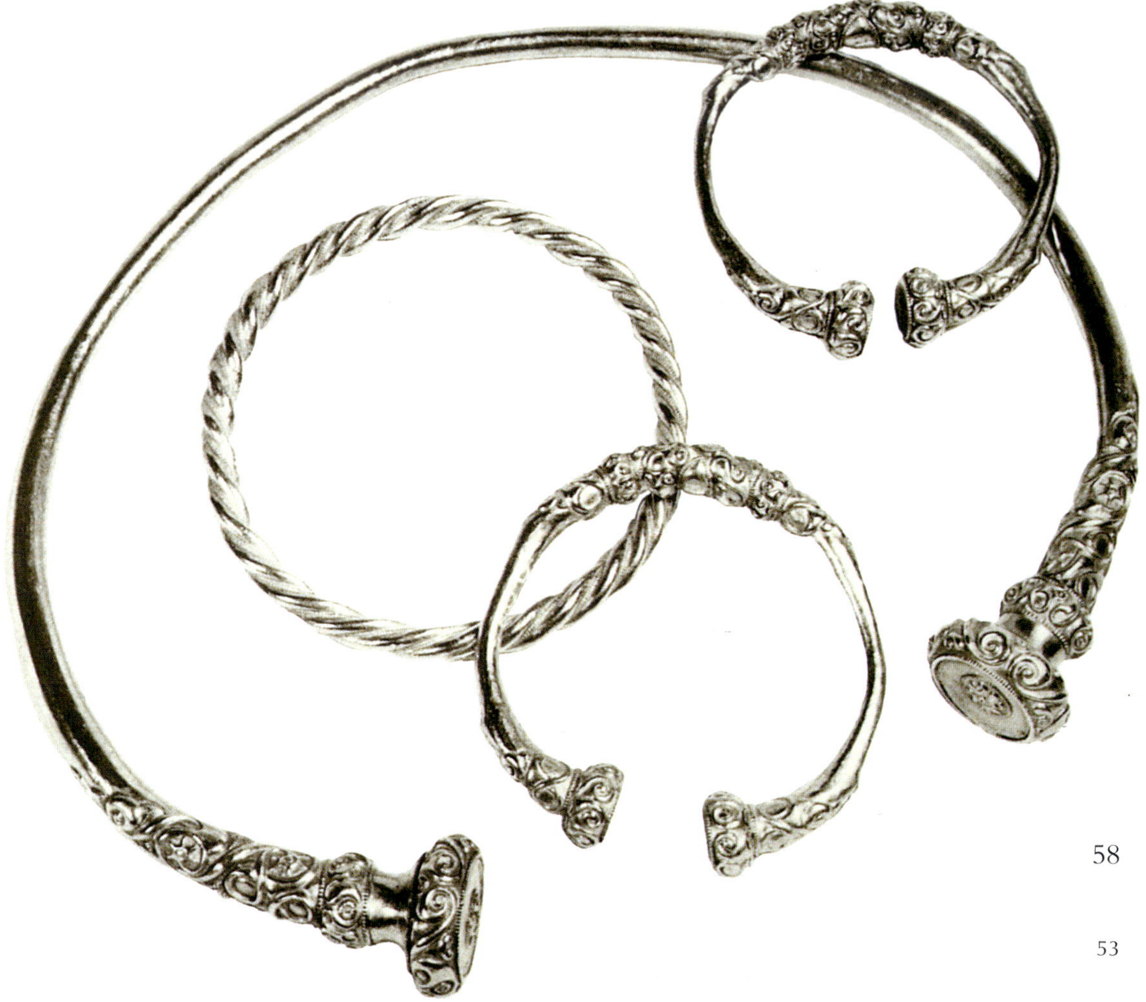

58

These will be examined in more detail in **59** and **60**. In both examples, two heads meet on a Borderline. In both, there are spirals that suggest excitement.

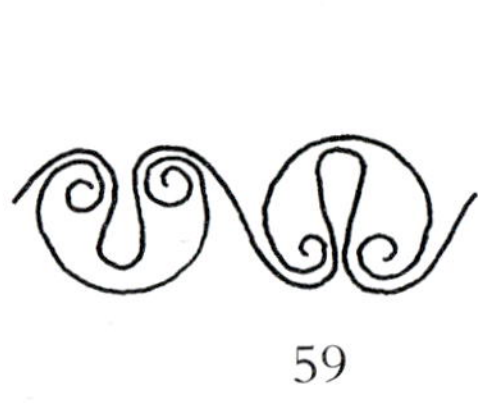

59

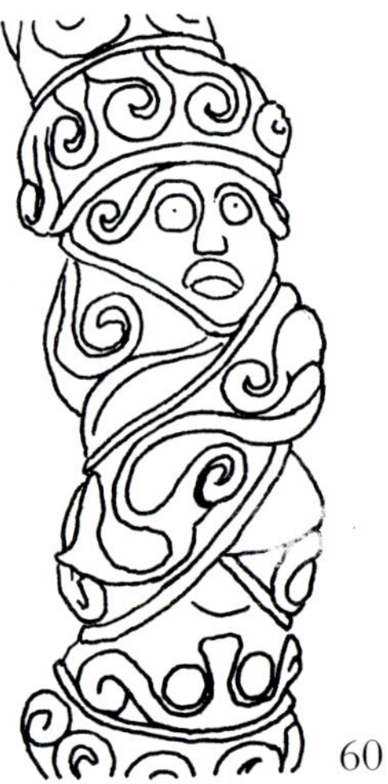

60

The torques and bracelets from Reinheim (**61**, **62** and **63**) are in a symbolic style. They are less abstract than figures **58–60**, but they are equally exciting.

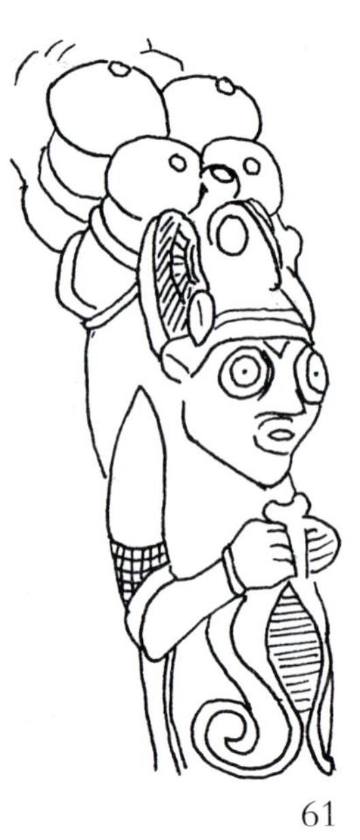

61

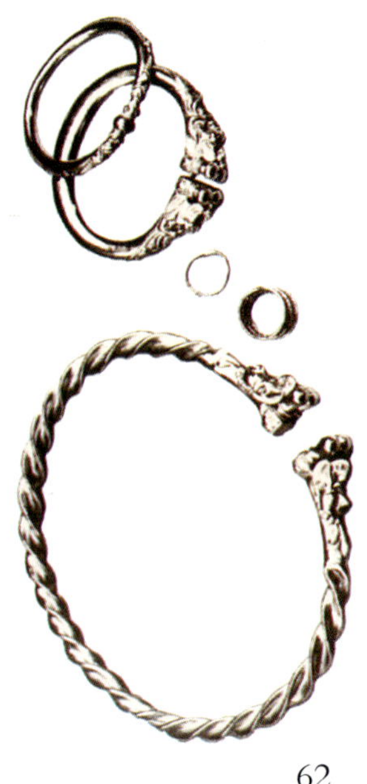

62

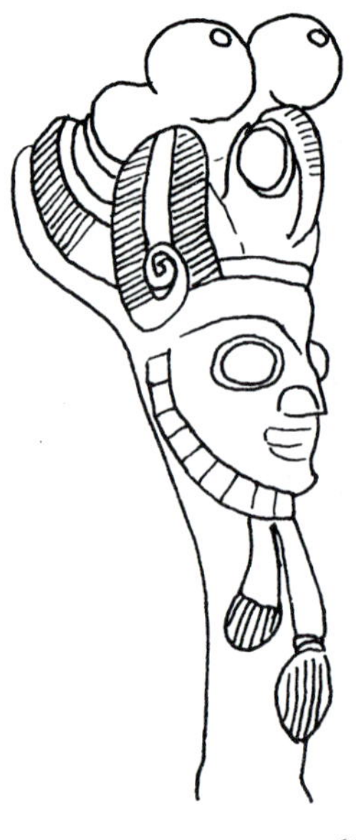

63

On the heads there are patterns like breasts that emerge from a woman, and a bird – one that is like an owl. There is a spiral on the Lower Region of the female. The framework of the bracelets is similar. Indeed, the same framework is also found on rings.

The same framework is found on the bronze torque from Dumfries (**64**) although the pattern is of an unusual form.

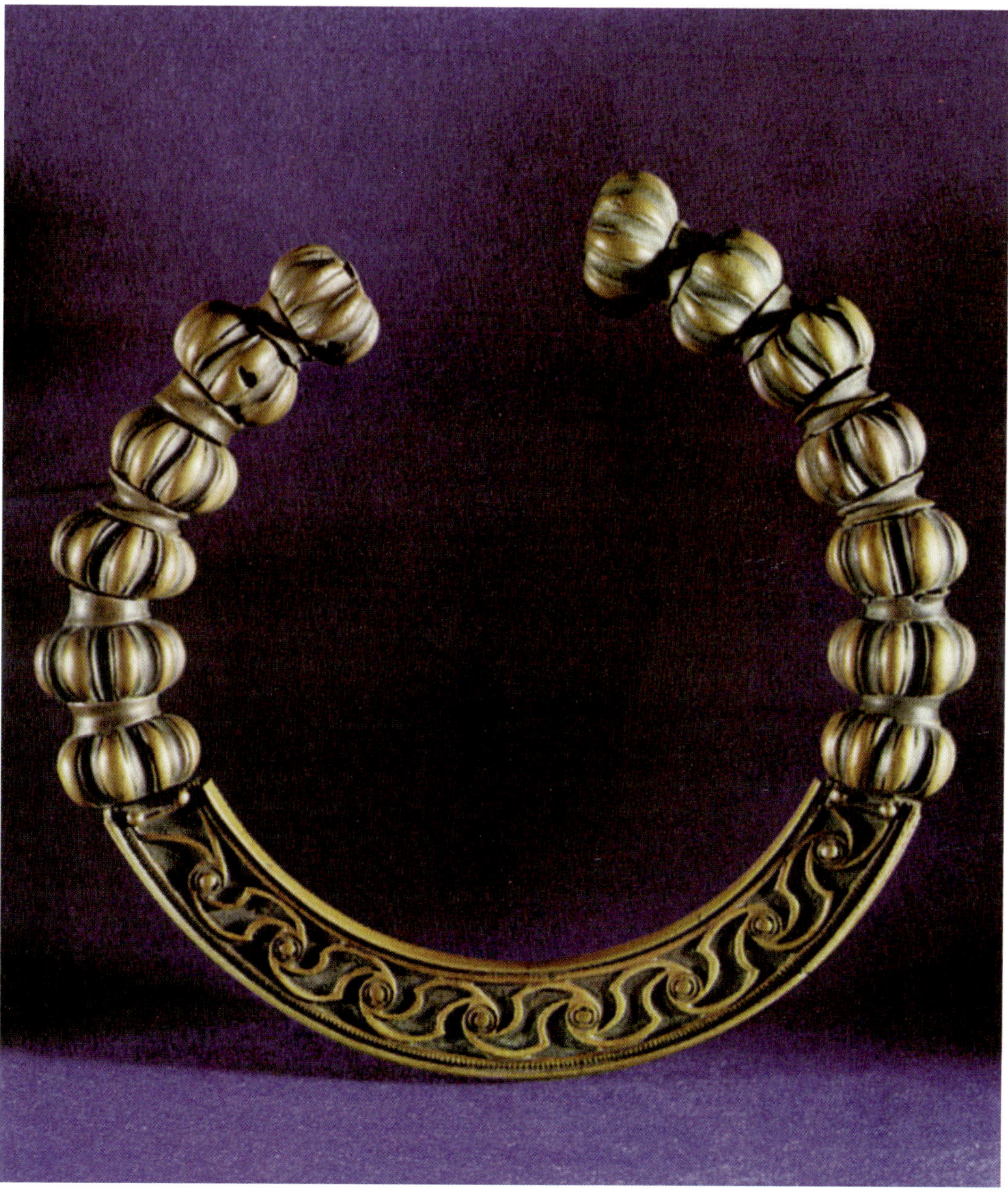

64

The two terminals appear as six extremities and seven extremities, with a spiral upon a flat piece of bronze between them.

On the gold torques from Ipswich (**65** and **66**) there are restless wire lines in spirals around a strong circle.

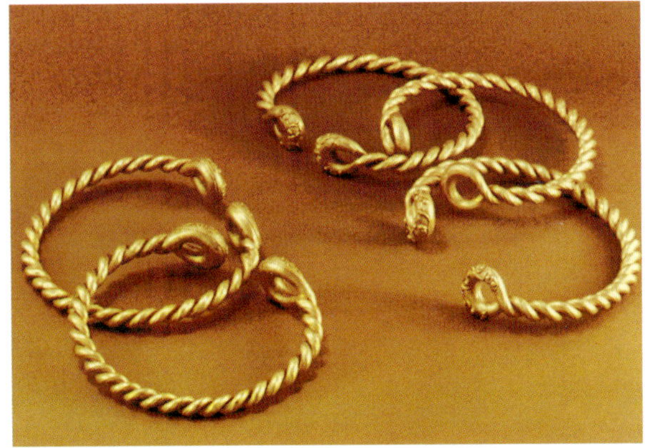

65

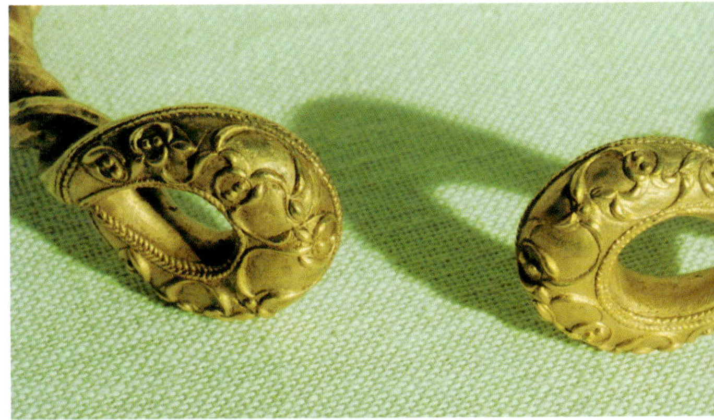

66

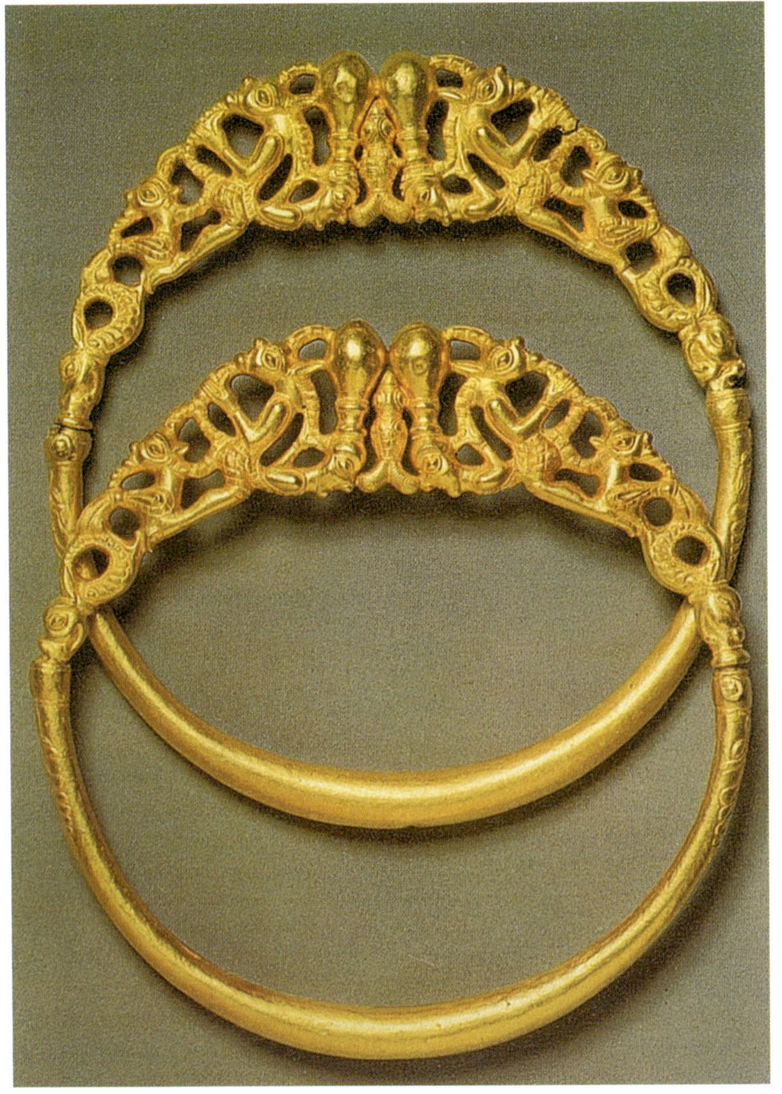

67

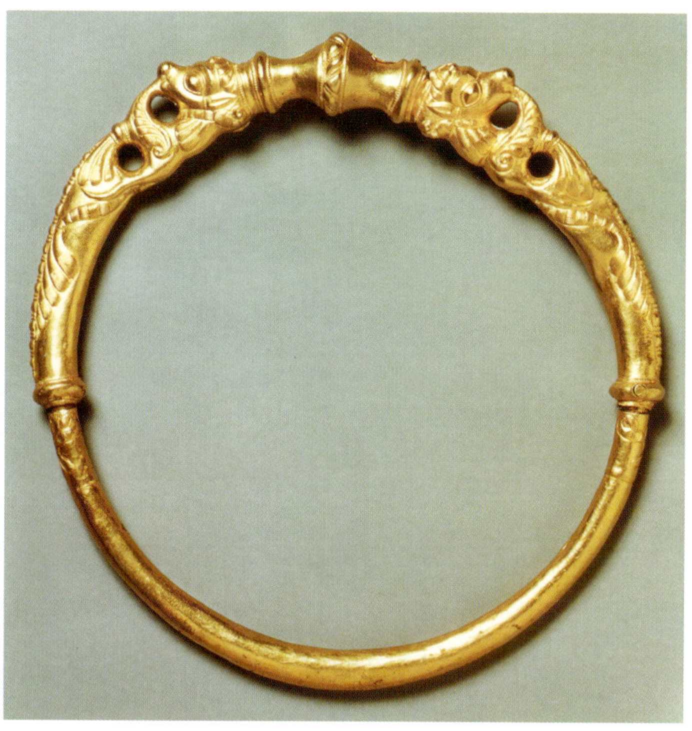

68

Figures **67** and **68** show three torques from Switzerland.

The framework is more of a narrative in these. On torques **67** there are two heads downwards, and two upwards. The former represent the descent to death; and the latter the ascent to life. Torque **68** has two human heads among wings, an image which represents the experience of ascent, the rebirth. These torques denote descent and ascent, the two aspects of Spiritual Transformation.

Figure **69** shows a figure wearing a torque. Beneath the Borderline on the torque there is a two-headed creature swallowing human figures – this represents the experience of being swallowed by death. Above the Borderline we see the upraised arms of a being that holds two vanquished creatures: this symbolizes that the might of the destroyers has been overcome.

In all of these torques Spiritual Transformation is usually represented by two heads, and by a spiral. Wearing a torque is a sign of attaining a state of tranquil meditation. One could expand by tracking down the various styles that various tribes had for representing the Transformation. And one could hazard a guess that the most sophisticated torques conferred a higher status than those that are more plain.

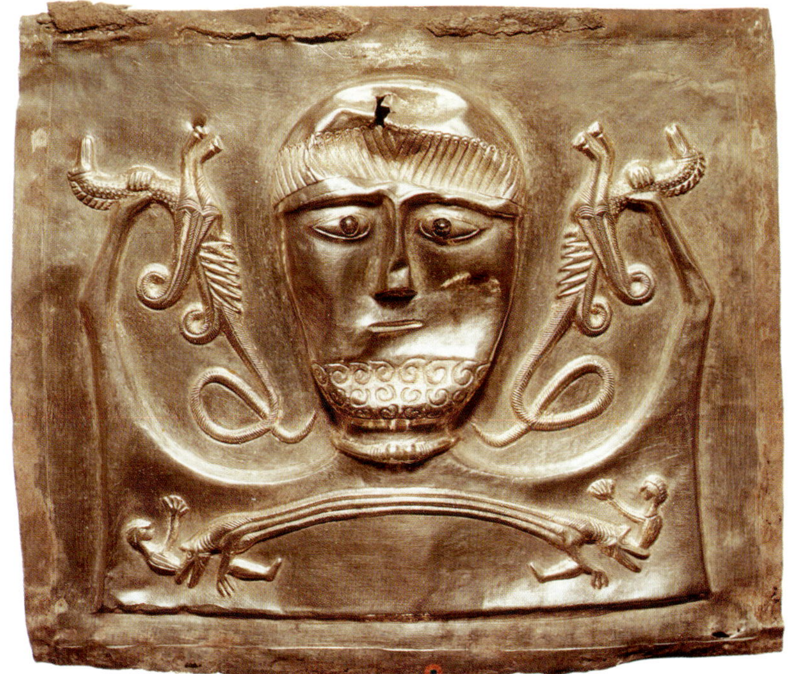

69

Dualities

What needs to be emphasized is the prominence of duality in the imagination of the Celts, as that imagination is manifested in their art

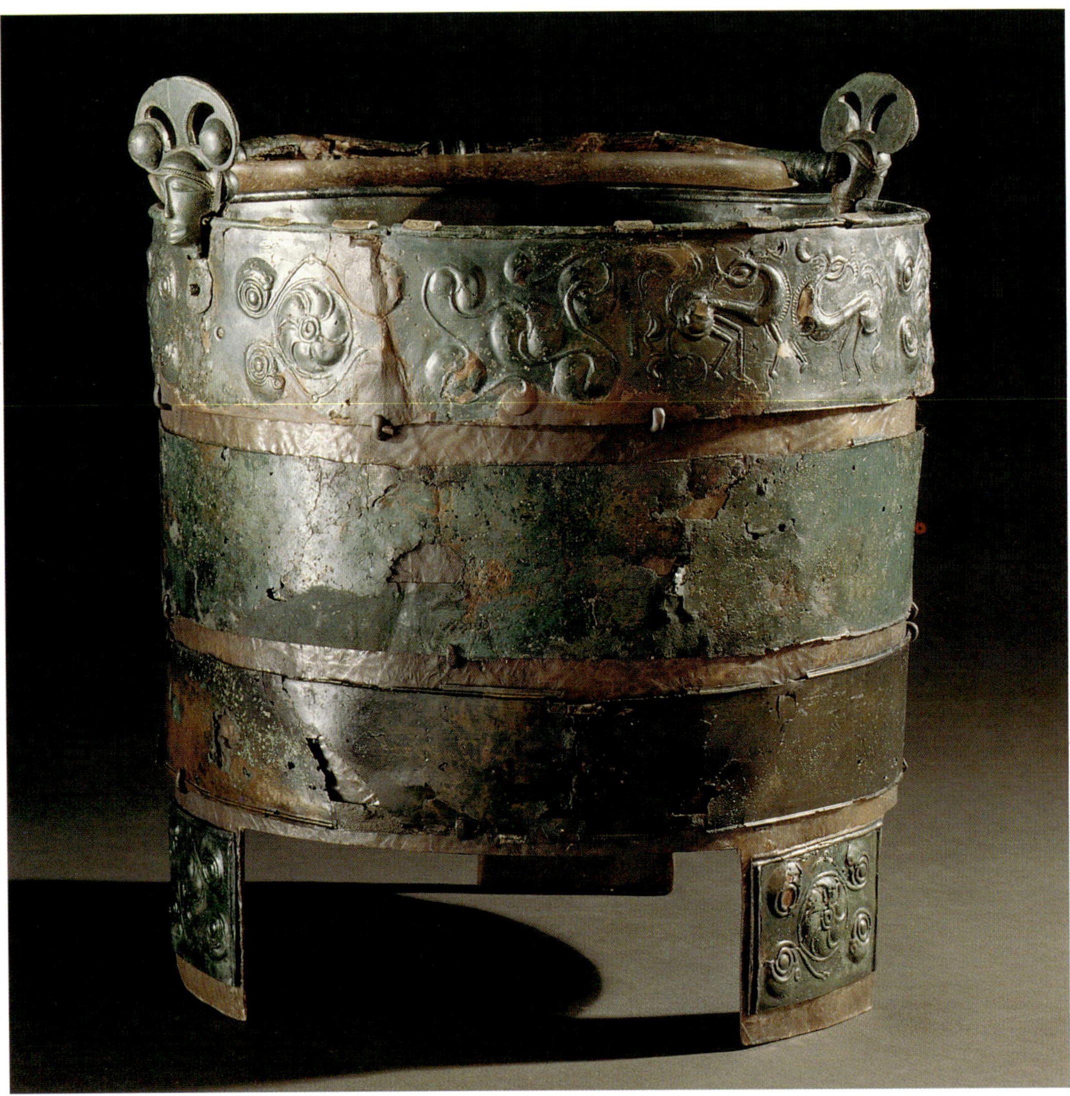

70

By now we are familiar with the main duality of the art of La Tène, that is, the Upper Region and the Lower Region, or the Deep, on both sides of a Borderline. We are also familiar with the two great powers of death and birth (and rebirth) that are presented in this art. The two opposing powers are often represented by shapes like leaves, some of which are falling and symbolizing death, and some are ascending and symbolizing birth and rebirth. We could go on to associate the falling leaves with darkness, and the ascending leaves with light. We could also connect the falling leaves with the feminine Deep, and those that ascend with the Upper Region where the masculine heads are found. What needs to be emphasized is the prominence of duality in the imagination of the Celts, as that imagination is manifested in their art. The following diagrams illustrate this.

These diagrams show some dualities (**71**).

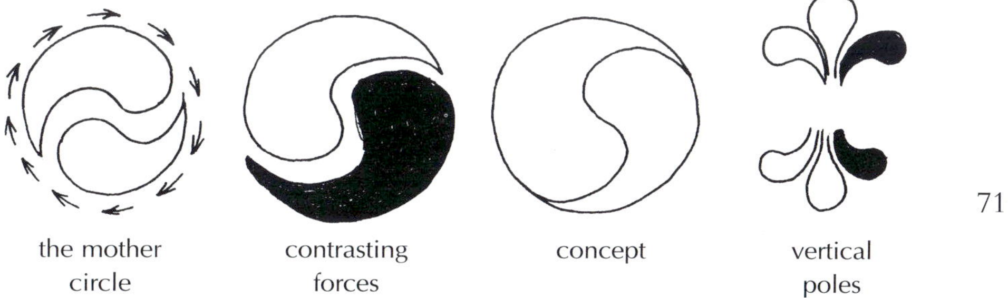

71

Now we shall consider examples of duality in specific works of art. First, there is the Aylesford bucket, **70**. On the bucket, in the middle, we can see two leaves opposite one another forming a circle: that is one duality. On the right are shapes like two creatures, with birds' heads, opposite one another. There are two round shapes about the form of a human head, which forms part of the handle. The two leaves and the two round shapes form a circle (denoting death and rebirth) in the Deep beneath the Borderline, which is the rim of the bucket. The two handles of the bucket are shaped like two male heads in quiet contemplation, above the agitation of contrary powers that can be seen in the leaves below them.

Figure **72** shows in more detail the duality of the leaves:

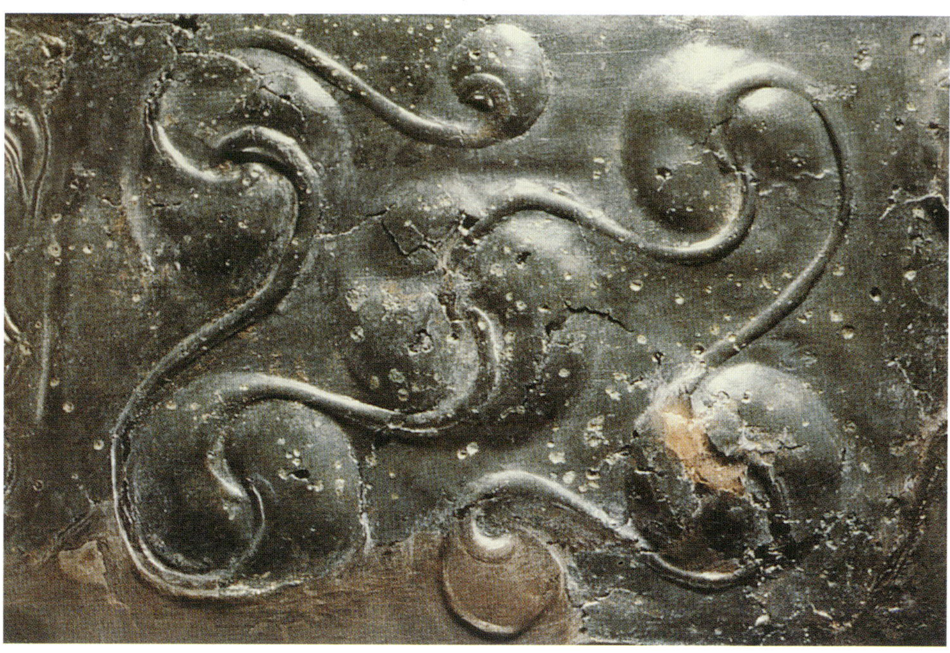

72

In the upper part there is a leaf which turns into a long, restless, 'S' shaped line. On each side of this line there are two leaves that come together to form a circle – indeed, to form five circles, the largest one in the middle. The restless line comes to a point at the bottom. It represents one aspect of the Borderline between two opposing forces.

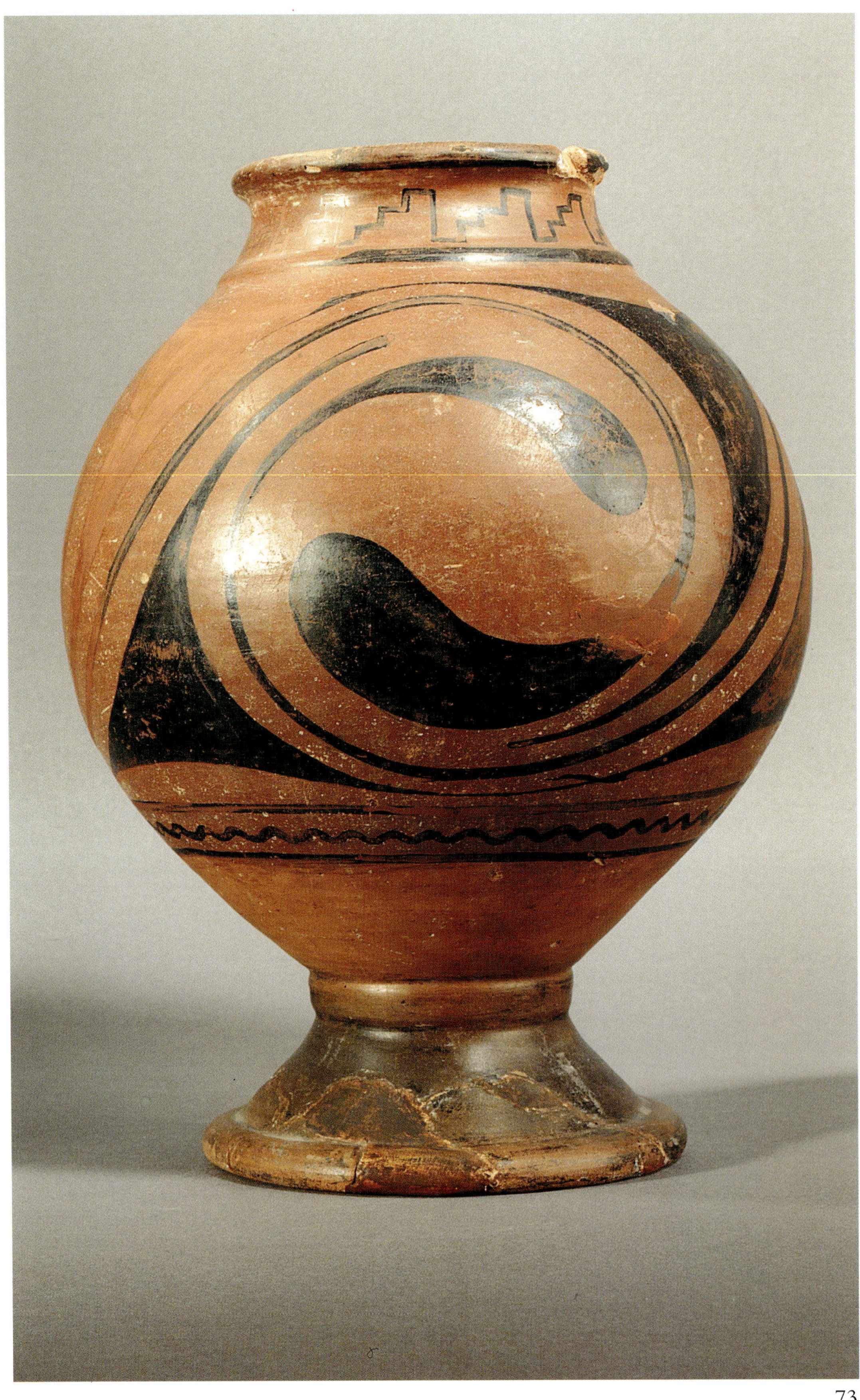

73

In the piece of pottery, **73**, we see another example of the same pattern.
In **74** is another example, a variation of abstract dualities in the shapes of (dark) red leaves, and (light–coloured) leaves within a circle.

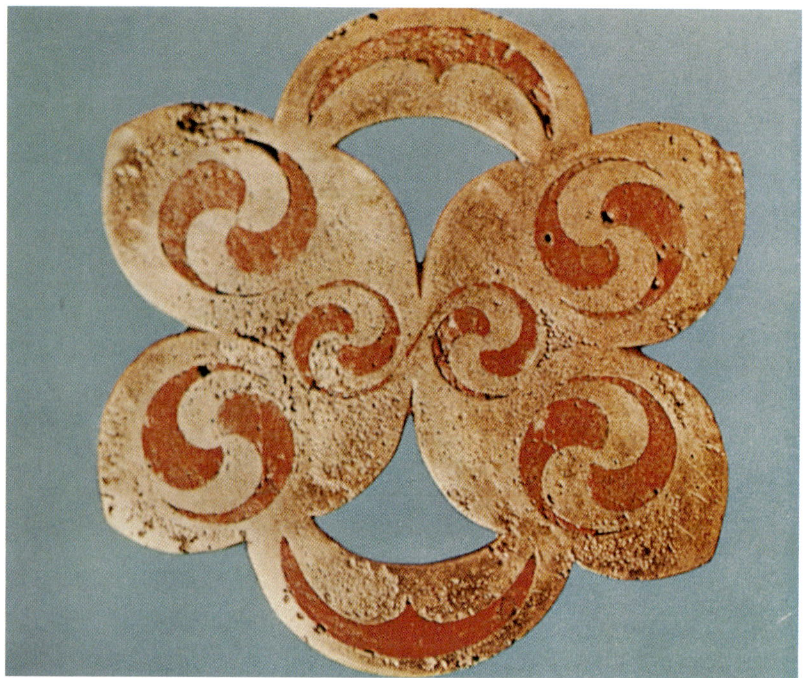

74

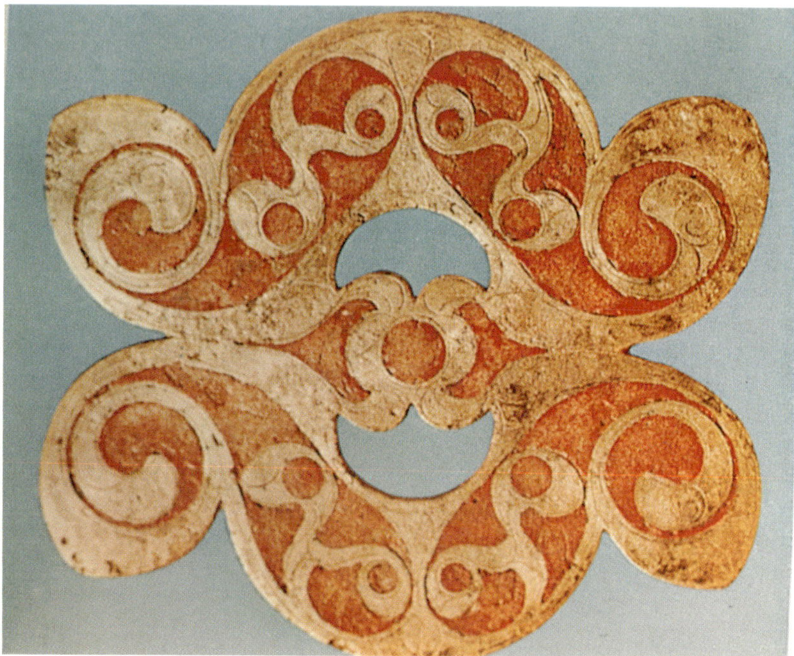

75

In **75** there is a more complex pattern of duality.

Other examples are seen in **76** and **78**. A representation of the Tal-y-Llyn plaque (**77**) has been placed between them in order to show that these dualities are of a wider significance than those discussed earlier.

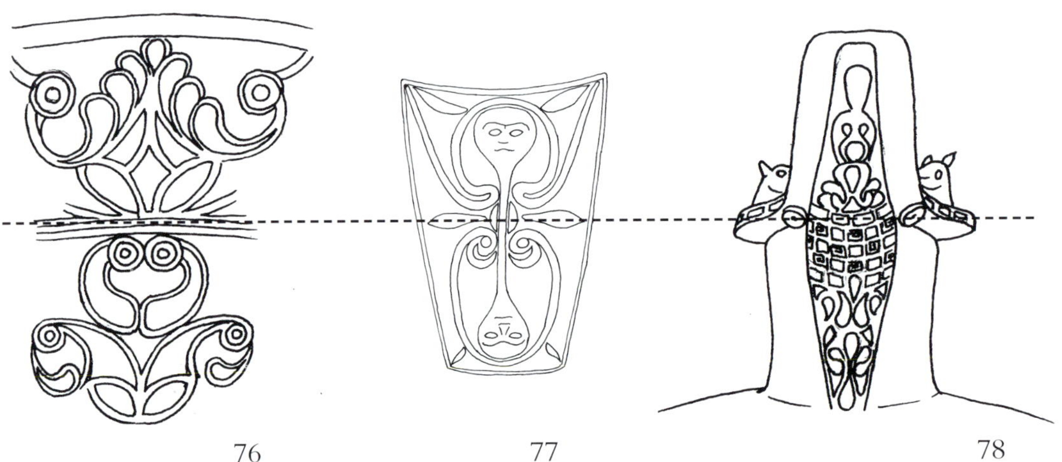

76   77   78

On the neck of the wine flagon from France, **76**, are leaves in a broader context: they represent the descent and ascent within the body of the Mother.

Figure **79** is the bowl of which **76** forms part of its decoration.

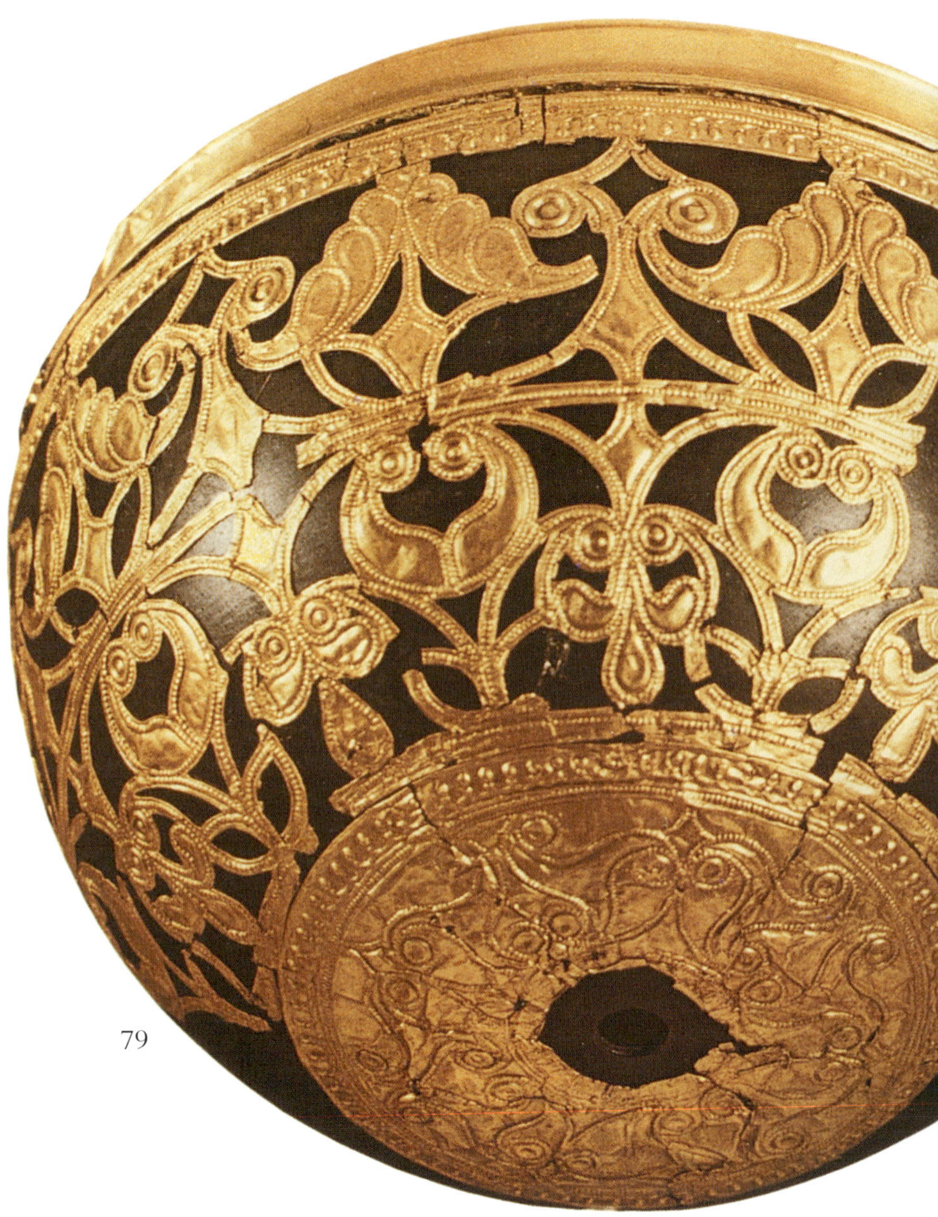

79

The highest leaf has a particularly upward aspect; its lightness suggests that it is ascending. Below the Borderline there are two leaves that seem to be descending: they are turned downwards and appear to be heavy.

Figure **80** shows an enamelled bronze ornament from England.

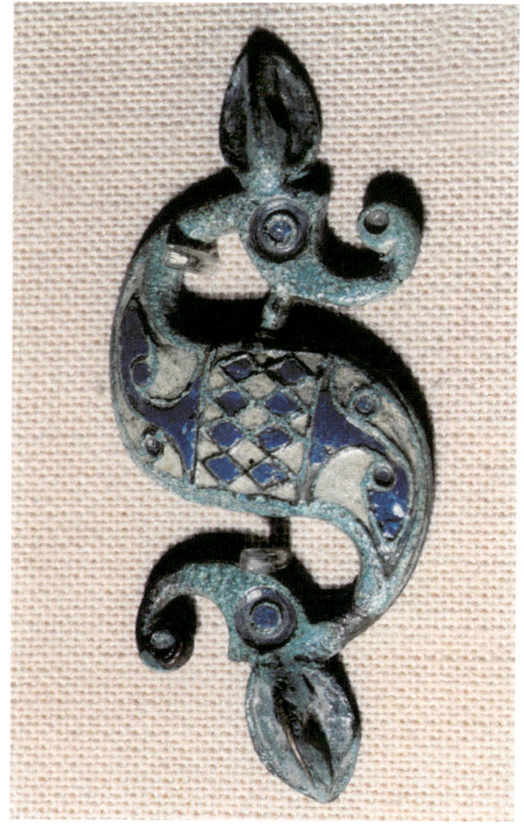

80

The duality of its pattern is obvious: there are two leafy heads with noses on each side of a Borderline. In the Borderline are two leaves or buds on each side of four diamond shapes.

In the bowl mount, **81**, there are two metal heads (of a more natural aspect than is usual) on each side of a Borderline.

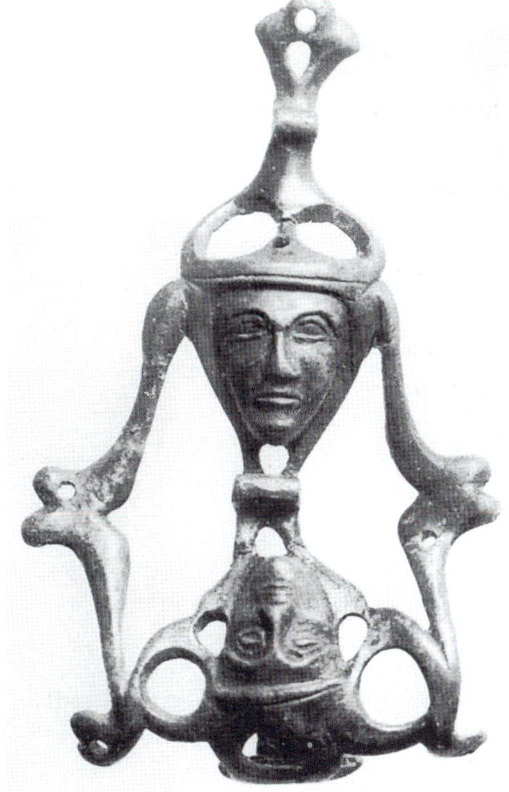

81

The belt buckle, **82**, shows opposing dualities placed on each side of a large head.

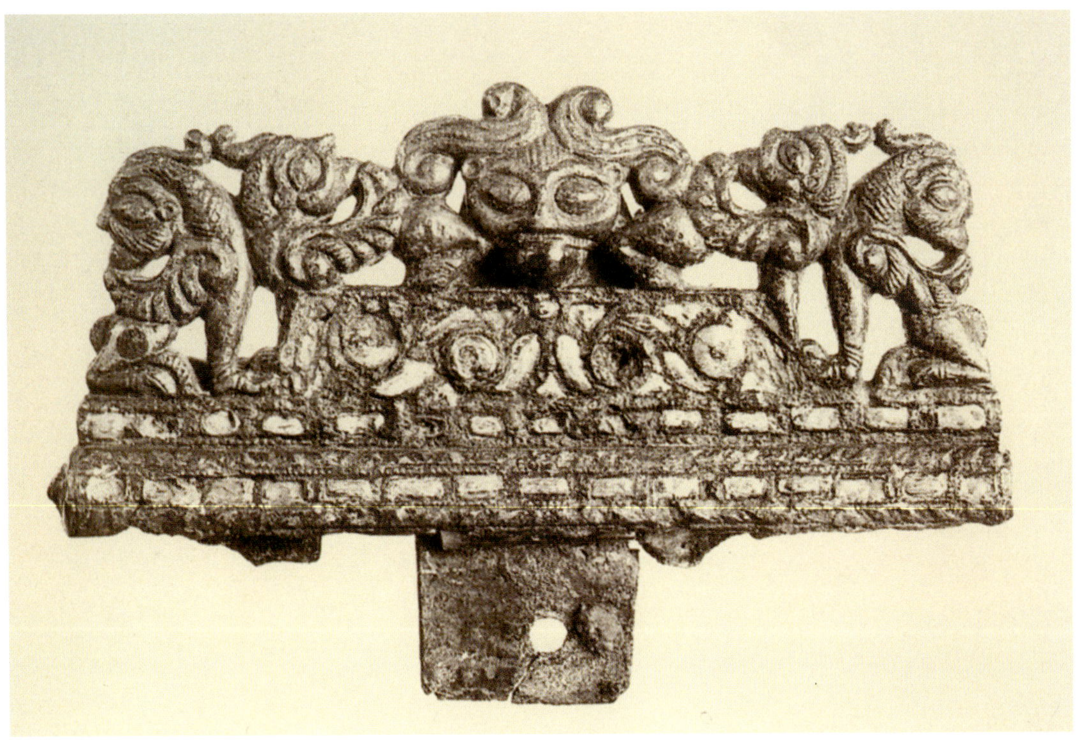

82

Beneath the head are signs of a spiral denoting the agitation of the Deep. Note that the head of one winged creature is turned upward, and is linked to the head by two 'S' shapes. The head of the other creature is turned downward. They represent the downward and upward forces. It may be that the significance of this work will be made clearer by Diagram **83**:

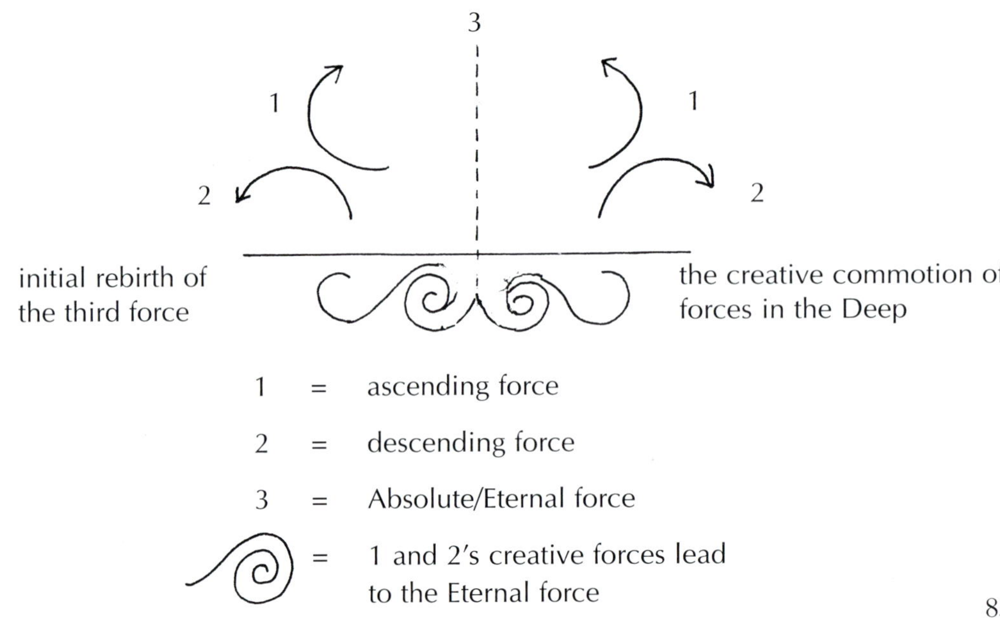

83

Simple and straightforward examples of duality are to be found on the pattern on the Trawsfynydd beaker, **84**:

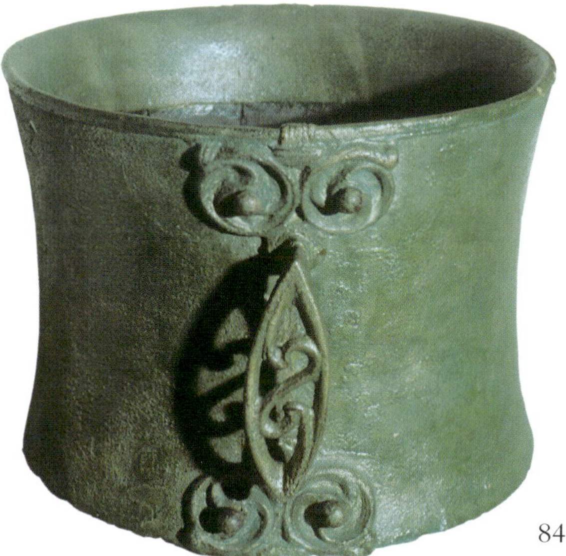

84

and the two limestone heads from Bouches-du-Rhone, France, **85**:

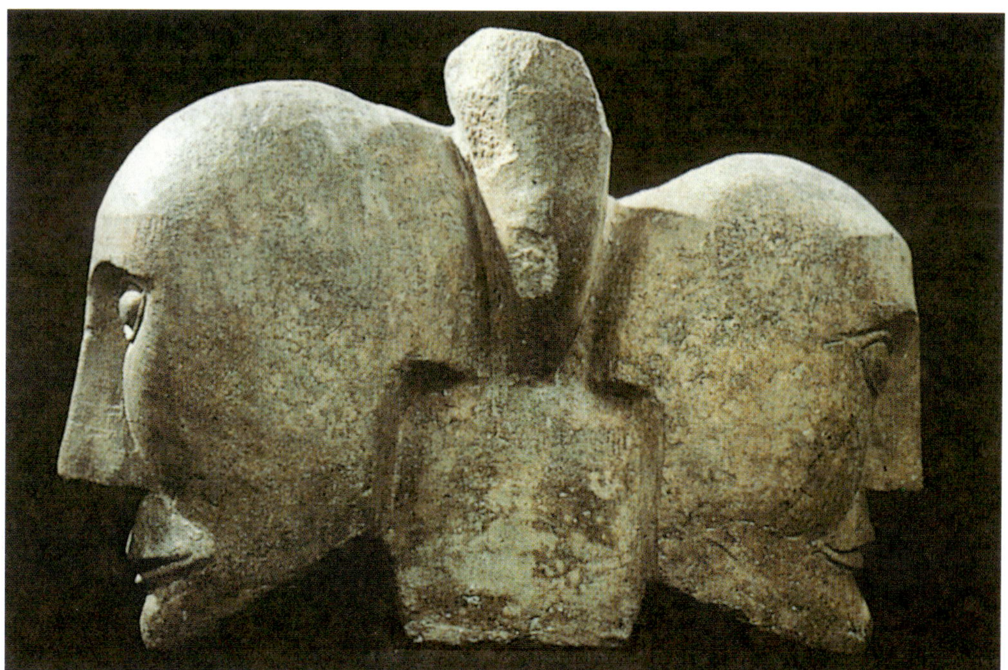

85

The two heads are back to back, and between them is something that may be – it has been suggested – the remains of the beak of a great bird. That would mean that the original work was larger than what we have today. It is worth noting that there is a hint of a smile on the head on the right, and a hint of sorrow on the head on the left. The head on the left is tilted downward. These two heads represent two opposing forces.

Figure **86** shows the iron hearth (*pentan*) of Capel Garmon. On each side of the hearth there are two bull heads facing in different directions.

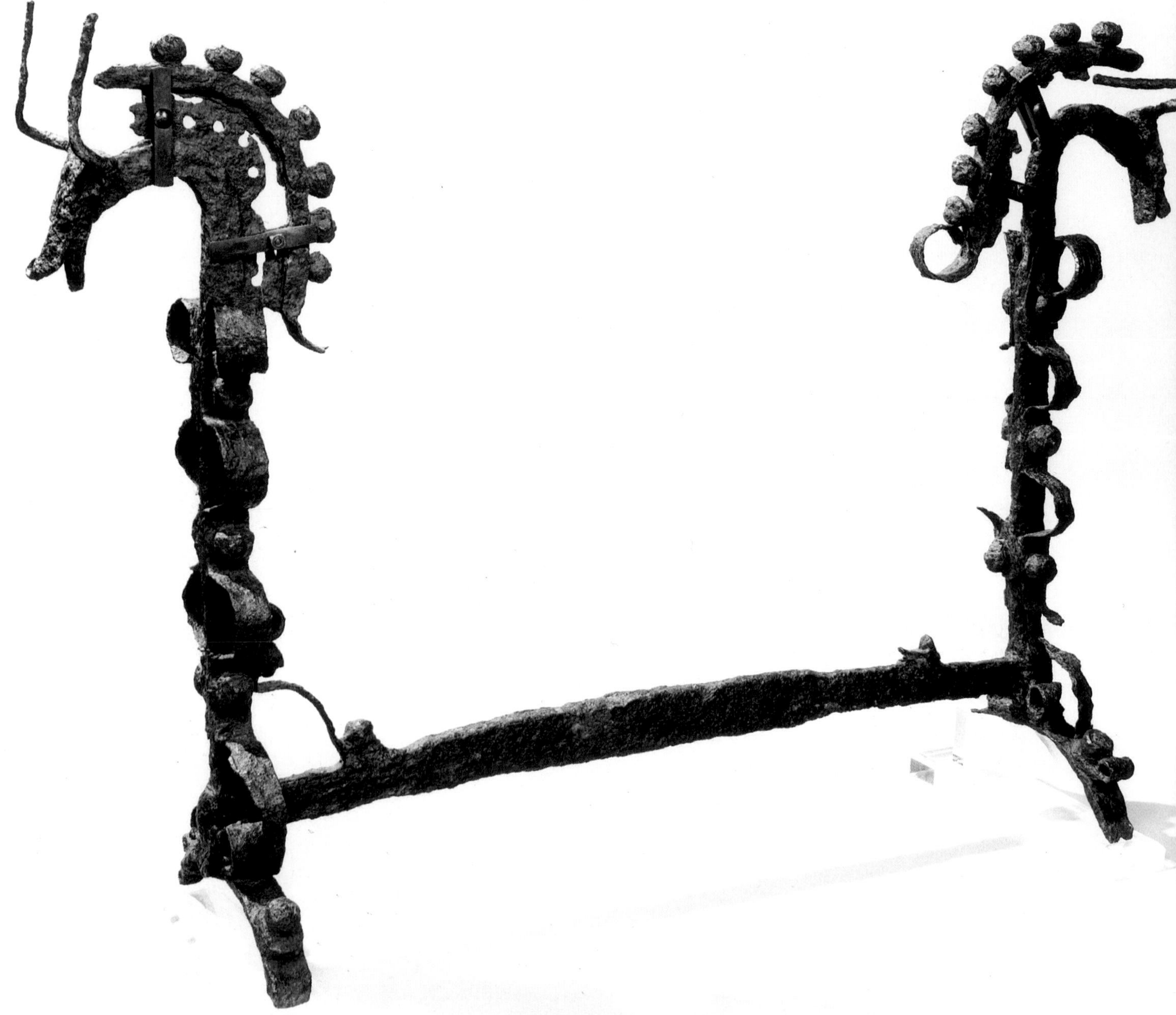

86

This is how Iorwerth Peate described this hearth:

The fireplace was in the centre of the floor in the houses of both the aristocracy and the labourers, and the hearthstone was behind it. The iron pentan was placed in front of the fire to keep the fire in. This was a piece of iron in the shape of an 'H', the two ends usually splendidly crafted, and the wood or peat would be propped against the bar of the 'H'. A splendid example of an iron pentan from the early Iron Age was discovered in the Capel Garmon area.[1]

It is worth noting that this hearth was an implement with a practical purpose. It is possible that those who gathered around it were aware of the customary significance of dualities.

Figures **87** and **88** provide further examples of dualities.

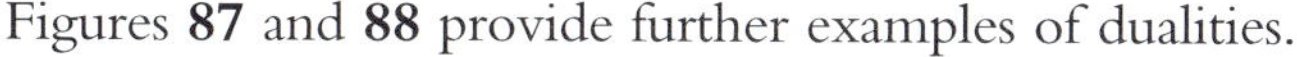

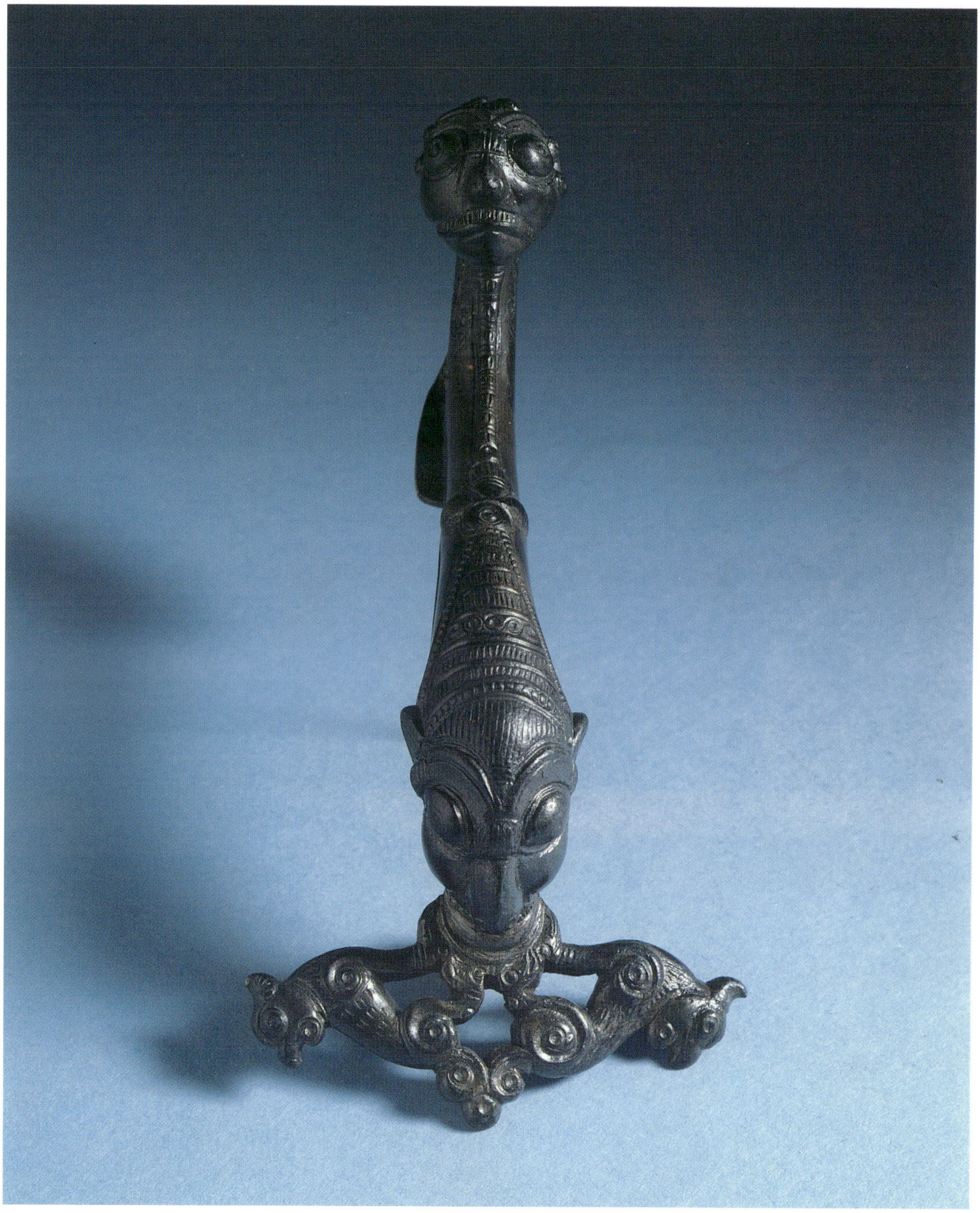

87

In the bronze ornament from Pasberg, Germany, there is a phallic head in the Upper Region. Beneath the Borderline are two terminals of a beast of prey in the middle of spirals. The Deep, which is here represented as something terrible, is being swallowed by the head of the fish.

In figure **88**, an iron lynch pin with a bronze head, from St Pölten, in Austria, we have a duality on either side of a large head.

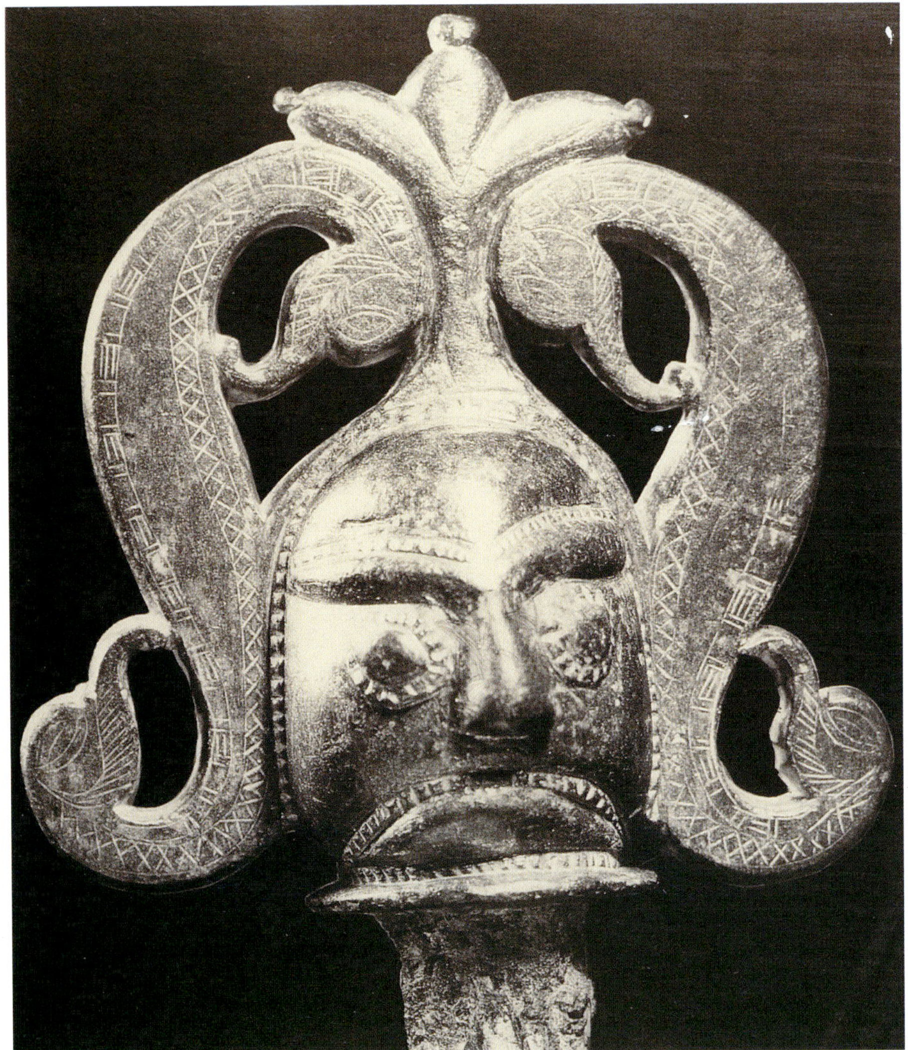

88

This duality is in the shape of the letter 'S', and there are creatures in the extremities. These represent contrasting powers on each side of the large head, which is also a bud and which signifies the quiet, magical meditation that is a consequence of Spiritual Transformation.

Many Welsh tales demonstrate the importance of dualities in the Celtic imagination. Let us consider Blodeuwedd, in the Fourth Branch of the Mabinogi, for instance. She is created from flowers and leaves, things that grow, and at the end of the tale she is transformed into an owl. When she is created she is the fairest and most beautiful maiden that anyone had seen; at her end she is a hideous owl, a bird that belongs to the night and darkness. She is an example of a duality in the imagination. It may be that she shares some imaginative characteristics with **89**, the head of a symbolic bracelet.

At one extremity of the bracelet there is a winged bird, a symbol of ascent, with breasts upon it: this is a positive image of fecundity. But the head is also an owl, a symbol of night and darkness. I suggest that whatever Celt wore this bracelet would have been conscious of its duality, and of the cycle of which that duality was a part.

Then we have the story of 'Culhwch and Olwen'. Culhwch has two mothers, his natural mother and his stepmother. The natural mother, Goleuddydd, made her husband promise that he would not marry again until he beheld a thorn with two heads on it, a duality, growing on her grave. The evil stepmother compels Culhwch to go through a process of Initiation by forcing him to face the giant Ysbaddaden in order to win his daughter Olwen's hand in marriage.

And what about Nisien and Efnisien in the Second Branch of the Mabinogi? These are just a selection of the dualities we find in Celtic tales.

In the pattern of dualities we find the same elements as in the basic pattern discussed in previous chapters. We have:

- An Upper Region and a Lower Region (the Deep)
- A descending and an ascending force
- A masculine and a feminine force

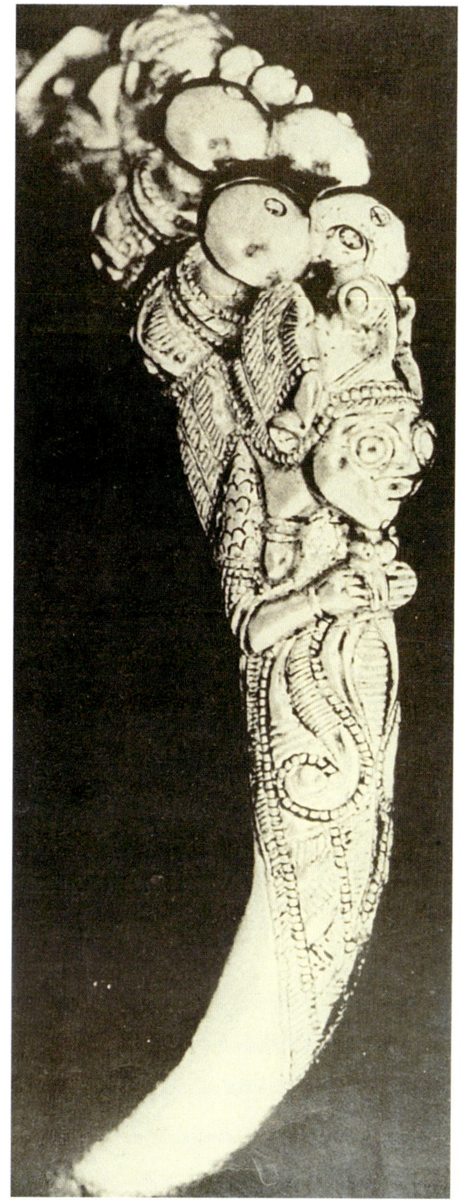

89

Celtic dualities remind one of the Ying-Yang (or Yin-Yang) of the Chinese, or the symbol which they call 'Tai-chi Tu'. Duality appears to be a basic concept in the human mind, what Carl Gustav Jung would call an 'archetype'. The following comments by Richard Wilhelm are relevant in this context:

This symbol has also played a significant part in India and Europe.[2]

In its primary meaning yin is 'the cloudy', 'the overcast', and yang means actually 'banners waving in the sun', that is, something 'shone upon', or bright. By transference the two concepts were applied to the light and dark sides of a mountain or of a river. In the case of a mountain the southern is the bright side and the northern the dark side, while in the case of a river seen from above, it is the northern side that is bright (yang), because it reflects the light, and the southern side that is in the shadow (yin). Thence the two expressions were carried over into the Book of Changes and applied to the two alternating primal states of being.[3]

We shall end this chapter by referring to the artist-craftsmen who made the works that we have been discussing. It is likely that they had a kind of 'priestly' function. Consider the blacksmiths in a Celtic society. It is certain that they would have had a knowledge of religious tales, and a considerable knowledge of the technique of Initiation. It is well-known that the education of the Druids and poets lasted for several years in Celtic societies. Here is a comment by Anne Ross:

A Druid-elect, as we know, took some 20 years to master and assimilate the secrets of his calling. Likewise, in Ireland, a fili ('poet', 'seer'), was required to study for from seven to twelve years in order to master orally the complex disciplines with which he was concerned.[4]

I think that the artist-craftsmen were seers of some kind. I refer again to the words of Anne Ross:

Below the king came his chief nobles who were highly aristocratic and powerful. This class included the priest ... Below them again were the non-noble freemen, like gentlemen farmers, owning land and property and including the finest craftsmen, especially the blacksmith who had a high position in early Celtic society; his craft was believed to have been of a semi-supernatural character and the smith-god held an equally elevated position in the divine society of the Celtic deities.[5]

This confirms my contention that the work of the artist-craftsmen shows a knowledge of Celtic religion, as well as instruction in that religion — though I cannot entirely agree with Anne Ross about a 'smith-god', and other Celtic gods. The Celts had a code of signs or symbols of religious powers and processes, and dualities were a part of that code.

I think that the artist-craftsmen were seers of some kind

Notes on page 114

8 The Third Force – Triads

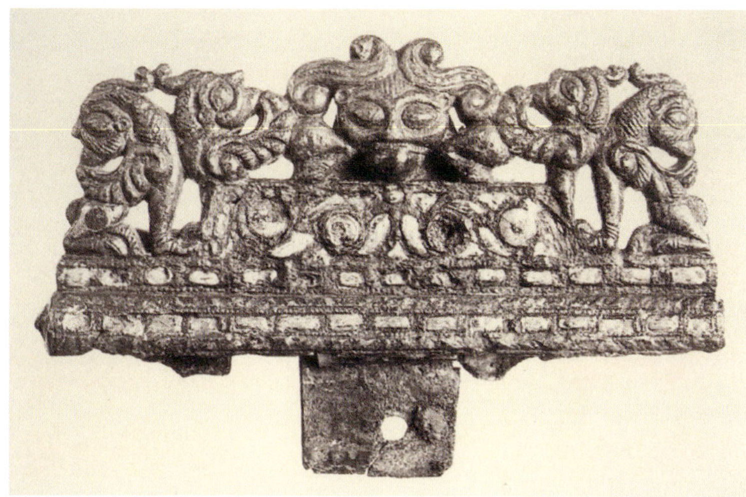

90

Dualities become triads. The third force is the tranquil meditation that is a consequence of experiencing the other two forces – death and birth (or rebirth)

We have discussed dualities in Celtic art. Between the two opposing forces represented by these dualities, in the middle, there is a third force. Dualities become triads. The third force is the tranquil meditation that is a consequence of experiencing the other two forces – death and birth (or rebirth). Let us examine again the belt buckle from Weiskirchen in Germany, **90**. In the centre, between the duality of agitated forces on each side of it, is a large, magical head that conveys stillness, the stillness that has transcended living and dying. In a way, this head conveys the unseen, an eternal, still presence that has risen beyond life and death. We sense this force by responding to the image with our imagination.

Let us consider other examples. Let us look again at one of the heads on the Aylesford bucket, **91**. The still presence of the head in meditation extends to its head-dress. There is a light, uplifting force in the shape of the head, which is at one with the circular, crown-like shape of the head-dress, which contains two balls (a duality) on either side. The head represents the third force.

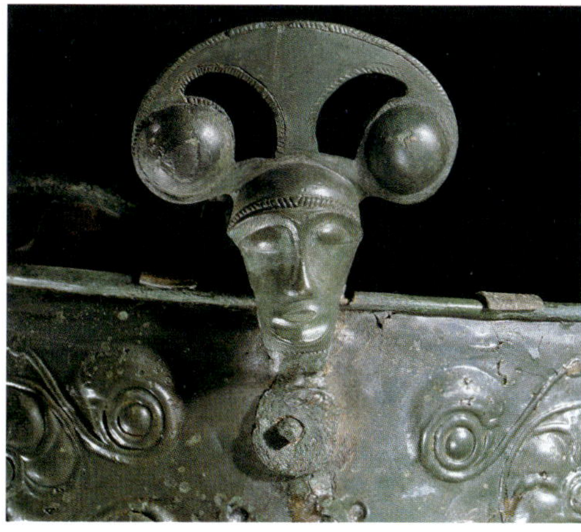

91

Figure **92** is an ornamental pin from Weiskirchen, Mainz in Germany.

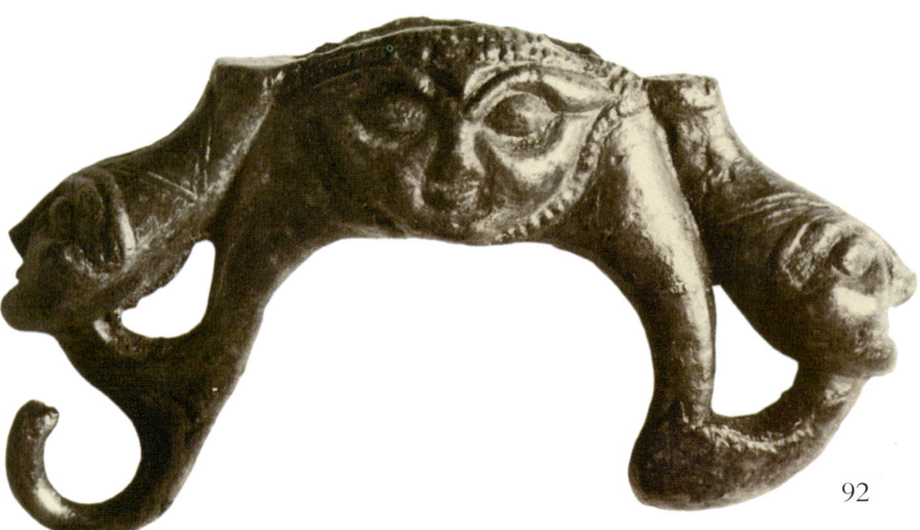

92

Three heads form one aesthetically attractive shape. The head in the centre is larger than those on either side of it. Those heads face in different directions and so convey opposing forces. There is a suggestion of a smile on the head in the middle. It forms a bridge between the two emotional states expressed by the two other heads, and is on a higher emotional plane than them: 'he who is the head, let him be a bridge' (*a fo ben, bid bont*), as the giant leader Bendigeidfran says in the Second Branch of the Mabinogi.

Figure **93** shows a gold bracelet from Rodenbach, in Germany.

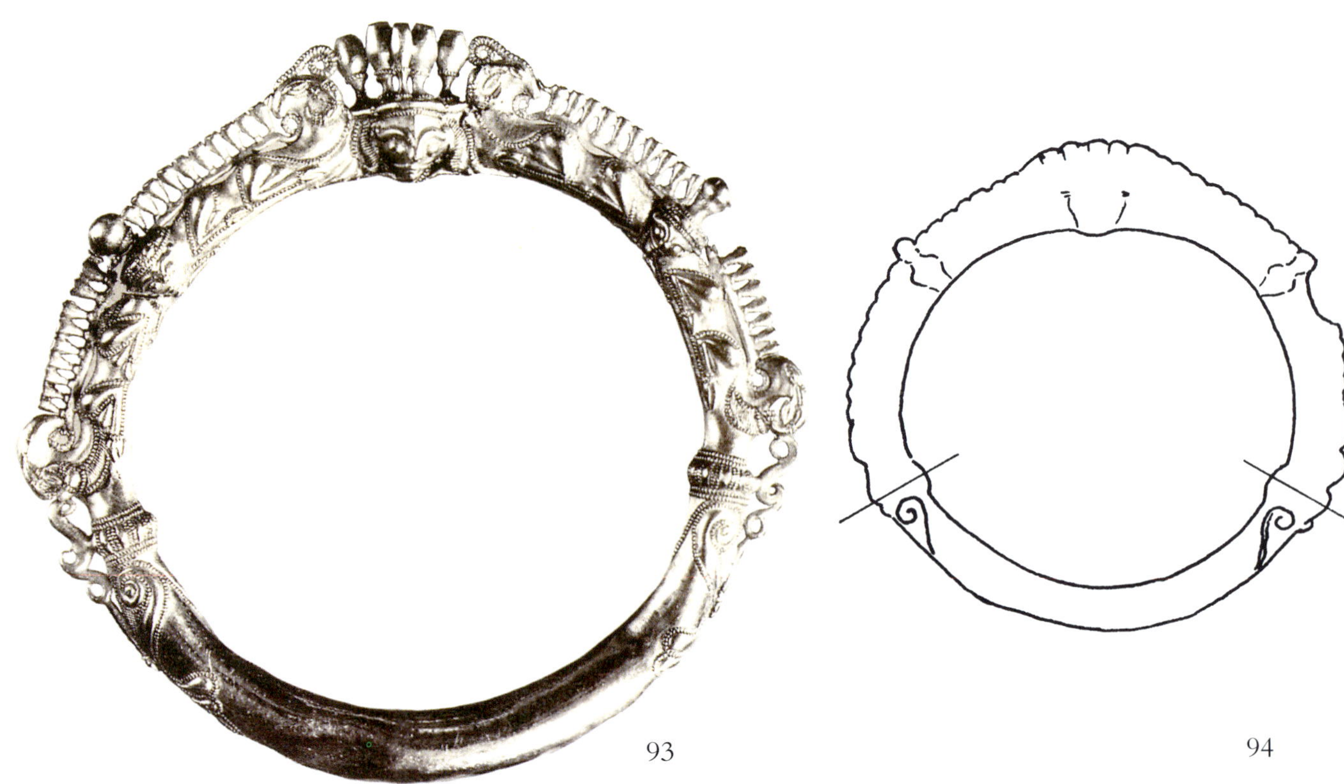

93

94

There are three heads on the bracelet. The magical head in the middle is larger than the other two, and the cluster of flowers or buds on top of it is larger than the clusters on top of the other two. It is also positioned higher. In the lower part of the bracelet there is a linear link in the shape of an 'S' between the two rams and the spiral beneath them. This bracelet conveys a complete experience of Spiritual Transformation, and it is easy to believe that wearing it would have been a sign of religious distinction.

Figure **95** is a simple, symbolic image of the three forces that are by now so familiar to us.

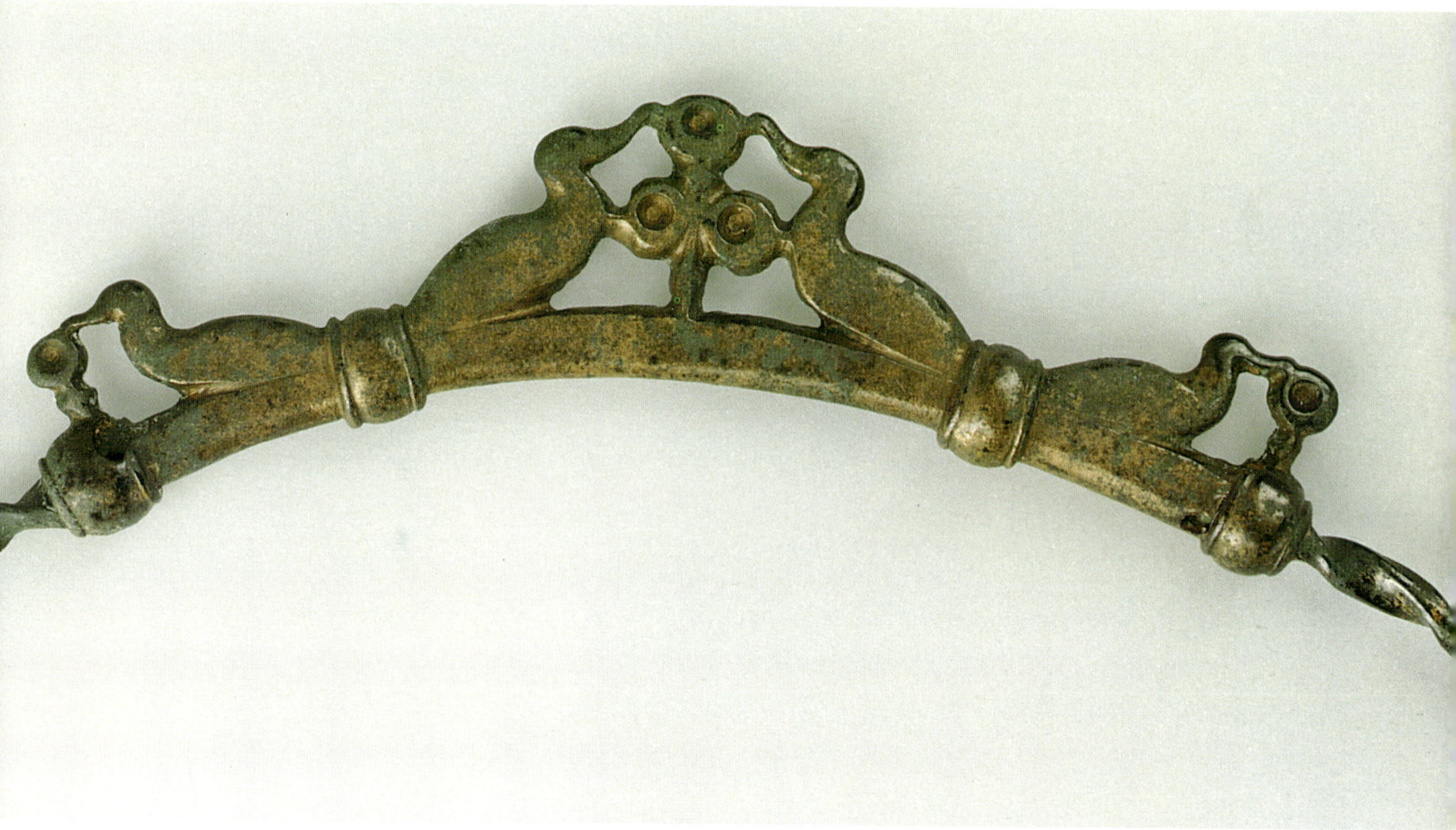

95

On both sides a bird faces a magical symbolic tree; the two face in different directions. In the middle are two birds facing each other and sustaining a tree; this makes a triad of the whole. Note that the two birds are linked to the spiral that completes the circle of the torque and conveys the excitement of the experience of the Deep. The fullness of the Spiritual Transformation is expressed here yet again.

In **96** we have a torque with three knobs on the outside of its circle. Every knob is the same shape; they are all circular. But note that the shape of the uppermost knob is bigger than the other two. On this torque there is a triad of threes, and each individual triad gives prominence to the third force.

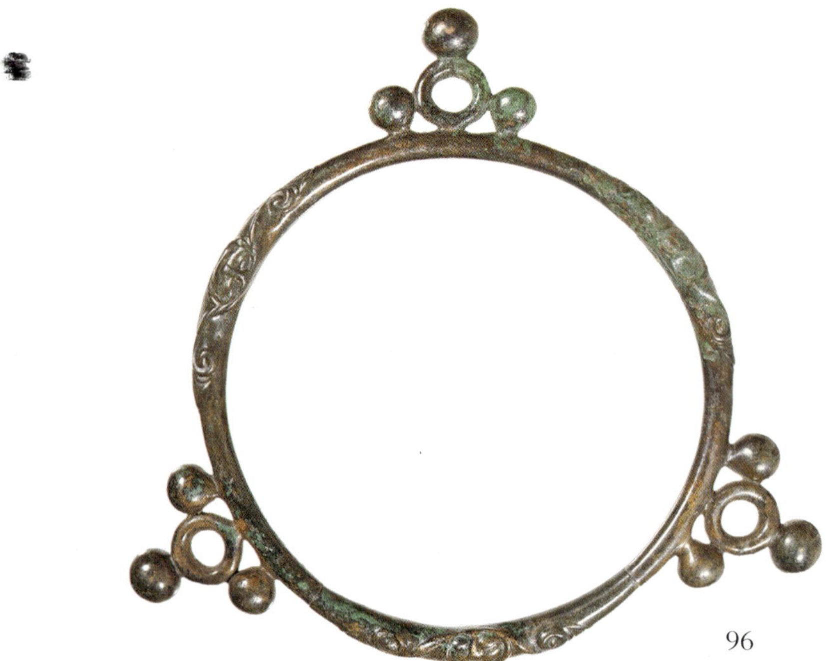

96

Triads are also found on the scabbards of swords. In **97** we have three horses by the mouth of a sword scabbard. Two of the horses are facing each other, they are head to head, and the third is in the centre, above them. Note that the stance of the third horse is freer and that it forms a bridge between the other two.

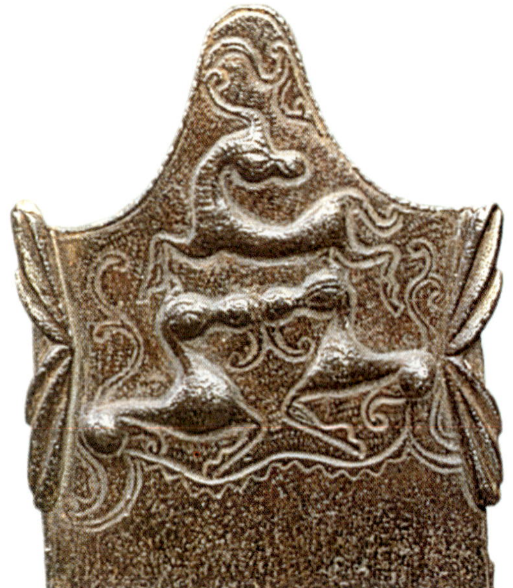

97

Figure **98** shows another triad, this time of the heads of birds and with no difference in their sizes. This triad is also situated by the mouth of a scabbard.

This is a simple logo of a triad: it is simple because the three heads are the same size – though one appears to be higher than the others. These two triads are found on scabbards: a scabbard is feminine in shape – it is like a womb. It will be remembered that the Deep is feminine, the dimension where death and rebirth occur. The images on the scabbards would have brought comfort in war, as surely as the belief of the Celts that death was not the end of life's journey, a belief to which Caesar refers and a belief that he claims made their warriors exceedingly brave in battle.

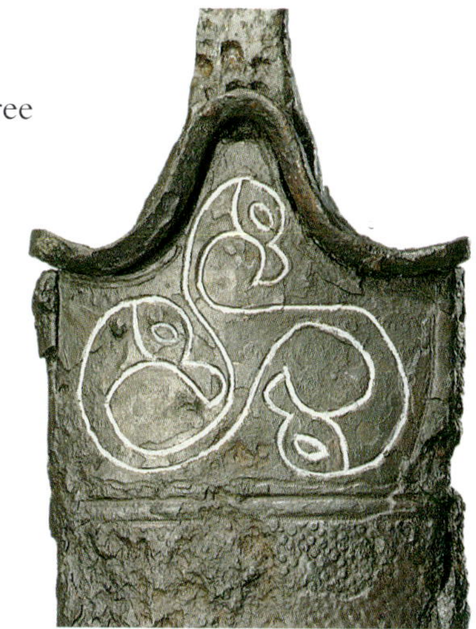

98

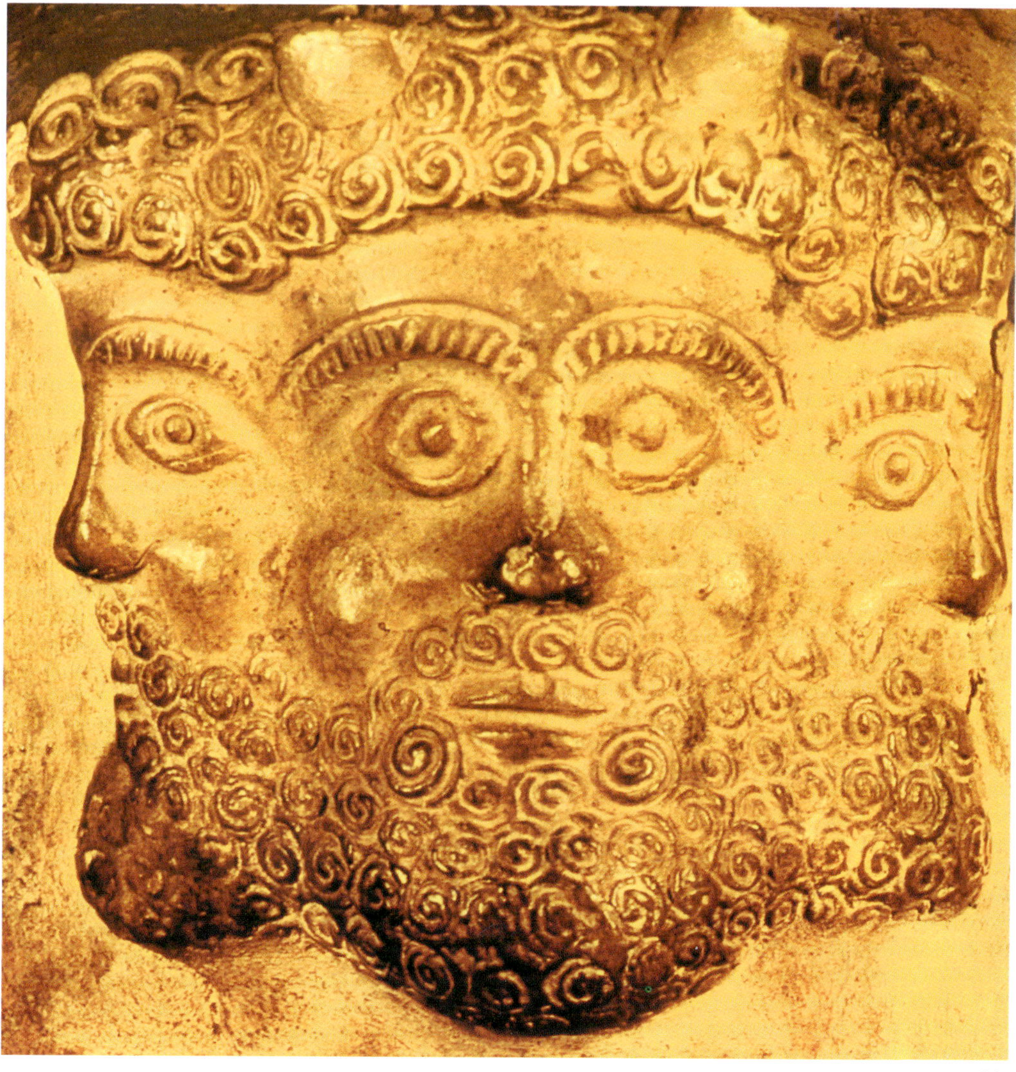

99

Let us now turn to triads of heads, **99** and **100**.

Figure **99** shows three magical faces. The spirals on the heads create a magical effect – in spite of the fact that there are Roman features on this sculpture, such as the imitation of cheeks. In the middle, a face looks straight at us. This one conveys meditation. The other two faces represent the opposing forces on its two sides.

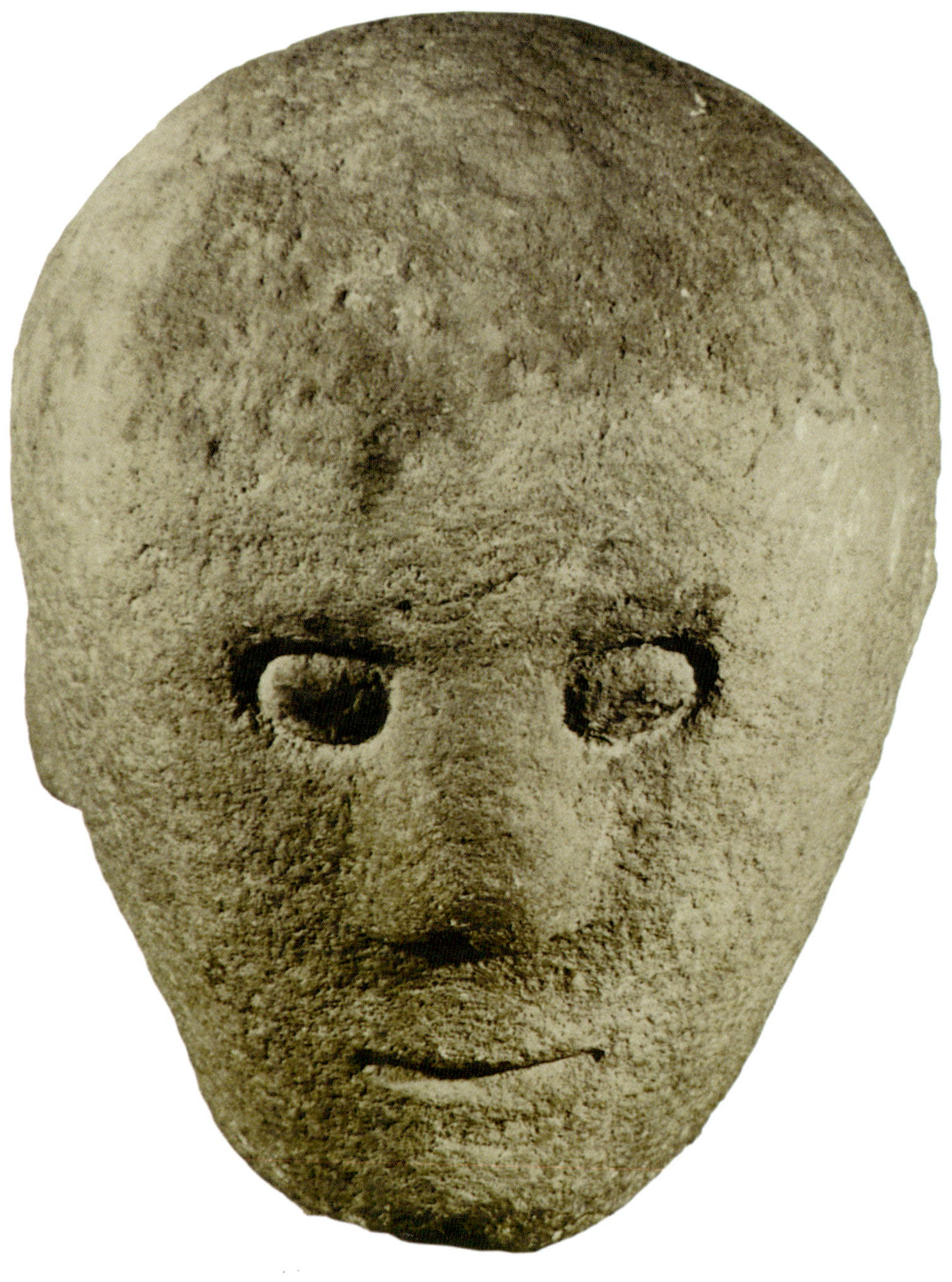

100

The three heads in **100** and **101** form one phallic head and are carved out of a stone with a hole in the bottom. All three heads have a meditative aspect but the one in the middle (**100**) best expresses a quiet meditation, without showing joy or grief. Figure **101** draws attention to the two heads on either side of it: the one on the right appears to be in meditation and the one on the left expresses wonderment.

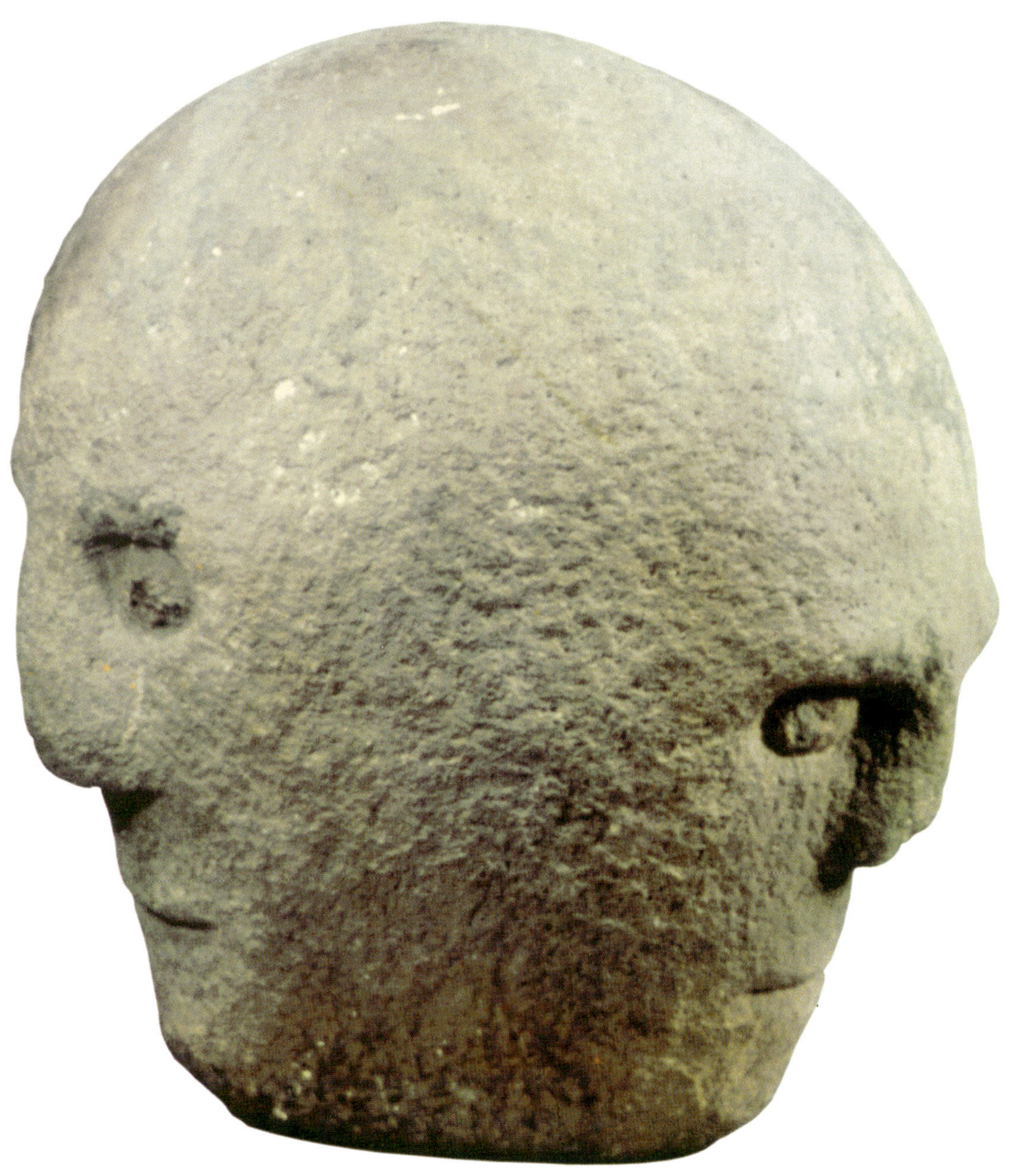

101

Lastly, let us examine the head in **102**.

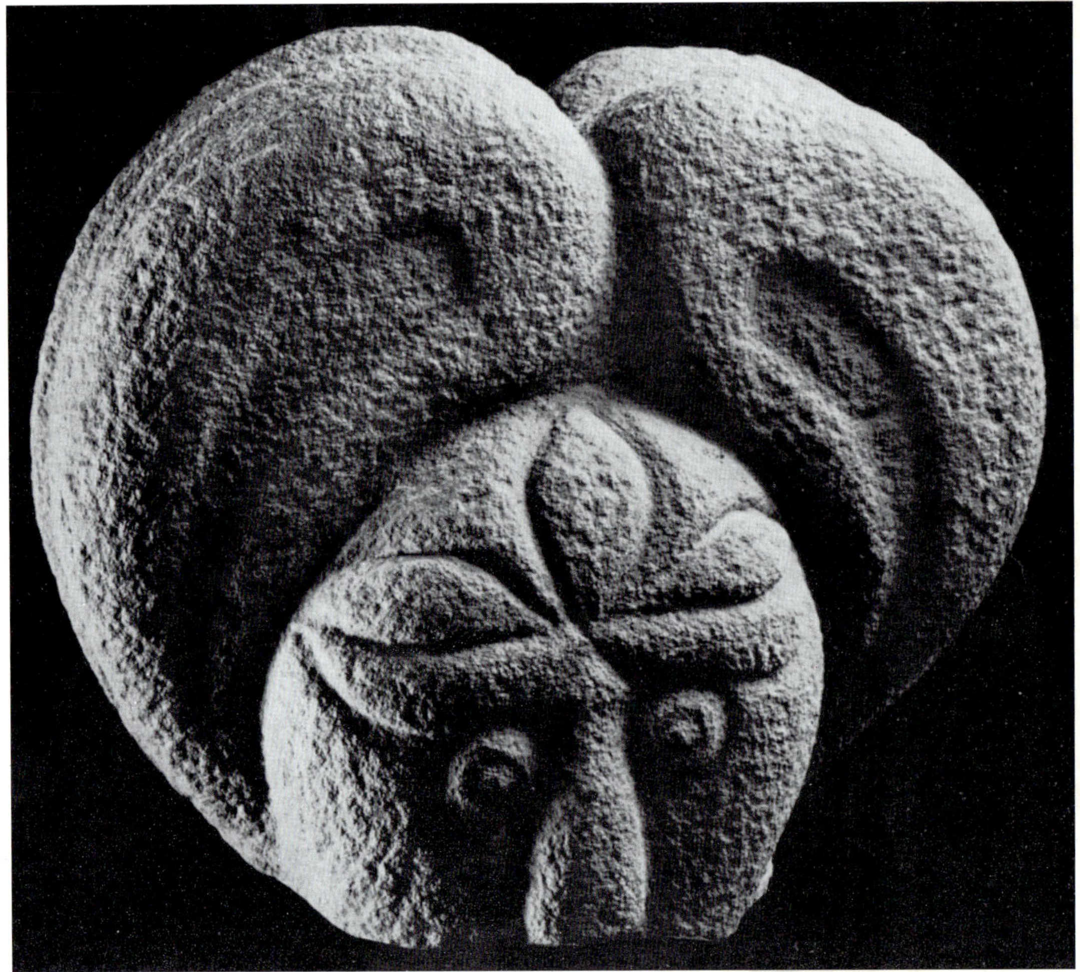

102

It has already been said that this is a magical symbolic head. It is a phallus and it is also a leafy plant. On its forehead we see three leaves, and the one in the middle is bigger than the other two and placed higher. This leaf, one of three, represents the same kind of force as the head itself.

Whoever is familiar with medieval Welsh and Irish literature knows the importance of triads in them. There are references to them in tales and poems. For example, there are the three birds, the Birds of Rhiannon, that comfort the weary warriors who returned to Harlech after terrible warfare in Ireland:

… there came three birds and began to sing to them a certain song, and of all the songs they had ever heard each one was unlovely compared with that.[1]

This triad signifies supernatural power.

The presence of triads in the old art signifies the completion of Spiritual Transformation, Initiation, as a complete unit

Then, there are the three magic drops that Little Gwion swallowed in the Tale of Taliesin, a swallowing that leads to Spiritual Transformation and the bringing of Taliesin into being again:

… the **Three Drops** were safely inside Little Gwion and, because of that, he knew all that had been, what is, and what will be.[2]

The new being, Taliesin, has supernatural knowledge, as he says to Gwyddno, the father of Elffin, who discovered him in a bag on a seashore:

'I can say more than you can ask me.'

'Let me know what you can do,' said Gwyddno.

'All the arts of the world,' said Taliesin, 'are in force in my belly, for I know what has been and will soon be.'[3]

In Wales there were collections of triads, now edited as a book by Dr Rachel Bromwich. As Dr Bromwich notes, these triads were meant to serve as a means of instructing and educating the poets:

The argument has been advanced elsewhere that Trioedd Ynys Prydain, like the Trioedd Cerdd, were evolved as part of the teaching given by the bardic schools; pupil bards being required to learn the triad sequences by heart. As such, the various groups of triads originated simply as mnemonic devices; and Trioedd Ynys Prydain came into being as an aid to the collection of the repertoire of narrative material which the young bard was in the process of mastering.[4]

It must be asked whether the poets and storytellers, who learnt about triads centuries after the period of La Tène Celts, and after Christianity had supplanted their religion, had lost sight of the power of the old triads.

The presence of triads in the old art signifies the completion of Spiritual Transformation, Initiation, in a way that conveys its elements — death, birth or rebirth, and the attainment of a state of tranquil meditation — as a complete unit. This is the essence of the Celtic idea of a three which is also one.

Notes on page 114

9 Celtic Art: The Visual Code

The main proposition of this book is that Celtic art presents a vision of existence. That vision is a religious vision. In the Foreword, it was claimed that this art is a source of information about the Celts and their religion, the only direct source that we possess.

In the Foreword, too, I said that there is no direct testimony that the Celts had any gods; they have images that convey their religious vision. This matter needs to be investigated in more detail, and a reasonable question could be asked: Am I claiming here that the heads of the art of La Tène are not the heads of gods? Not exactly. I believe that the Celts, originally, thought about religion in a different way from the ancient Greeks and Romans, and that it is likely that they came to think about 'gods' under the influence of the Greeks and Romans.

The Framework of the Religious Code of the Celts

Their art bears testimony to the fact that the Celts thought of existence as life, death, and rebirth, and that an imaginative experience of this gave way to a tranquil meditation. We have called the experience of going from life to the Deep and being reborn a Spiritual Transformation. We have also called it Initiation. The following diagrams (**103**) explain the various ways of conveying this vision.

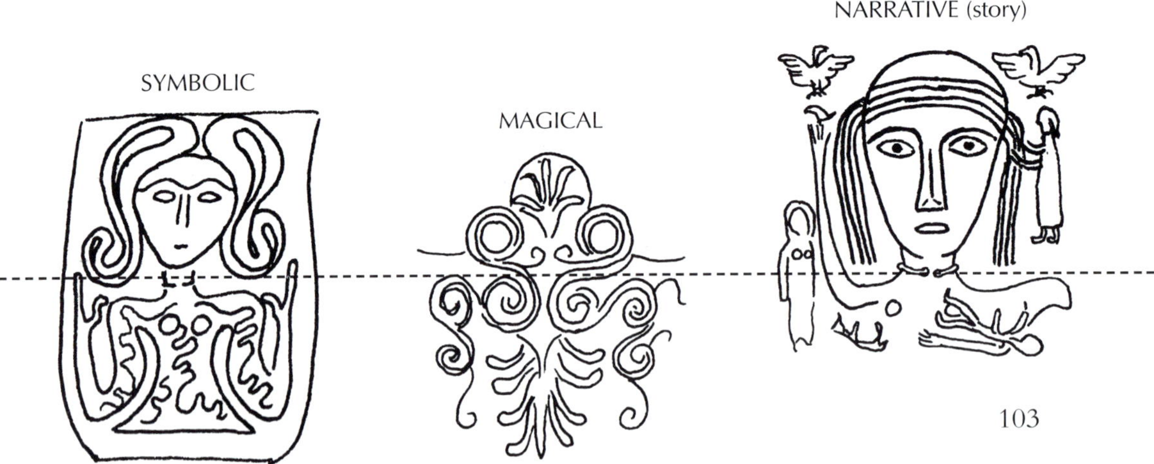

The main emphasis of Celtic religious experience is to be found in symbolic images that lead to a quiet, transcendental meditation. More often than not, the heads in Celtic art are a means to express that meditation. That is why I am reluctant to acknowledge that, originally, the Celts thought in terms of gods.

> The heads in Celtic art are a means to express that meditation. That is why I am reluctant to acknowledge that, originally, the Celts thought in terms of gods

Another reason is the similarity, already alluded to, between Celtic religion, as conveyed in its art, and aspects of Shamanism. Shamanism is the technique of ecstasy, and ritual journeys are a part of it: the two things are to be found in the art of La Tène. Mircea Eliade, the great authority on Shamanism, does not mention that it is necessary to have a concept of a god in Shamanism before Initiation can be accomplished. But Eliade states that 'seeing' spirits shows that a person has overcome the profane human condition.[1] Eliade describes 'initiation dreams' of tribes in Asia and Siberia where a spirit appears to the one undergoing the Initiation and he refers to the strange images that he sees, images like big birds carrying the soul to another dimension or to another world and back again. He also describes some of the terrifying visions of the one undergoing the experience, visions of his own body being torn, or of his heart being ripped out of him. He writes, too, of pleasant visions, like the vision of a beautiful woman. We ought to take special notice of Eliade's summary of the whole process of Initiation:

Taken together, they represent a well-organized variant of the universal theme of the death and mystical resurrection of the candidate by means of a descent to the underworld and an ascent to the sky.[2]

A vision of images is also a feature of the art of La Tène.

The Misinterpretation of the Religion La Tène

Without understanding the basic code of the religion of La Tène it is easy to misinterpret features of it. For instance, there are the references to some of its images as examples of sacrifice. Where did references to sacrifice come from? From the works of Greek and Latin authors. Frightening and terrible assertions have been made about Celtic 'religion', like the claim that rituals included human sacrifice and hanging and burning people. Julius Caesar even describes tribes in Gaul burning human beings in great structures made of wicker![3]

This is the response of the archaeologist Barry Cunliffe to allegations of this sort:

Convincing evidence of human sacrifices is surprisingly rare in the archaeological record.[4]

And here is the comment of the historian Ronald Hutton on the remarks of Caesar in general:

... he devoted very little space to describing his enemies, and when he did so he had a powerful motive for disparaging them in order to justify his aggressive warfare against them.[5]

And his comments on the remarks of Classical authors in general:

The ... texts are at first sight relatively numerous, representing between them a dozen authors, some of whom quote others. But their value diminishes considerably upon closer inspection. Virtually all were written between about 150 BC and AD 100, when the Celtic world was in the process of alteration and adaptation. Most referred only to the tribes of Southern Gaul, modern Provence and Languedoc, which may have been very atypical.[6]

Putting Their Existence in Order

The order seen in the images of the religious code of the art of La Tène is remarkably consistent all over Europe. We catch a glimpse of this order in some of the old Welsh tales. There is a striking example in the tale of 'Pwyll Prince of Dyfed'. The following is a brief summary of the relevant part of it – key words are indicated with bold type:

One day, whilst he was out hunting, Pwyll Prince of Dyfed got into great difficulties. He started to quarrel with Arawn, king of **Annwfn** (the Other World) about a stag that he had claimed from him. Pwyll had to make amends for this by consenting to help Arawn to rid himself of the oppression of Hafgan, another king of **Annwfn**, from a kingdom that was opposite to that of Arawn. Pwyll was to do this by exchanging kingdoms with Arawn. Pwyll went to **Annwfn**. Whilst he was there he slept with Arawn's wife, but he turned his back to her every night, and did not touch her. But, one night, Pwyll came face to face with Hafgan in a ford. Pwyll dealt him one mortal blow, and succeeded in putting that **underworld kingdom** in **ORDER**, in spite of danger to himself. The task involved an **experience of death**. Then Pwyll and Arawn met again and strengthened the good relationship between them. The outcome of it all was that Pwyll brought **ORDER** to the two kingdoms, or the two worlds, although they were so different:

'And by reason of his sojourn that year in Annwn, and his having ruled there so prosperously and united the two kingdoms in one by his valour and his prowess, the name of Pwyll Prince of Dyfed fell into disuse, and he was called Pwyll Head of Annwn from that time forth.'[7]

Pwyll comes into contact with the Other World, Annwn; he undergoes an experience of Spiritual Transformation. That contact brings better order to him and his kingdom.

The Deep and Annwn

Is the Deep the same place as Annwn (or Annwfn)? Is Annwn a place or a dimension? The following is a summary of suppositions about the place:

Annwn is the Other World, or in full Annwfn from the negative an- and dwfn (world) as I prefer to interpret it. This is the Not-World, the world that is not this world. The other explanation of Annwn is that it was an Inner World, within the earth: but that is a limitation on the meaning of the word, as can be seen. From the evidence available, it is difficult to conceive what kind of place it was or where it was. The beliefs of the Celts about the Other World were influenced by ideas about an Other World in other religions, especially by Classical and Christian ideas. Indeed, 'Annwn' became another word for 'hell' in Welsh.[8]

The concept of the Deep is itself a duality: on the one hand, it is a place to die and, on the other a place to be born or reborn. These are some ideas about the nature of Annwn in Welsh and Irish literature:

There are many names for Annwn, and all of them give us some idea of what kind of place it was. There is Tir na n-Og (Land of the Young), Tir Tairngiri (Land of Promise), Tir na t-Samhraidh (Land of Summer), Magh Mell (Land of Joy), Tir inna mBeo (Land of the Living) and so on in Irish. In Welsh we have Caer Siddi (Land of the Síd: in Ireland these are underworld fairies), and Caer Feddwid (Fortress of Intoxication).[9]

Many of these features are similar to the features of the Deep in the art of La Tène. It should be borne in mind that, like the Deep, the Welsh Annwn had another aspect, a negative one. Originally the Deep was a dimension, and it is likely that Annwn was also a dimension.

The Circle and the Centre

In this book we have often referred to the main framework of Spiritual Transformation. In diagrams, the Borderline between the Upper Region and the Deep has been shown by a horizontal line, and the tranquil meditation by a vertical line. We have also mentioned torques and circles with significant patterns upon them. Here are some more details of the circle and the centre.

The two diagrams, **104** and **105**, show the framework with a horizontal Borderline, vertical meditation and a circular framework.

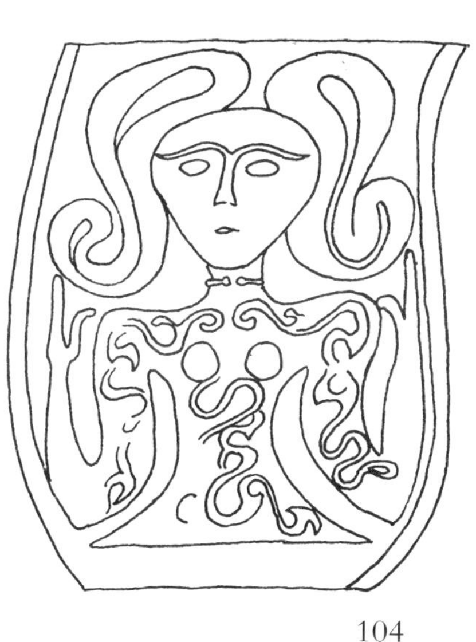

104

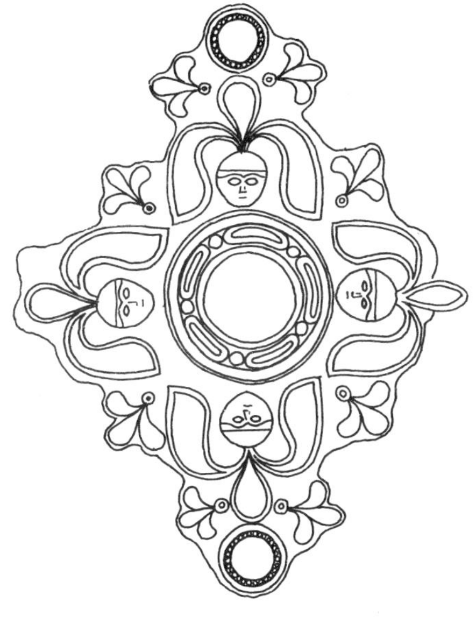

105

If we imagine that we are looking at figure **104** face to face, then we are looking down at figure **105**. There are four leafy heads in four extremities around a circular centre, all in a commensurate pattern. In this centre, we find the quiet, eternal meditation. But the pattern of Transformation is also to be seen in the heads. Note that there are three leaves (bear in mind the triads) on each head, two in a downward direction and one in an upward direction – the one in an upward direction has a phallic aspect. The leaves suggest descent and ascent, and the quiet meditation is found in every head, not only the one in the middle. In fact, we have five versions of Spiritual Transformation here, one represented by the whole, and four by the four leafy heads, see figure **106**.

The importance of the centre is obvious in some tales, as in the tale of 'Pwyll Prince of Dyfed'

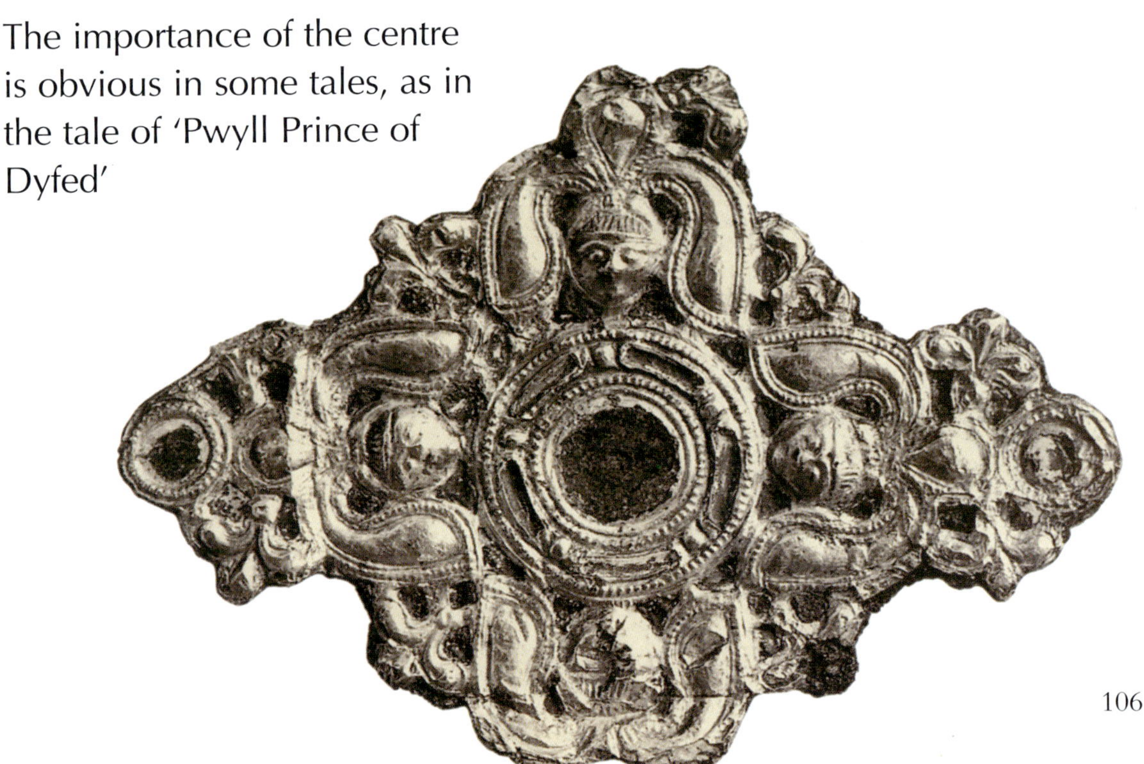

106

The importance of the centre is obvious in some tales, as in the tale of 'Pwyll Prince of Dyfed', the First Branch of the Mabinogi. The relevant part of the tale follows, with the significant words indicated in bold type:

And on the morrow in the young of the day he [Pwyll] arose and came to Glyn Cuch to loose his dogs into the wood. And he sounded his horn and began to muster the hunt, and followed after the dogs and lost his companions; and whilst he was listening to the cry of the pack, he could hear the cry of another pack, but they had not the same cry, and were coming to meet his own pack. And he could see a clearing in the wood as of a level field, and as his pack reached the edge of the clearing, he could see a stag in front of the other pack. And towards the **MIDDLE** of the clearing, lo, the pack that was pursuing it overtaking it and bringing it to the ground.[10]

It is towards the centre of the clearing that Pwyll has his wondrous vision.

If we consider the importance of the centre, it is interesting to note that the Celts had a word, *nemeton* (in Welsh *nyfed*), to signify a 'sacred glade'. To them the centre was the most sacred place. The archaeologist Jean Louis Brunaux comments in this way on the centre of the later 'temples' of the Celts, temples which were of a rectangular shape:

Inside the enclosure, the most sacred area was the centre. This was often determined geometrically and was then occupied by a post, a pit, or a building.[11]

The plan shown in **107** is an example of a sanctuary in Gournay, in Belgium. According to Brunaux it has an entrance and a centre that he considers to be particularly sacred. In their art and their sanctuaries it is clear that, for the Celts, the centre was a very special place.

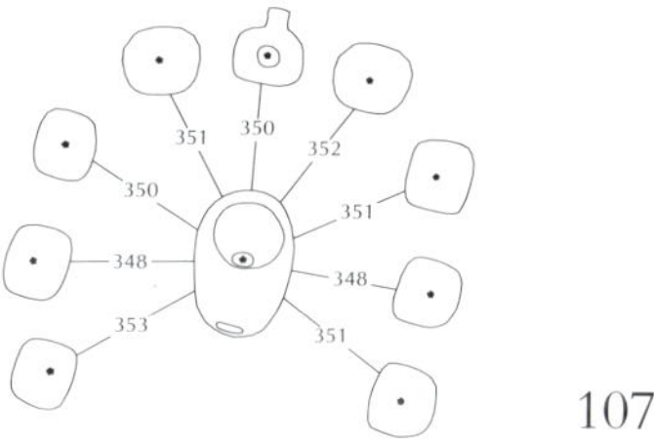

107

Figure **108** and the diagram of it, **109**, show another example of the circular framework.

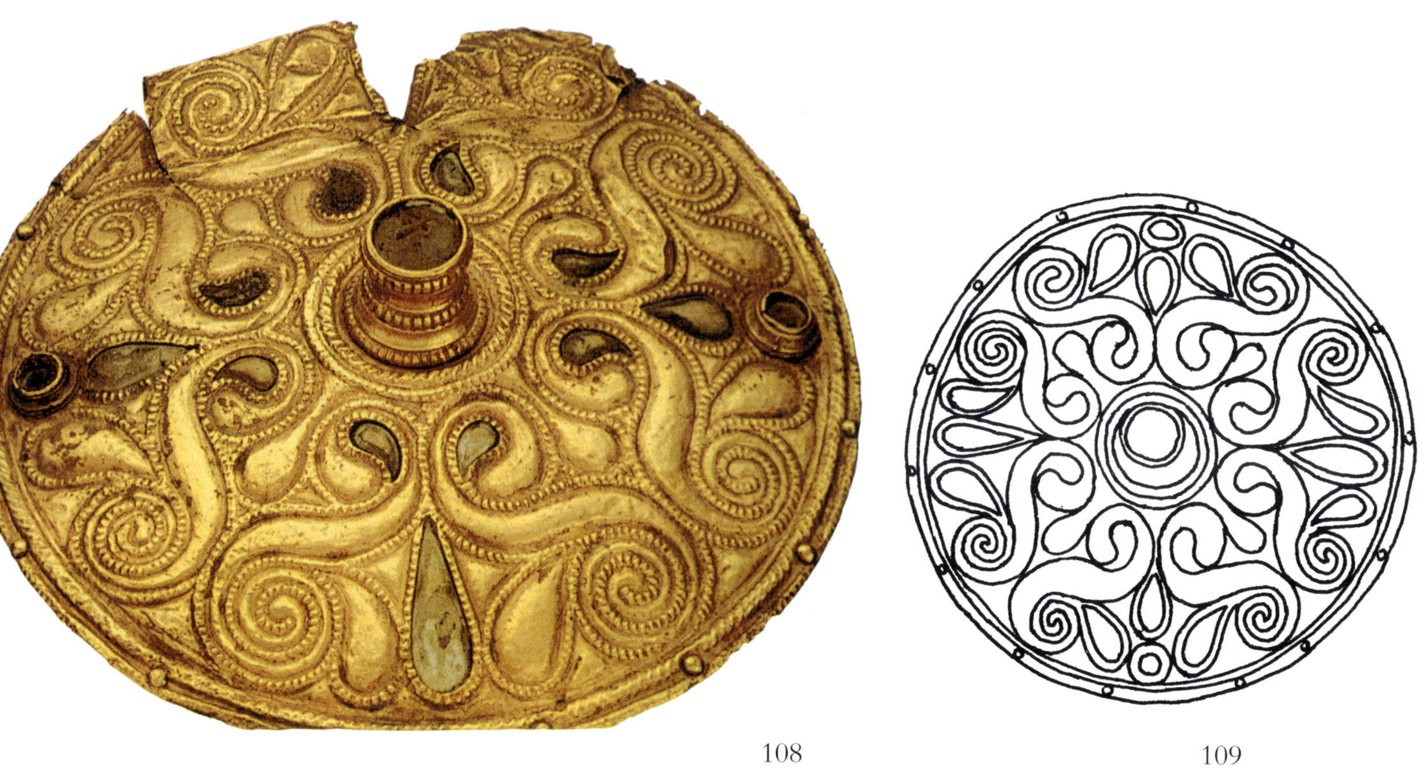

108

109

It should be remembered that the centre represents the Deep. Note how we are drawn towards the centre by the spirals. Here we have four pairs of spiralled circles, in the shape of an 'S', leading to the Deep. From the circles in the centre, phallic shapes arise. We see that there are triads of leaves on the rim of the complete circle, two downwards (representing the descending force) and one upwards (representing the ascending force). Once again we have five versions of Spiritual Transformation, one represented by the whole, and four in the patterns within the outer circle.

It is worth considering whether there is a relationship between these circular patterns and the ritual interest of the Celts in openings into the earth, such as holes or pools.

Figure **110** shows a burial mound with a circle of stones around it.

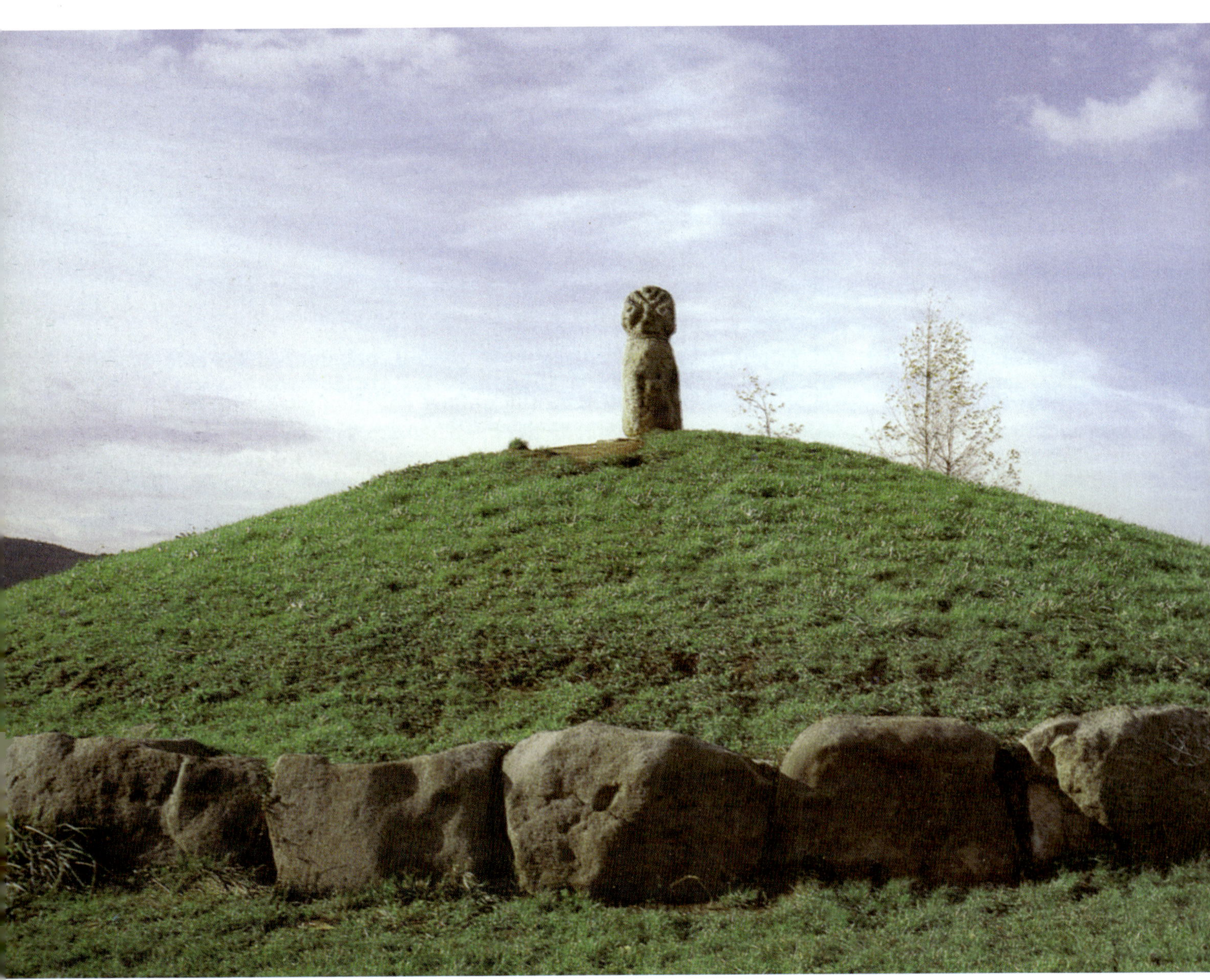

110

In the centre of the mound is a sculpture with a two-faced head, each face looking in a different direction. The complete head is phallic. Although this was the grave of a soldier and a girl, this head was not meant to portray either of them; it is a symbolic head. Here we find a consciousness that the circle and the centre were sacred places. The sculpture was placed in the creative womb of the earth. There is a mixture here of death and life, in accord with the pattern of Spiritual Transformation.

Figure **111** shows a disc with two circles of symbolic heads.

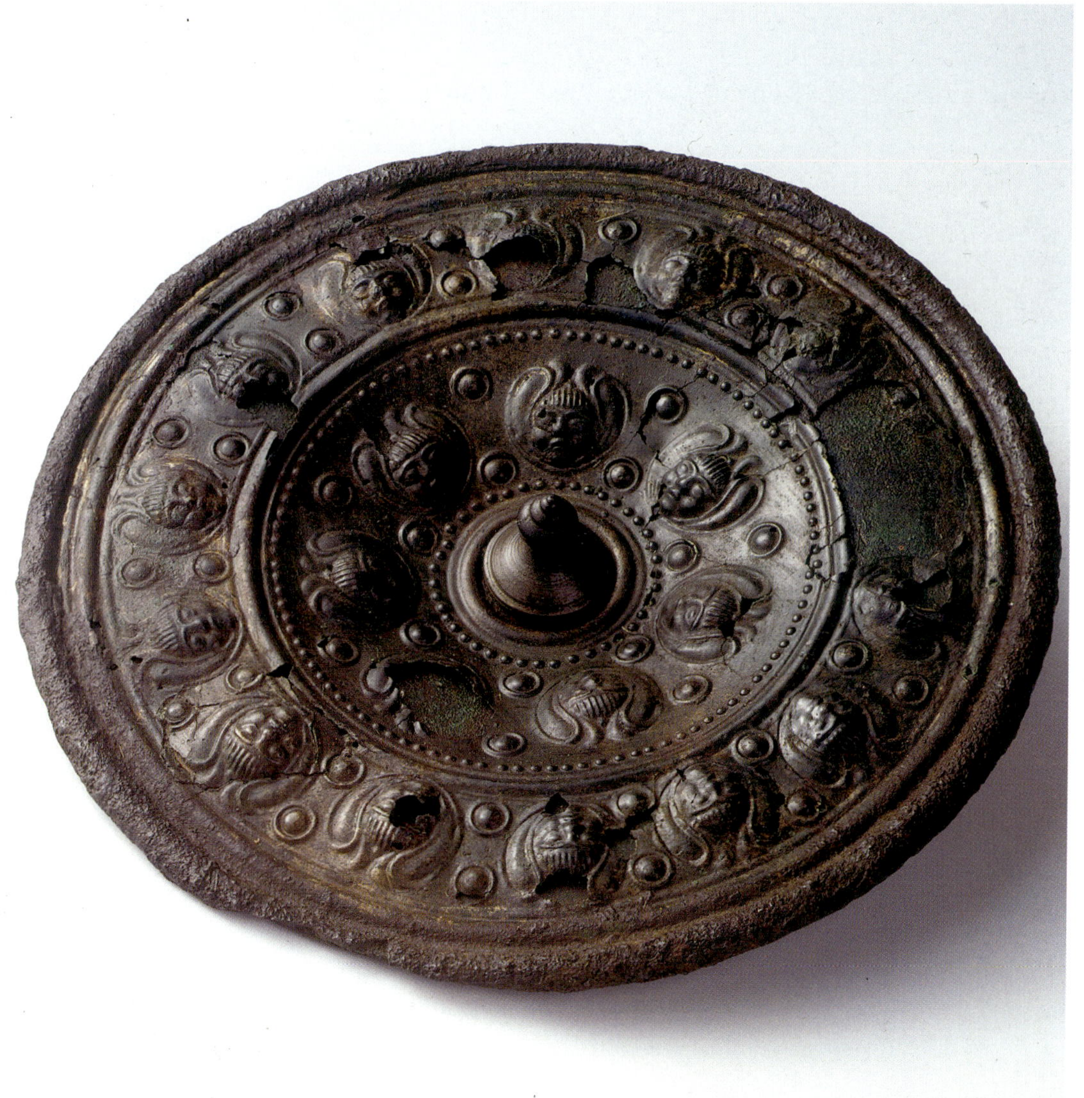

111

These shapes represent the spirit or soul of a group of people engaged in a religious rite. Note how light and uplifting these circles are.

Spirit and Soul

The words 'spirit' and 'soul' are used for the belief of the Celts about a person's immortal essence. It must be asked whether the Celtic belief in the existence of the soul after the death of the body accounts for their obsession about depositing objects in holes and in pools, that is, depositing them in the Deep. Did they believe, literally, that what was cast into a grave went into the womb of the earth to be reborn? This is possible. It may be that the ritual of Transformation that is present in the art of La Tène is a code for communal meditation, a rite held in the open air to cast objects down into shafts, graves, wells and so on, that is, into the Deep. (Of course, there could be other reasons for depositing arms, namely to prevent them from going into the hands of the enemy.) Remember the remark made by Julius Caesar concerning the belief of the Druids, that the soul did not die but 'passes from one body to another'.[12]

The Head

It is a common assertion that the Celts' obsession with the human head issued from their belief that the soul dwells in the head. In their art the head is the most prominent symbol of quiet, spiritual meditation.

Figure **112** shows skulls in a pillar in a temple at Roquepertuse, and **113** shows carvings of heads in a pillar in a temple at Entremont, the two places being in southern Gaul. Their location in sacred places suggests their importance.

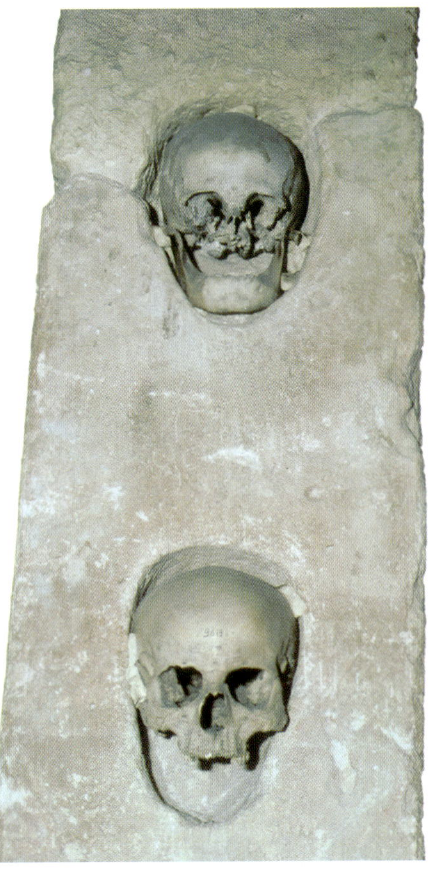

112

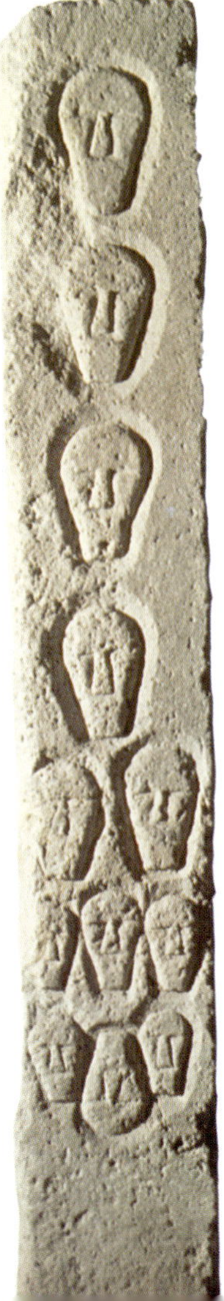

113

We can see that one head at the bottom, in **113**, is upside down: this suggests that the heads went down into the Deep and then up again.

Diodorus Siculus' well-known descriptions confirm how important the human head was to the Celts:

They cut off the heads of enemies in battle and attach them to the necks of their horses. The blood-stained spoils they hand over to their attendants and carry off as booty, while striking up a paean and singing a song of victory; and they nail up these fruits upon their houses, just as do those who lay low wild animals in certain kinds of hunting. They embalm in cedar oil the heads of the most distinguished enemies, and preserve them carefully in chests, and display them with pride to strangers, saying that for this head one of their ancestors, or his father, or the man himself, refused the offer of a large sum of money.[13]

If the soul was in the head, then the Celts possessed the souls of their enemies by possessing their heads.

The Welsh tale, more than any other, that shows clearly that the old idea of the importance of the head remained after the age of the Celts is the tale of 'Branwen daughter of Llŷr', the Second Branch of the Mabinogi. In a savage war in Ireland between the warriors of Britain and the Irish, the British giant-king, Bendigeidfran, was wounded. He ordered his warriors to cut off his head and carry it with them back to Britain. Here are his words – I have drawn attention to some things by putting them in bold type:

And you will be a long time upon the road. In Harddlech you will be feasting seven years, and the birds of Rhiannon singing unto you. **And the head will be as pleasant company to you as ever it was at best when it was on me.** And at Gwales in Penfro [Pembroke] you will be fourscore years; and until you open the door towards Aber Henfelen, the side facing Cornwall, you may bide there, and the head with you uncorrupted. But from the time you have opened the door, you may not bide there: make for London to bury the head. And do you cross over to the other side.[14]

The soul was in the head although it had been cut off from the body.

This is testimony from a tale from the Christian era. There are other testimonies concerning the lasting significance of the head in the old Celtic countries, such as the evidence of the half circle of phallic heads found in two Christian churches from about the twelfth century AD – figures **114** and **115**. It is likely that the old belief about the soul being in the head was still alive, centuries after the age of the 'Celts' had passed away.

Notes on page 114

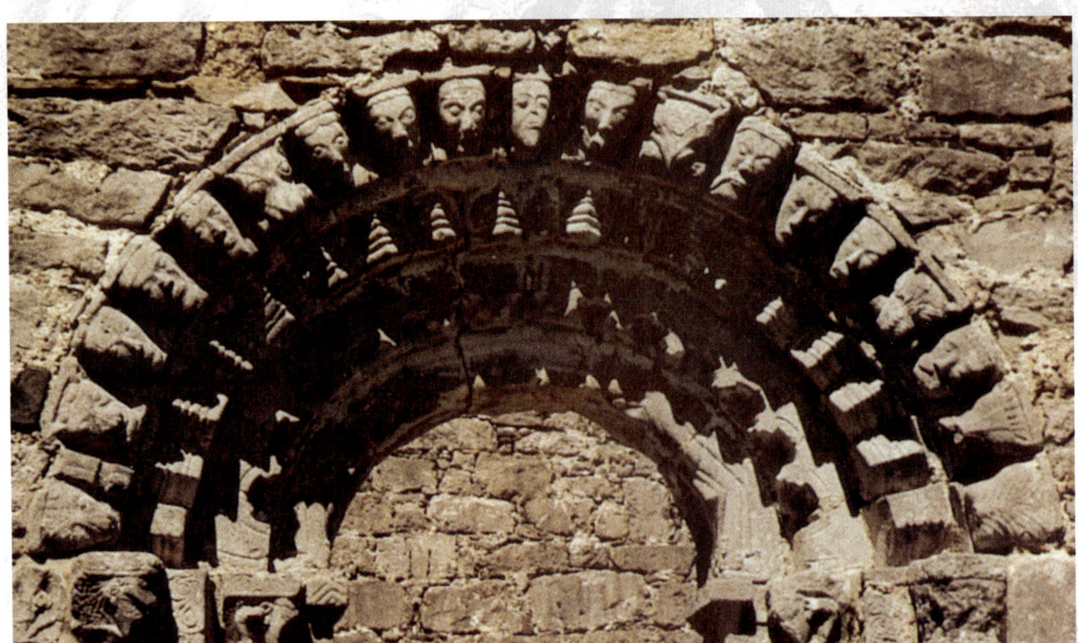

114

Evidence of the half circle of
phallic heads found in two
Christian churches from about
the twelfth century AD

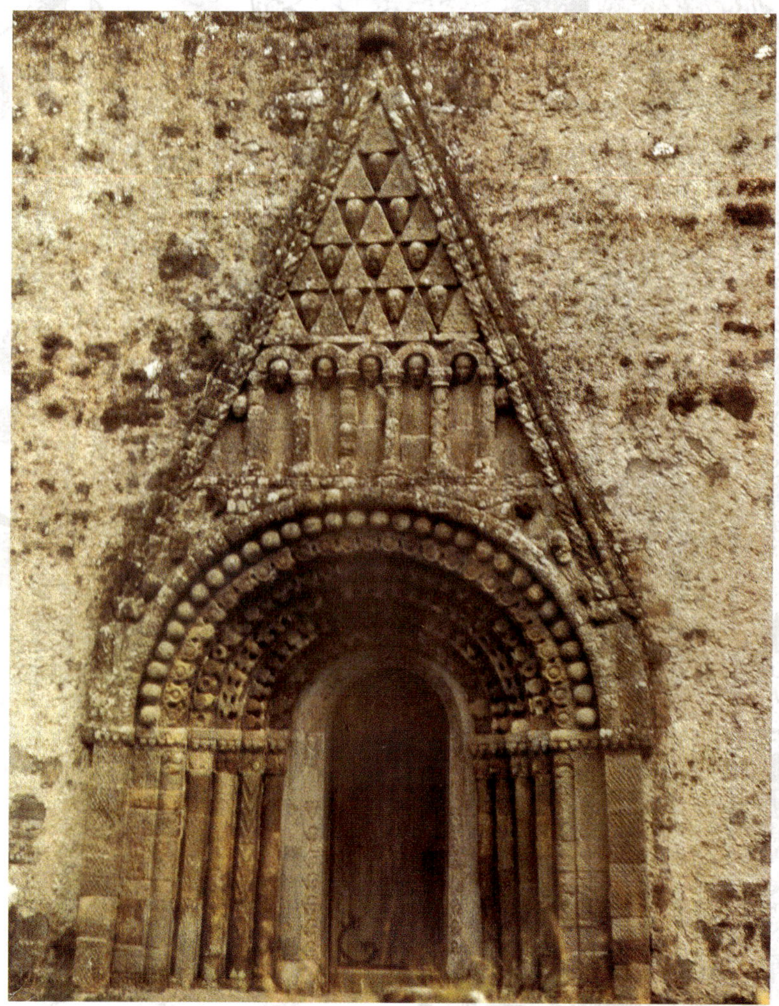

115

10 The Art of War

The Celts were renowned for their warlike nature. Imagine yourself going into battle in the old world in an army and facing a horde of Celts. In front of their host would be warrior lords, advancing to challenge the bravest of your warriors to single combat.

Imagine the Celtic war leader wearing a ceremonial helmet, **116**. On top of the helmet there is a bird of prey, with red eyes, whose wings flap as the leader issues his challenge. All of this would cause fear and trembling.

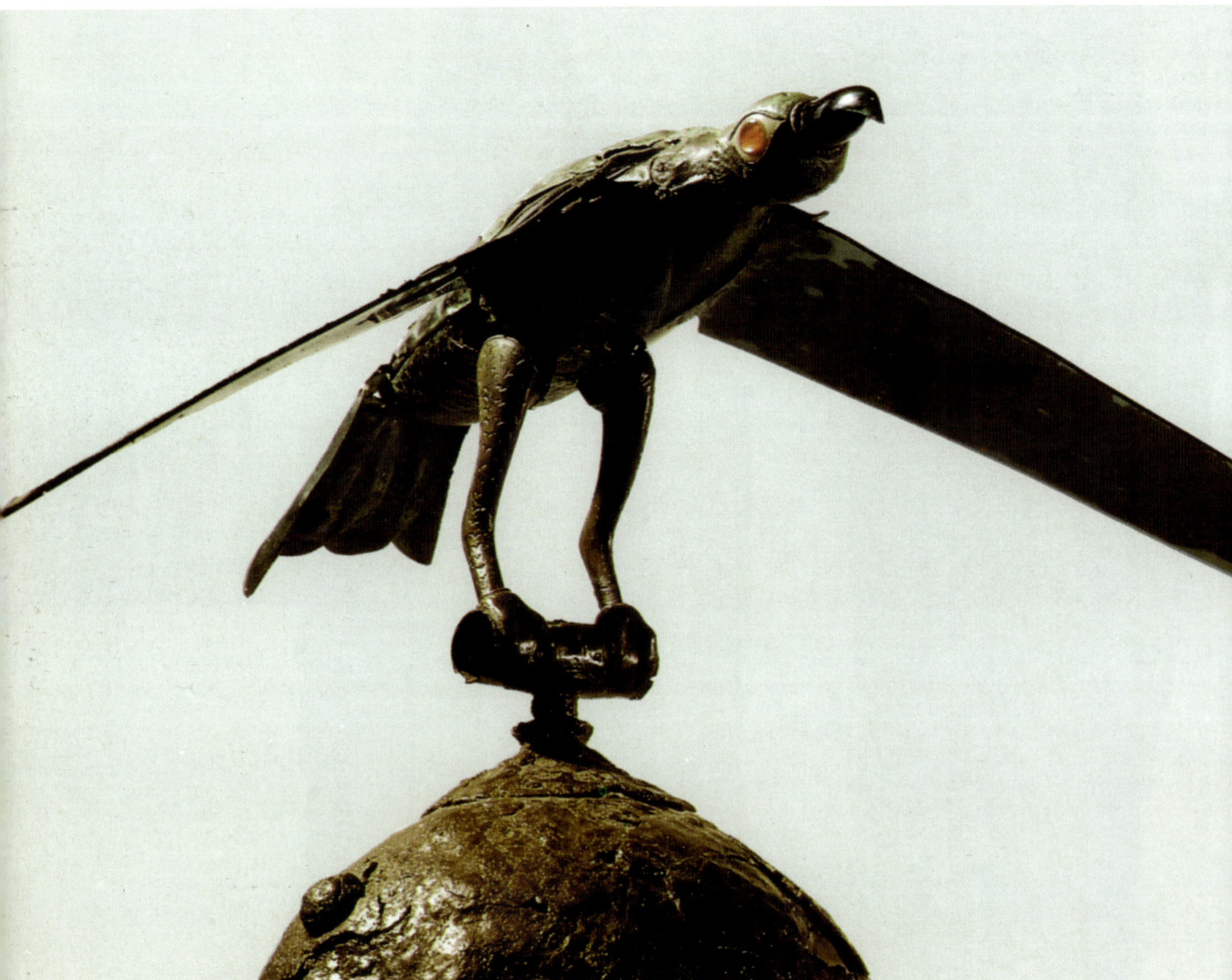

116

The following is Diodorus Siculus' description of the preparation for battle:

When the armies are drawn up in battle-array, they [the Celtic leaders] are wont to advance before the battle line and to challenge the bravest of their opponents to a single combat, and at the same time brandishing before them their arms so as to terrify their foe. When someone accepts their challenge to battle, they loudly recite the deeds of valour of their ancestors and proclaim their own valorous quality, at the same time abusing and making little of their opponents and generally attempting to rob him beforehand of his fighting spirit.[1]

Imagine the boastful shouting and taunting challenge of the Celtic leaders!

But this is not all that there would be on the battlefield. There would be periods of terrifying and deafening sound, some of it created by horns called 'carnyx', **117**. Just think of the frightening sounds that would emanate from the head of the boar with its savage mouth and terrifying eyes at the end of the horn.

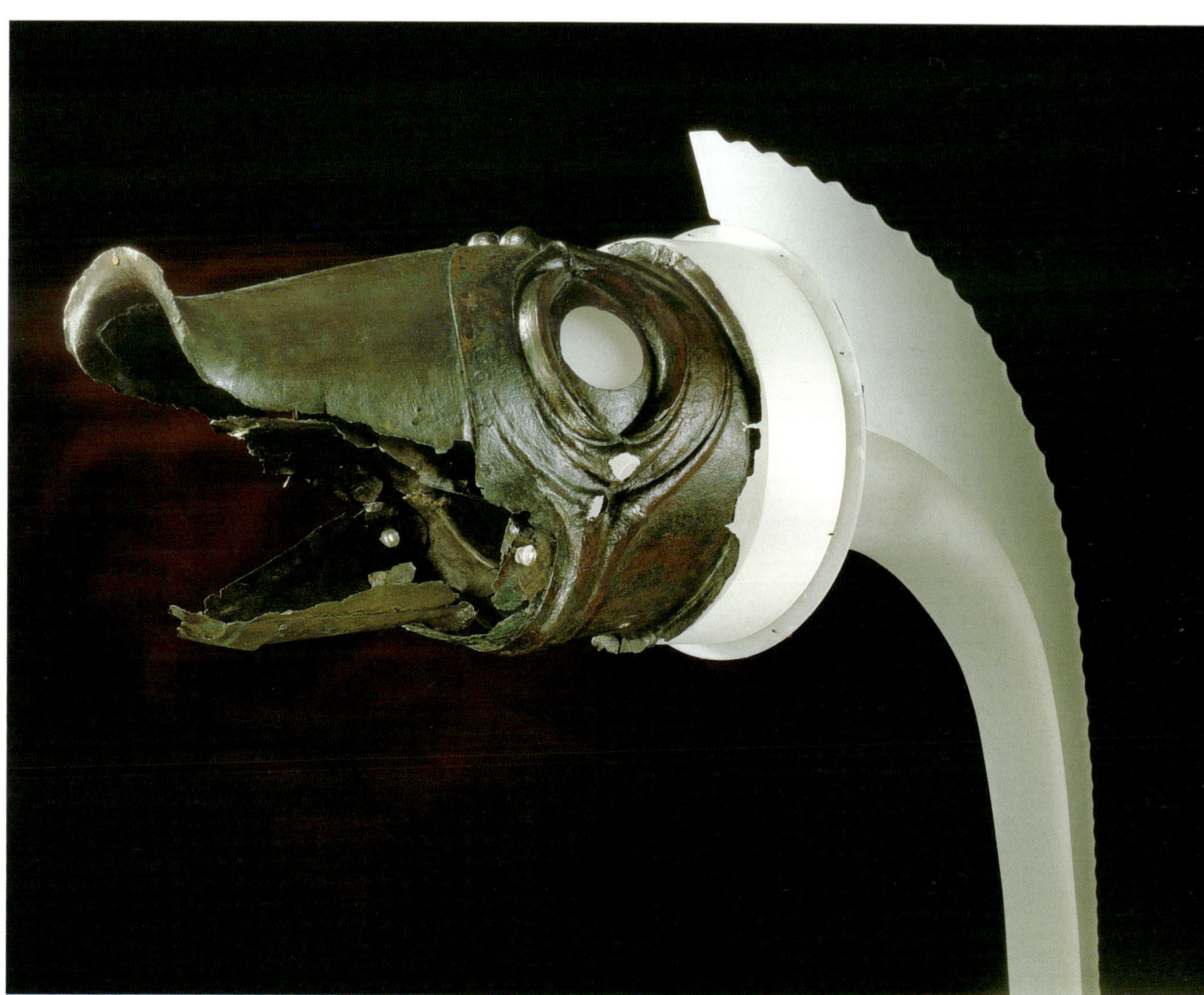

117

The following is a description by Polybius of a battle circa 225 BC:

They [the enemy] were terrified by the fine order of the Celtic host, and the dreadful din, for there were innumerable horn blowers and trumpeters, and the whole army was shouting their war cries at the same time: there was such a tumult of sound that it seemed that … all the country round had got a voice and caught up the cry. Very terrifying too were the appearance and gestures of the naked warriors in front, all in the prime of life and finely built men, and all in the leading companies richly adorned with gold torques and armlets.[2]

Figure **118** gives us a Classical impression of a Celtic warrior, naked except for his helmet, his torque and belt.

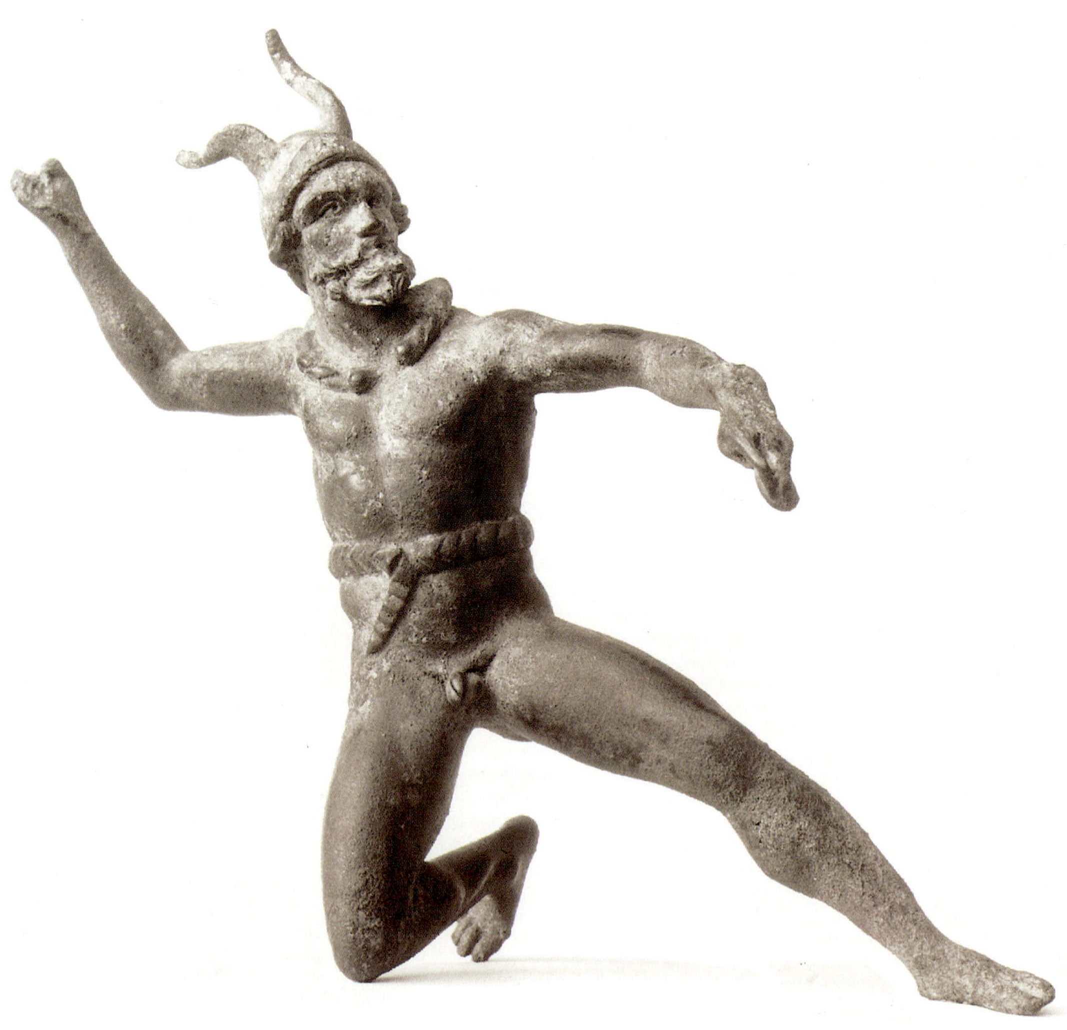

118

Many examples of Celtic helmets, torques, belt buckles, shields, swords, scabbards, and chariot gear have survived. Many of these were used in battle, but several of them were, it is thought, ceremonial gear – as, for example, **116**. The art of the Celts is found on their weaponry, especially their ceremonial gear, and it can be said that the Celts – in this context, especially Celtic warriors – wore their art. Why? To terrify the enemy, certainly, but also to fortify themselves with signs of their religion to face terrible tasks.

Let us consider some remarkable examples of Celtic shields from England, **119** and **120**. Figure **119** is the famous Battersea shield, and **120** the Witham shield.

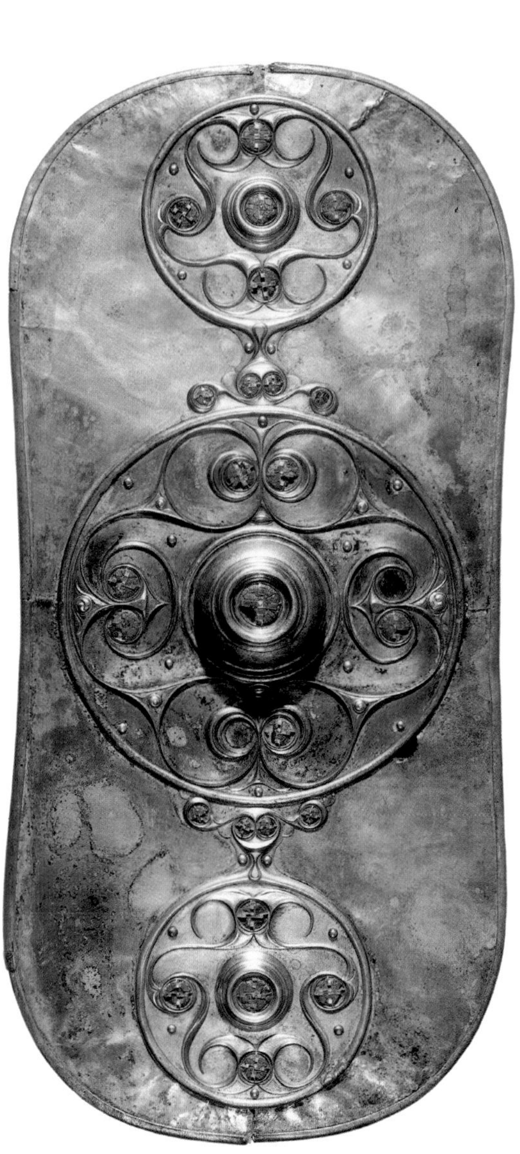

119

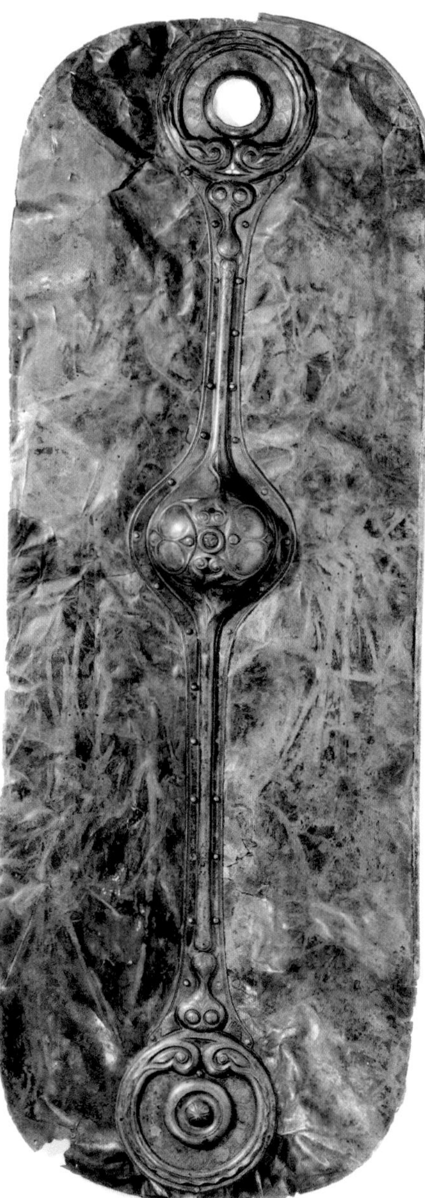

120

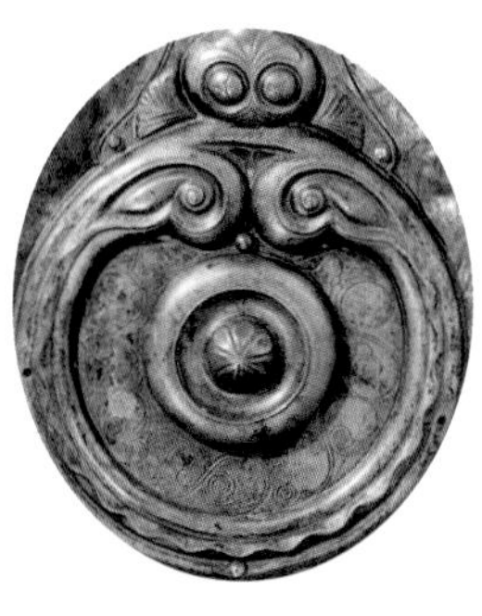

121

These shields would hardly be used in real battles. The archaeologist J.V.S. Megaw made
this comment on the Witham shield:

As to the use to which Witham may have been put, it can hardly have been defensive since even with
a wooden backing the thickness of the shield cannot have exceeded 0.5cm.[3]

The shields are covered with refined decorations which are also significant symbols. There
are spirals on the two shields. It will be remembered that in the art of La Tène spirals like
this signify agitation, especially stress on going into the Deep. Similar spirals are found on
various kinds of ceremonial battle gear. The purpose of these spirals is to remind warriors of
the Deep, the dimension of death, but also the dimension of birth and rebirth. For the
warriors this was a kind of insurance against death – once again we recall the words of
Caesar that their belief in immortality made Celtic warriors recklessly
brave in battles. Some archaeologists claim that there
is a boar symbol on the Witham shield: there
is a similar symbol on one of the
panels of the Gundestrup
Cauldron. A boar is an
animal that burrows: there
is a hint of burrowing
into the Deep in the
representations of
it.

Figures **122**
and **123**
provide
further
examples
of spirals.

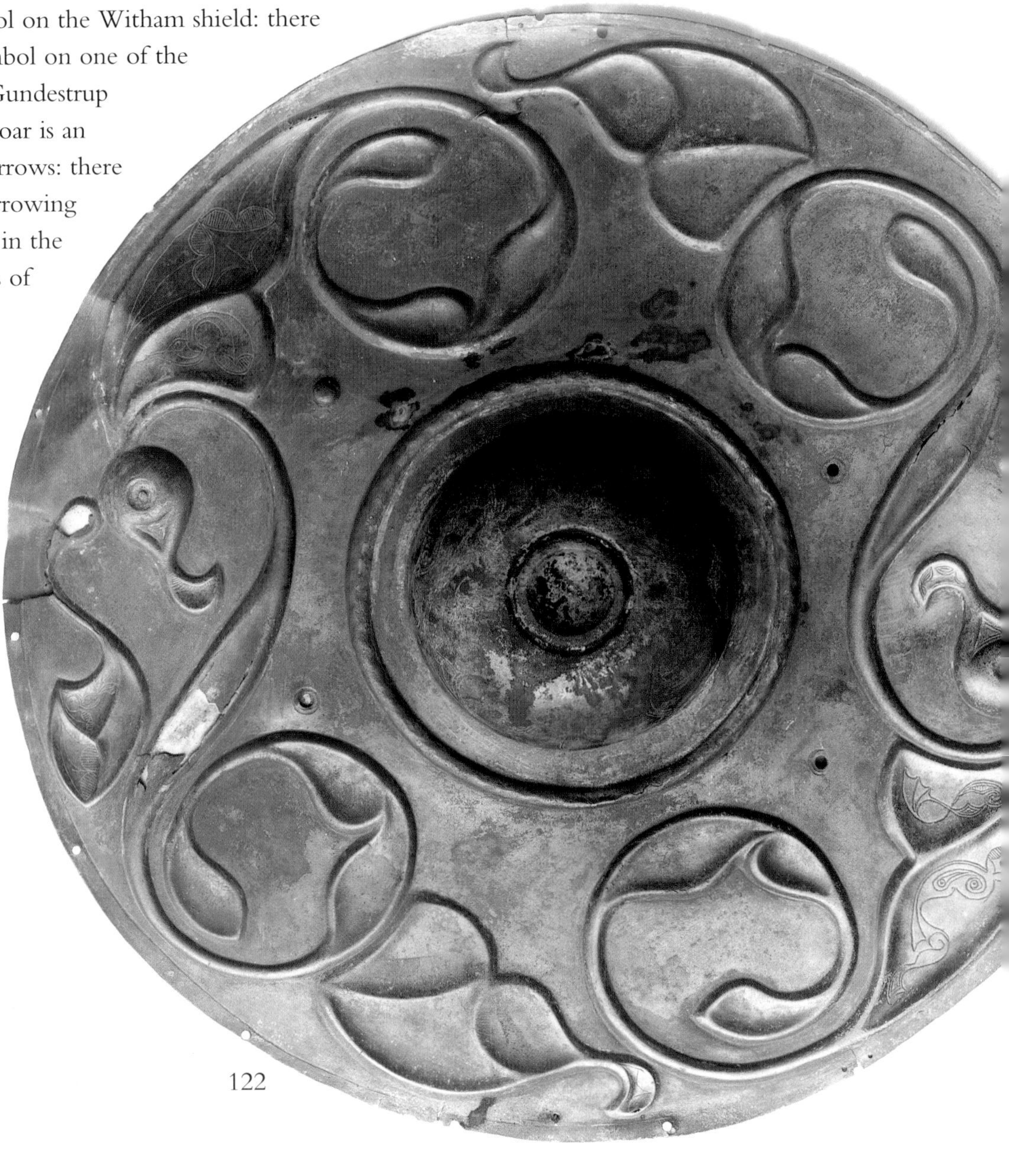

122

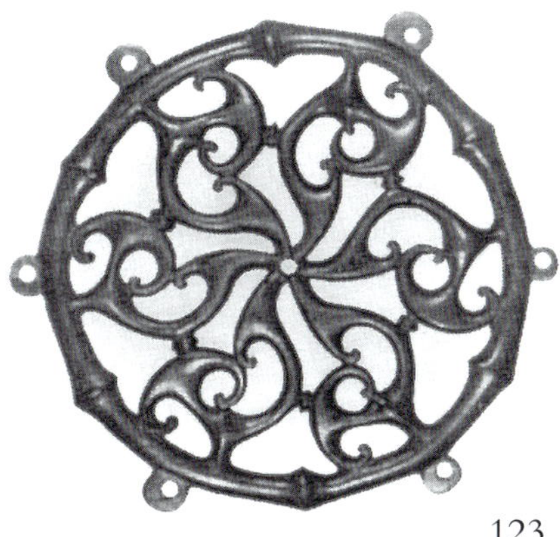

123

In **122**, in the boss or middle of a shield, there is a spiral line with the head of a dead bird of prey at one end of it, and buds or leaves, signifying birth, on the other end. Figure **123** provides an example of a spiral pattern around the Deep of the middle.

Figure **124** shows a pony cap from Scotland. There are spirals on it, and also spirals on its horns. On the end of one of the horns is the head of a bird of prey looking downwards. Again there is a hint of the Deep here.

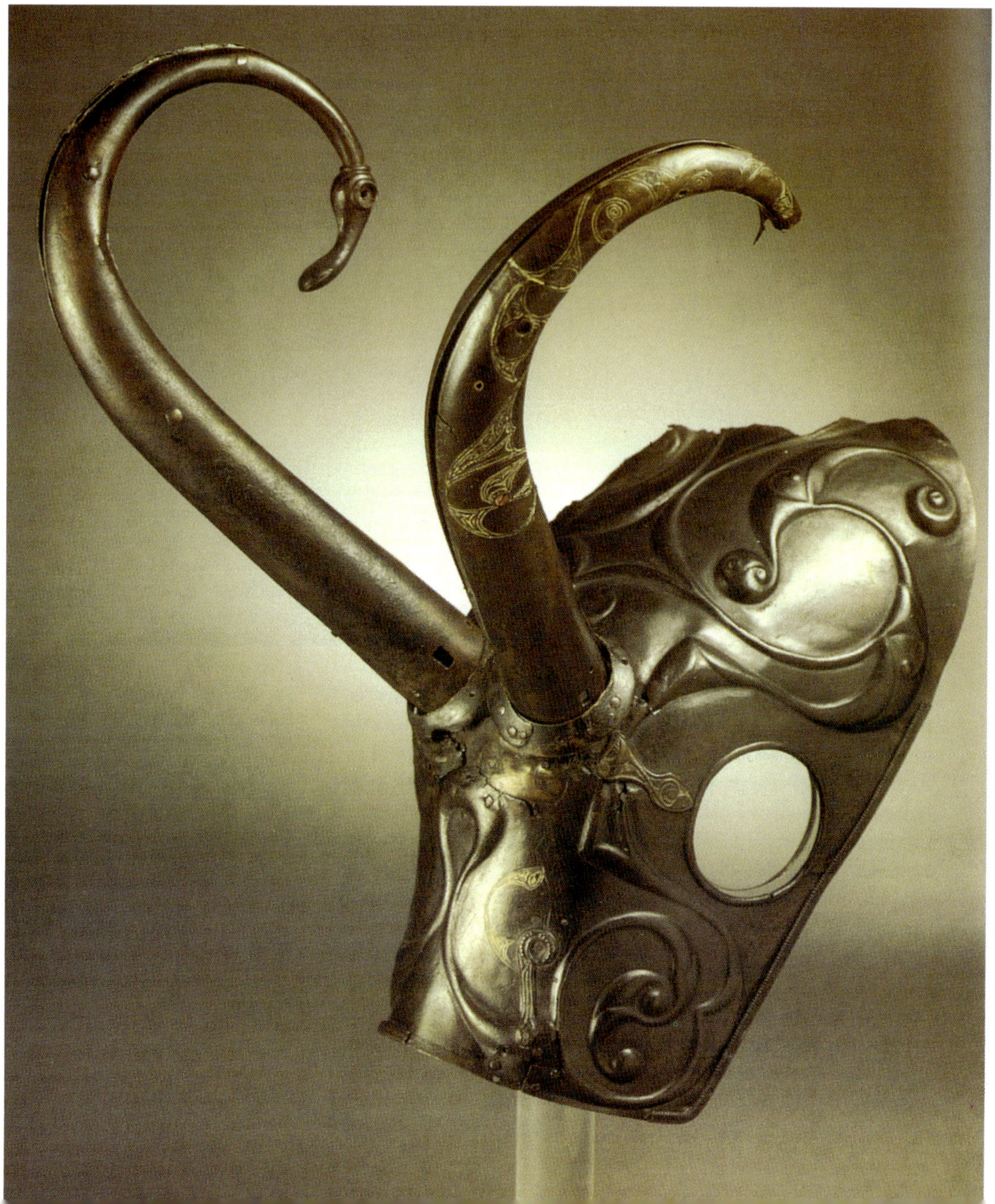

124

Figure **125** shows a part of the mount on a shield from Wandsworth. Its top is upright; it is likely that another part – now lost – was upside down. There is a hint of an owl in the head, a bird associated with darkness and the negative aspect of the Deep.

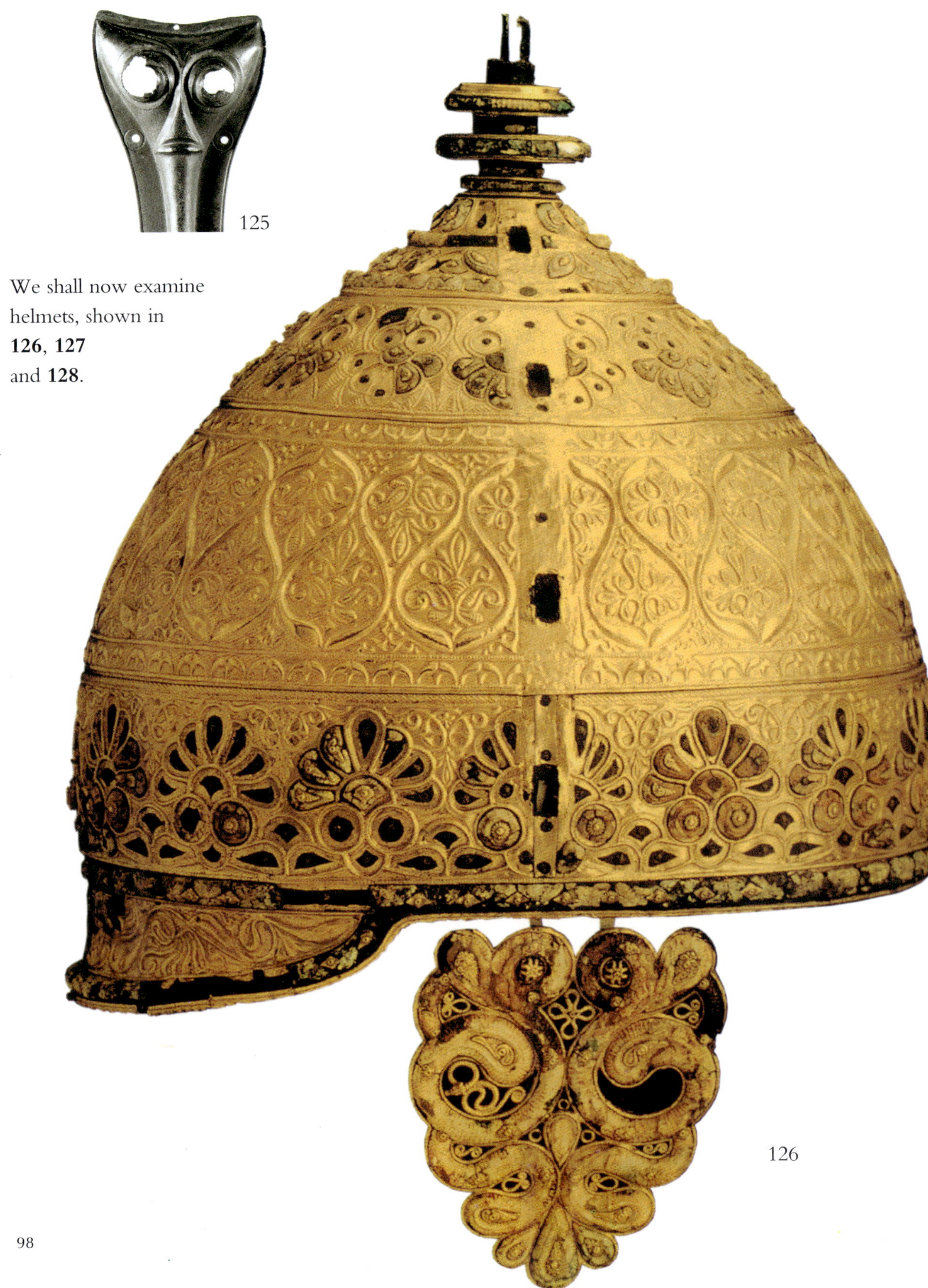

125

We shall now examine helmets, shown in **126**, **127** and **128**.

126

Figure **126** is an exquisitely fashioned helmet. It is covered with spirals of gold which, of course, represent the Deep. Upon the circular pattern at the top of the helmet are patterned images of an owl-like face, and also budding leaves. The owl has an association with the negative aspect of the Deep (darkness and death), and the buds a connection with the positive aspect (day and rebirth). On the middle strip is a pattern of contrasting shapes, up and down alternately. Within every shape is a plant, one with its head down alternately with one with its head up. The whole is like a labyrinth in the Deep. In the lowest strip are shapes, each like the head of an owl with large eyes, and also like a flower. On the tip of the helmet is a spiral and there are strange shapes on its ear flaps. The head of whoever wore this helmet would have been covered with signs of the Deep.

On top of **127** is a face not unlike that of an owl, leading through a spiral line to a spiral shape beneath. Underneath all of this is a spiral line. These are all reminders of the Deep.

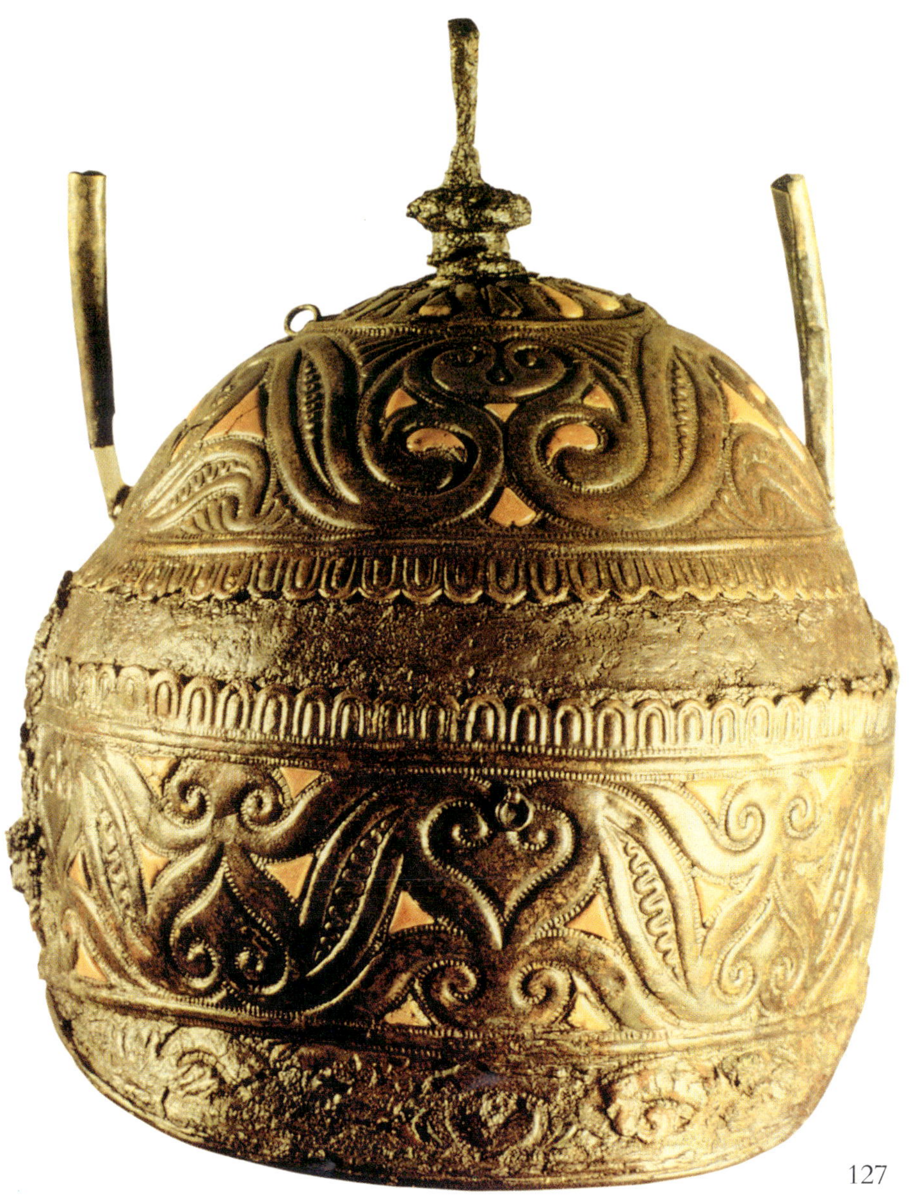

127

The helmet shown in **128** has some gold work on it. It is covered with spirals, and includes one spiral in the form of a triad.

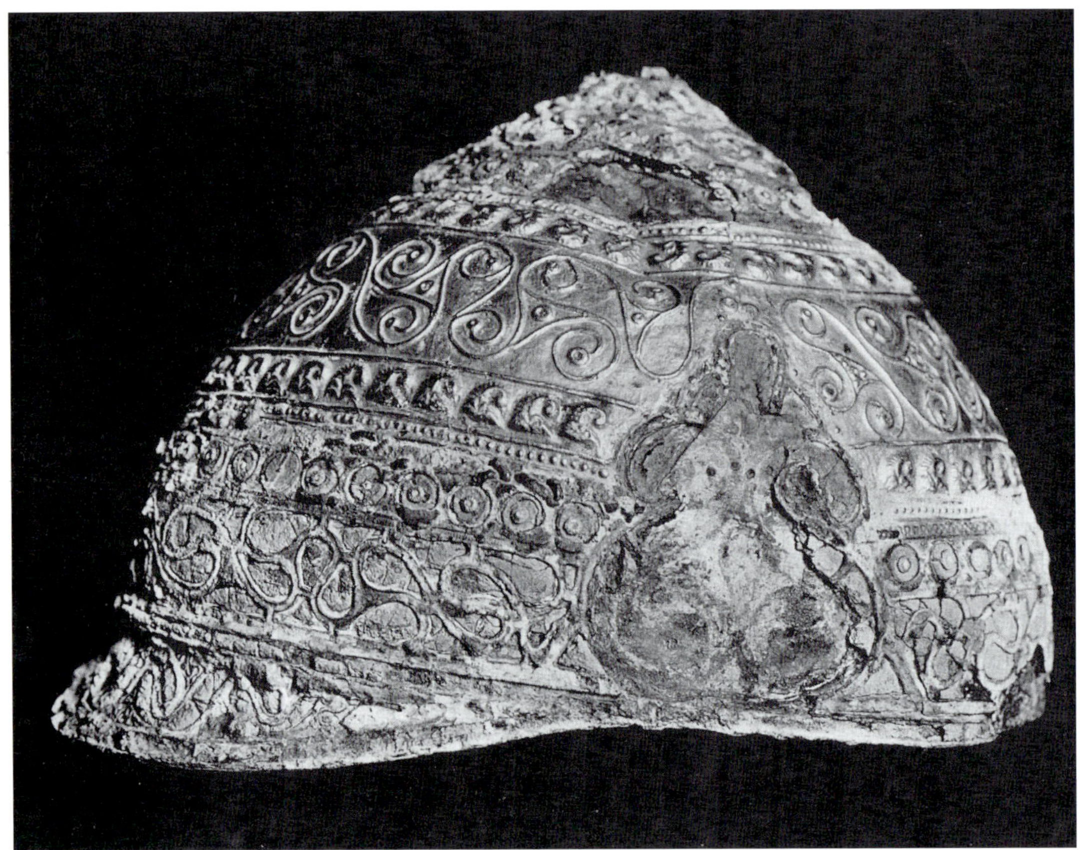

128

Numerous examples of sword scabbards covered with spirals could have been chosen, like **129**, for instance. But without the decoration on the sword handle which would have fitted into this scabbard, one cannot comment on the complete artwork. The scabbard – or sheath – of course suggests the feminine Deep.

129

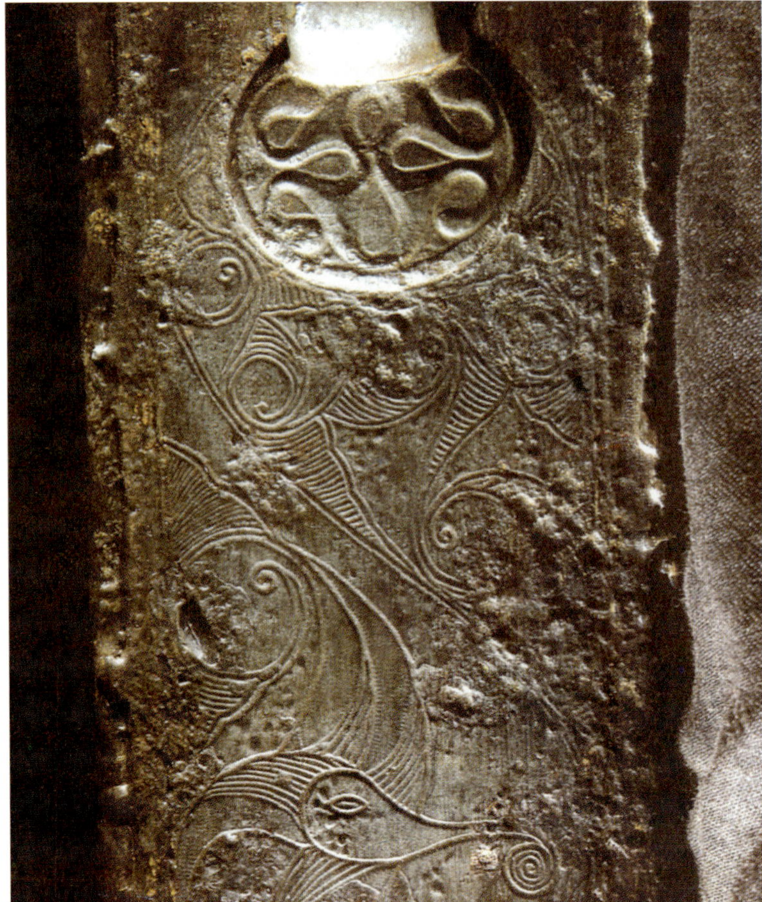

Figure **130** shows a complete handle and scabbard, though the handle is faded and worn. There is a horizontal row of spirals on the handle. On the scabbard is a spiral forming the shape of big owlish eyes. Below this is a decoration that suggests a plant upside down.

Last of all let us consider two axle pins from war chariots, **131**, **132**. On **131** there is a hint of an owl, the bird of the Deep. On **132** there is a spiral turning into a circle, and within that circle there are contrasting symbols, like ying and yang, acknowledged symbols of duality. The Deep is present here too.

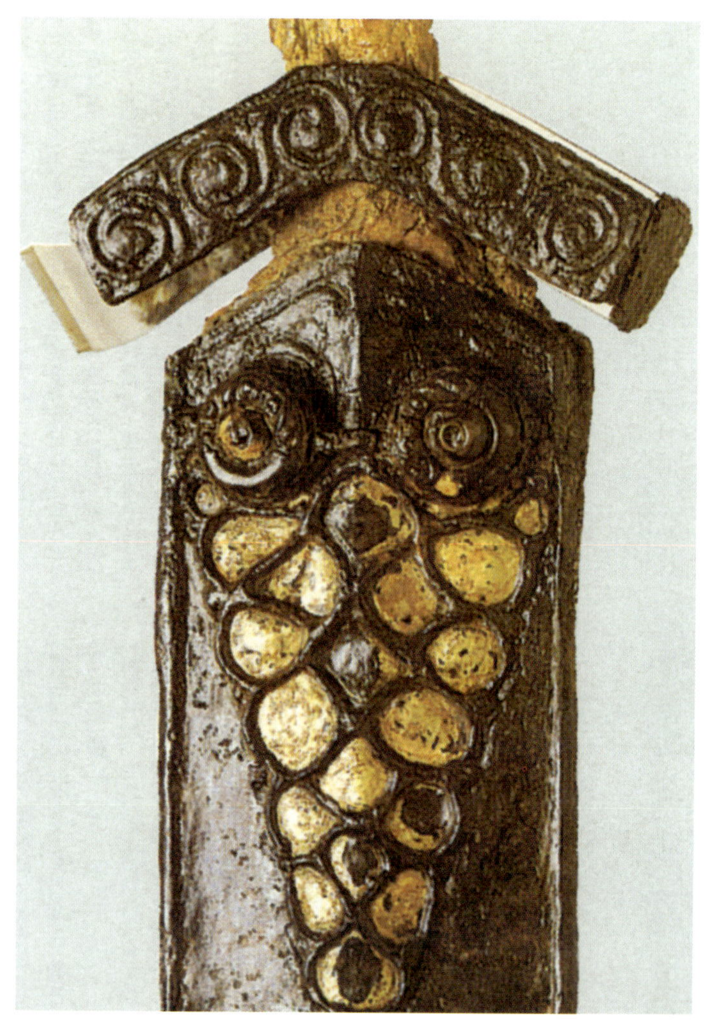

130

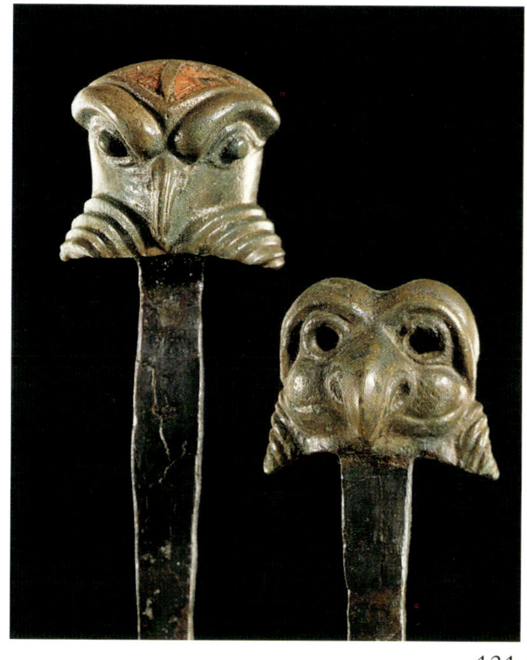

131

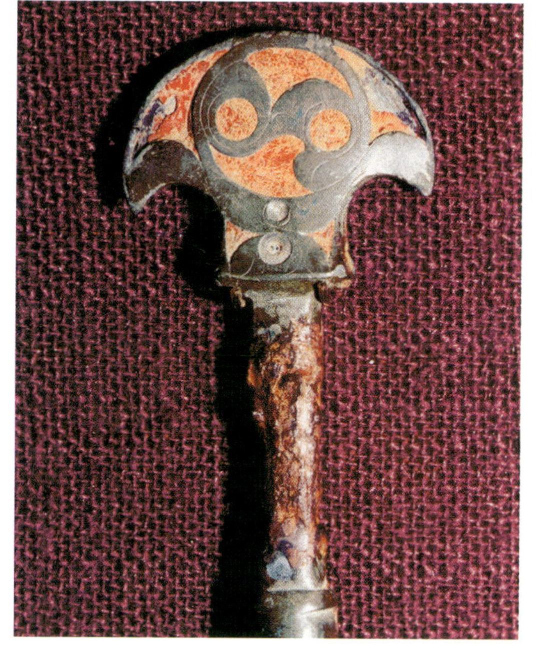

132

We shall conclude this chapter by referring again to one of the panels on the Gundestrup Cauldron, **133**, where the experience of Spiritual Transformation, or Initiation, is presented in the context of war. It is likely that we have here a glimpse of the confidence of Celtic warriors in the endless cycle of existence.

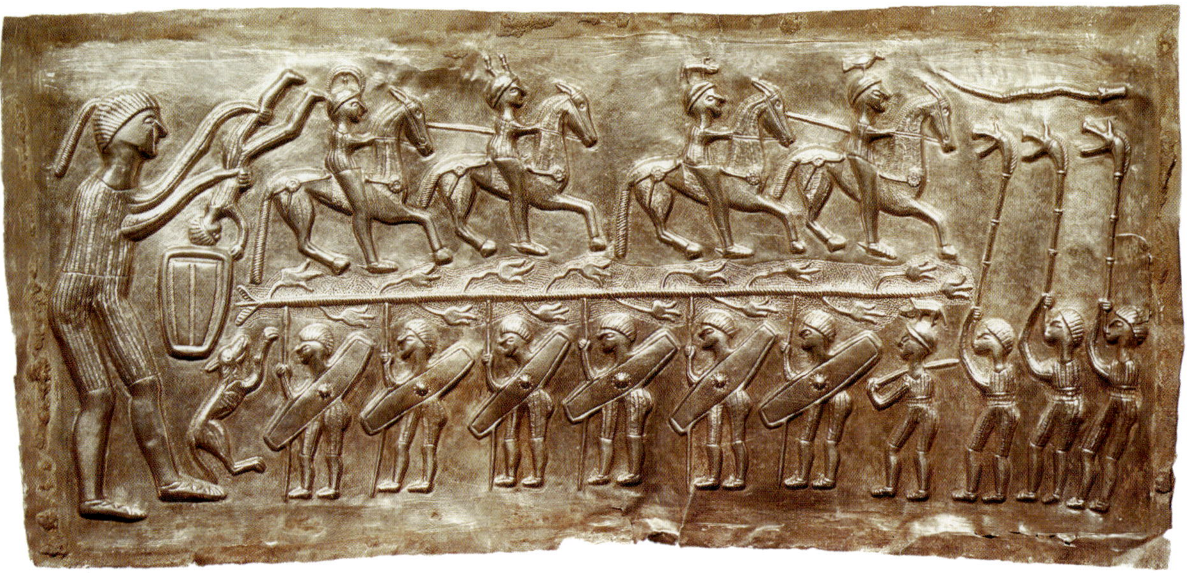

133

Notes on page 114

The Old and Original Art

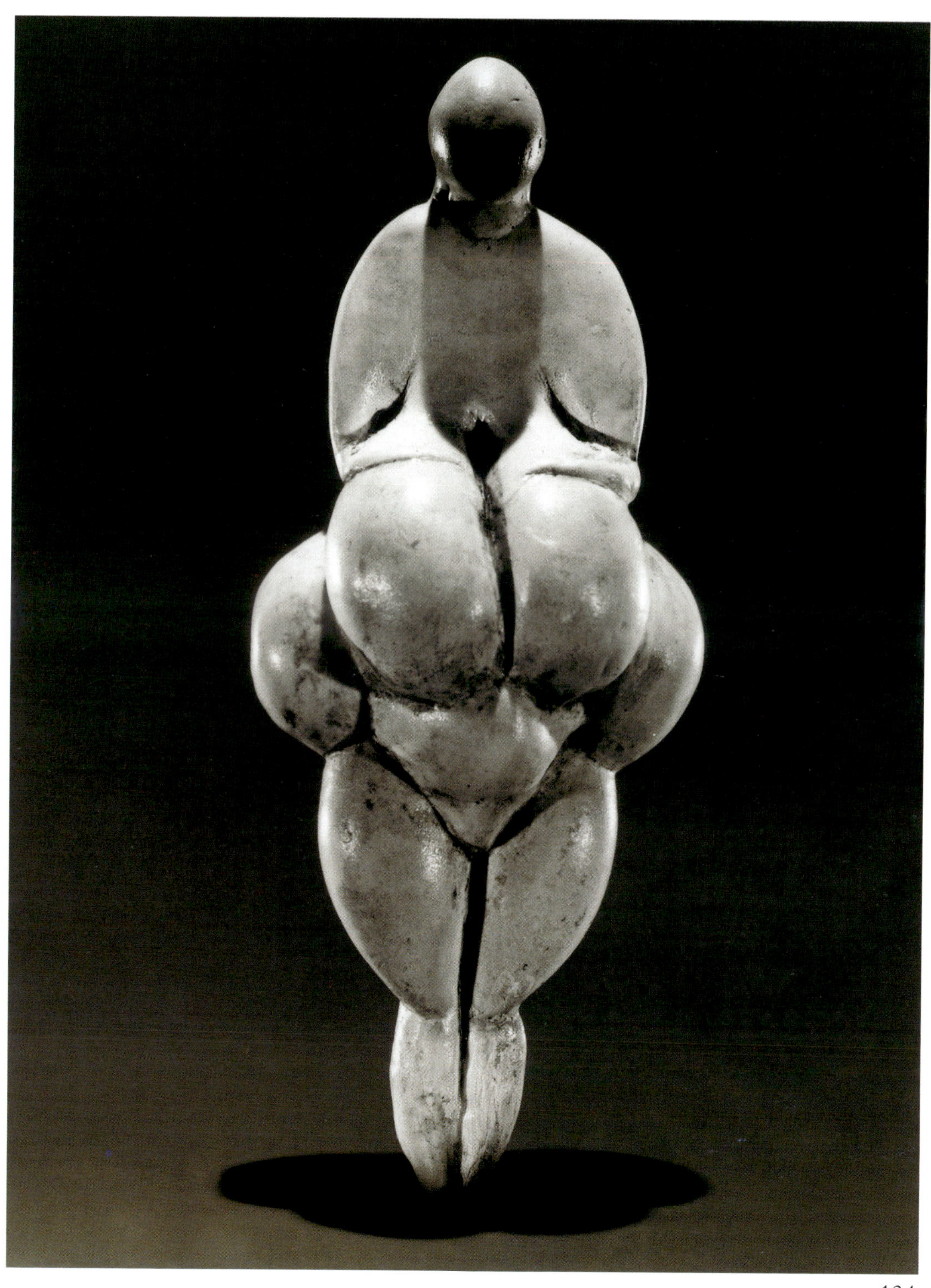

134

How far back can we go in search for the essentials of the art of the Celts? Back to the earliest art of Europe. Many commentators have referred to the influence of this or that art – the art of the Greeks, the Thracians, the Etruscans, the Romans – on the art of the Celts, and it is true that such influences can be detected here and there. But none of these influences have any real bearing on the true essentials of their art. If we are to search for the essentials we have to turn to the earliest art.

Figures **134** and **135** provide examples of this earliest art to which we shall refer.

These figures are from the Neolithic period… the uplifting element raises the artist's vision to a spiritual dimension, where the grandeur of existence is made manifest

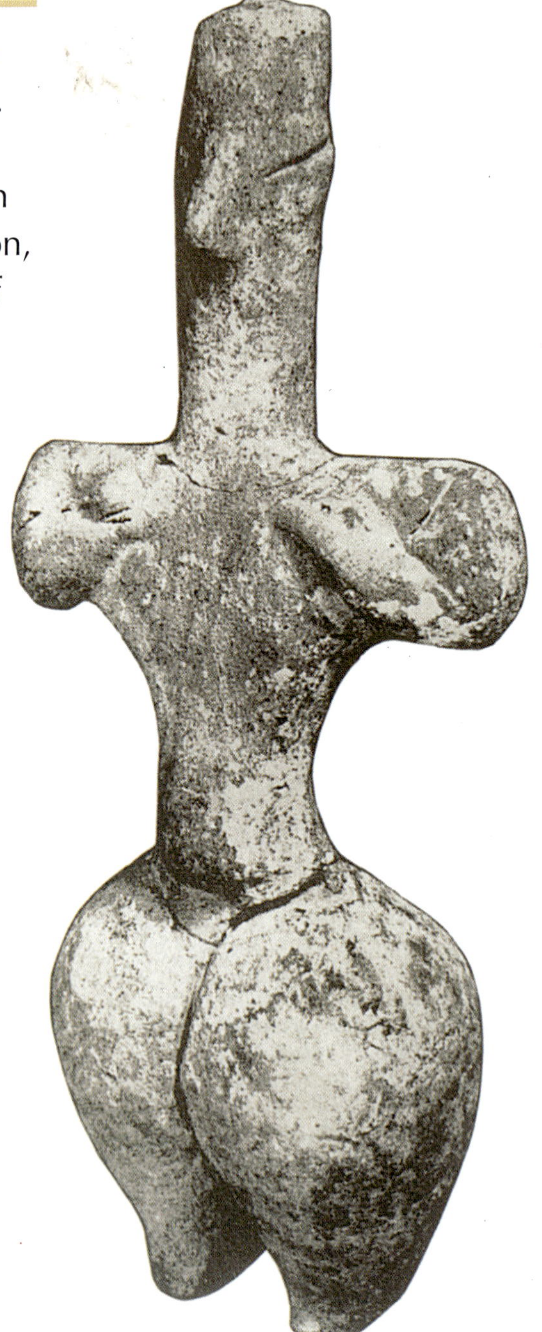

135

They show figures from the Neolithic period. Let us declare once again the main assertion of this book, that we do not find here imitations of the objects of our world; the art presents representations of the basic forces of existence. Both the figures shown have an Upper and a Lower part. The Upper Part presents a head that is also a phallus; it is an upraised form, that suggests spirituality. The Lower Part conveys a downward heaviness, femininity, motherhood, pregnancy, fecundity; the enormous thighs and buttocks, as well as the large breasts and belly, create an impression of flesh, sexuality and earthiness. The art creates a state that lies between the material – our everyday lives – and a sacred, eternal world. This is precisely what the art of La Tène does – it creates impressions through symbols. The sculptures suggest that the forces of life and death are part of existence.

The ancient artists were not incapable of drawing and creating realistic forms, likenesses of objects found in their world. Figures **136** and **137** demonstrate that early artists could create such pictures.

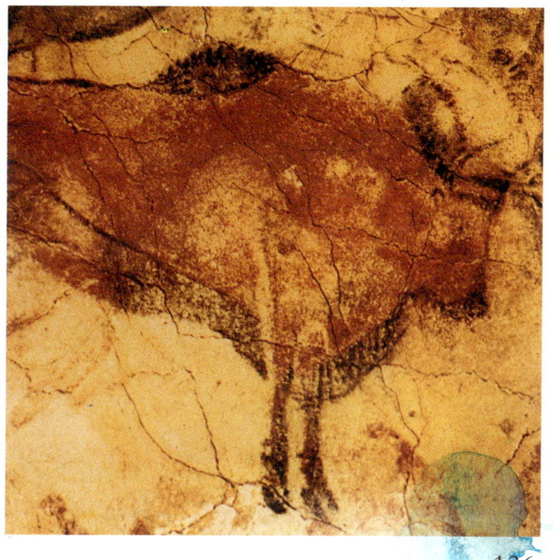

136

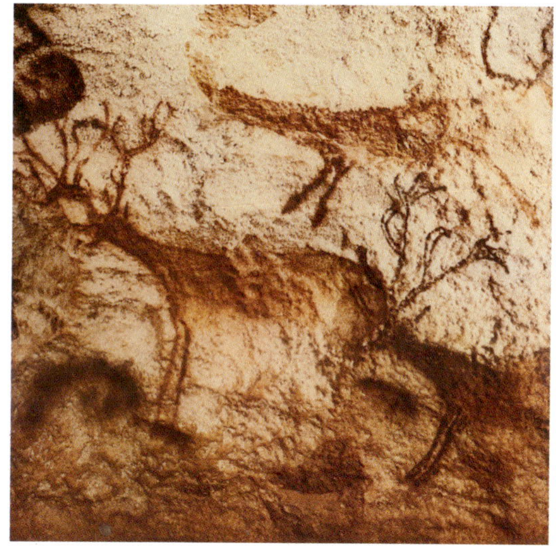

137

The truth of the matter is that the symbolic sculptures, **134** and **135**, are amongst the earliest examples of humankind's religious utterances. Why religious? Because they are the expression of an idea of an existence beyond material things and beyond the present, and because they present a vision of a whole society. This type of image continued to be creatively meaningful for over 5000 years, up to about 500 BC. In a way, such images are still meaningful.

The uplifting element raises the artist's vision to a spiritual dimension, where the grandeur of existence is made manifest. These early representations of Mothers are huge not only because they are pregnant, but because they are a symbol of the earth as an eternal and sacred Mother. Figure **138** presents various aspects of the same sculpture.

The head of this Mother shows a quiet, transcendent meditation: it gives a sense of lightness, as if it were meditating in the clouds. All of this is above the body and the womb, which are of the earth. And yet the body and the head are an inseparable part of one another. In this tranquil, symmetrical, complete work of art there is a spiritual awareness of the continuity of existence, in spite of death and the vicissitudes of this world. This sculpture shows that humankind was beginning to civilize itself.

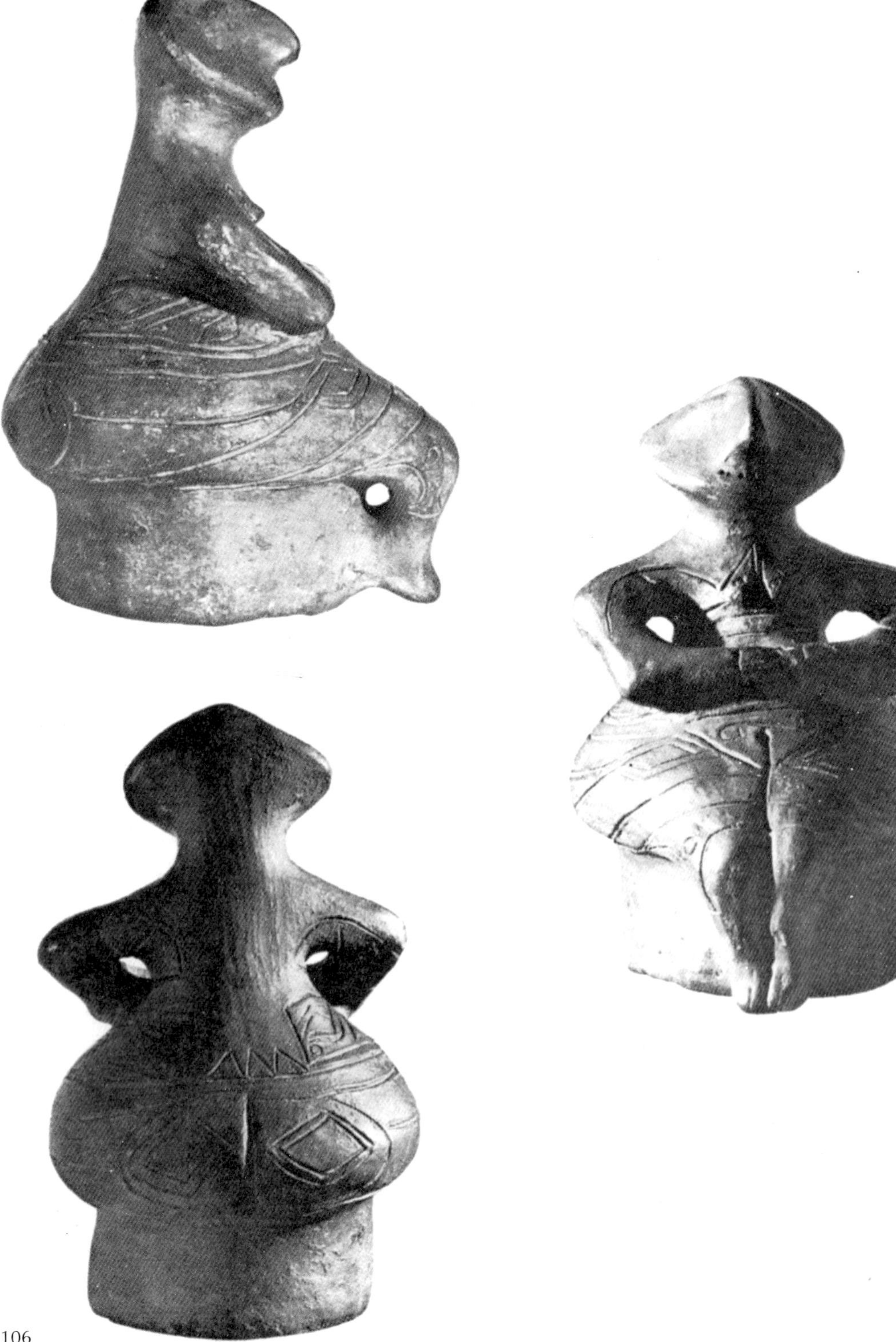

138

Only a short time before this sculpture was made, about 6000 or 7000 BC, man began to settle on the land and to cultivate it. This period saw the beginnings of agriculture in south-east Europe. After his time hunting animals and gathering his food, man settled down and began to sow and reap, and to rear animals. He came into a more direct relationship with the earth, and began to think of her as a Mother. According to Barry Cunliffe:

The spread of food production as a mode of subsistence, as opposed to food collection, was of vital significance in the development of European society. It freed man from the necessity to travel vast distance in seasonal pursuit of his food supply and allowed him, indeed forced him, to settle in hamlets and villages close to his growing crops. A more sedentary way of life led to the creation of larger communities, to a growth in population, and to craft specialization, thus paving the way for the eventual emergence of civilization.[1]

Man's wonder at the fruitfulness of the earth goes beyond his dependence on her for food and sustenance. It becomes an exaltation of her powers, a spiritual awareness. The numerous early sculptures of Mothers or Goddesses found along the length and breadth of Europe show that this awareness was widespread.

Marija Gimbutas has studied these great Mothers. Below, some of her comments are quoted. Concerning the great number and varieties of these figures, she concludes:

The reason for the great number and variety of Old European images lies in the fact that this symbolism is lunar and chthonic, built around the understanding that life on earth is in eternal transformation, in constant and rhythmic change between creation, birth and death.[2]

And concerning the immortality that they express, she has this to say:

Immortality is secured through the innate forces of regeneration within Nature itself. The concept of regeneration and renewal is perhaps the most outstanding and dramatic theme that we perceive in this symbolism.[3]

Of the great size of the Mothers she comments:

The pregnancy or the fatness of a woman or an animal was considered to be as holy as the pregnancy of the earth before her flowering in spring. Each protuberance in nature, be it a mound, a hill, on a menhir or on a female body – belly buttocks, breast, knees – was sacred.[4]

Gimbutas' next and final comment concerning the clashes between the old or primitive Europe and the later Indo-European influences are particularly important:

But the Old European sacred images and symbols were never totally uprooted; these most persistent features in human history were too deeply implanted in the psyche. They could have disappeared only with the total extermination of the female population.

The Goddess's religion went underground. Some of the old traditions, particularly those connected with birth, death, and earth fertility rituals, have continued to this day without much change in some regions; in others, they were assimilated into Indo-European ideology.[5]

The very essence of the framework depicting the great Mother includes a lower part suggesting feminine pregnancy. Her womb is like a vessel or a cauldron containing things. It is this womb that gives birth. In the upper part of the sculptures is the head, which has a phallic, masculine aspect. The following diagrams, **139–141**, explain all of this:

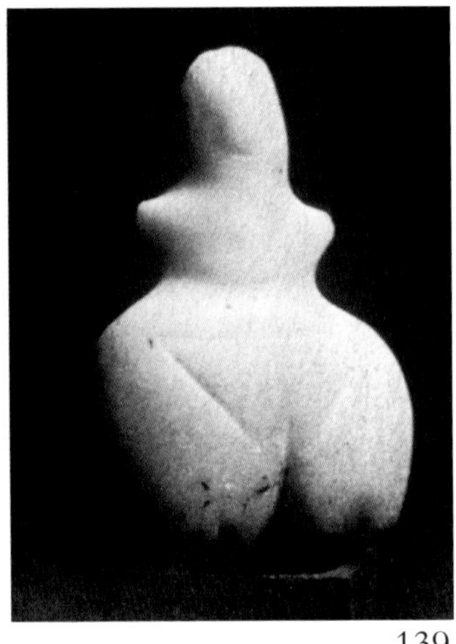
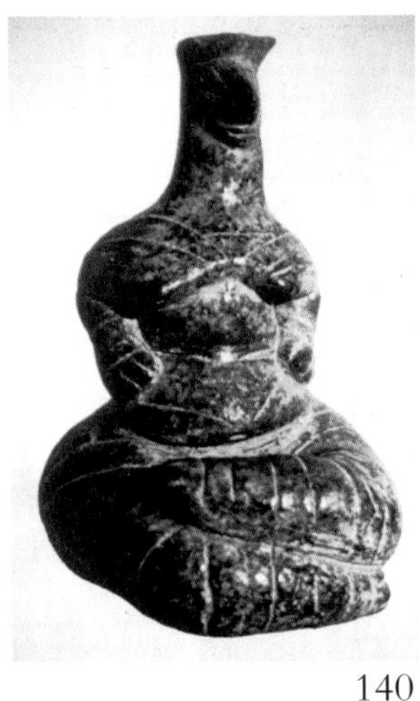
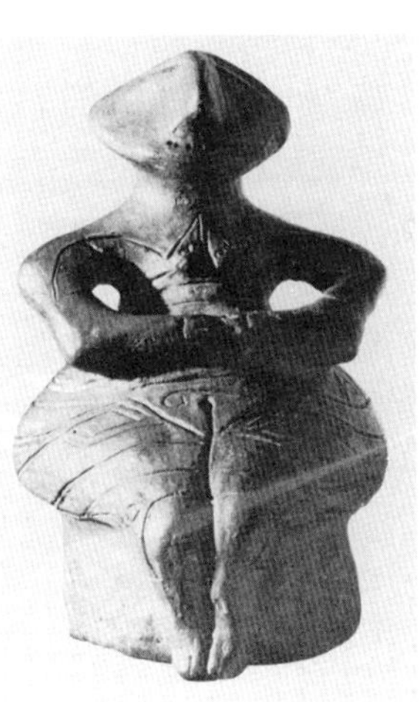

139   140   141

Two basic forces are represented here, a masculine force and a feminine force. The masculine force has a pole (or phallic) shape; the feminine force is like a womb. Diagram **142** shows the basic shapes of the two forces.

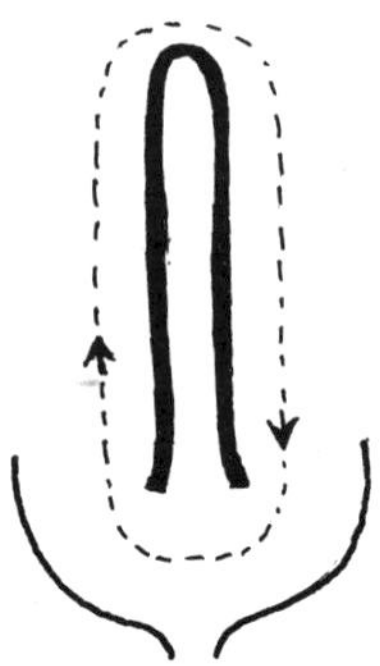
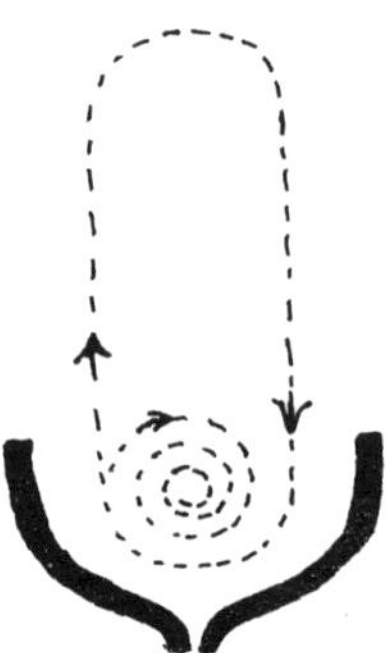

142

On some of these sculptures there are spirals on the womb, see the diagrams in Diagrams **143–145**.

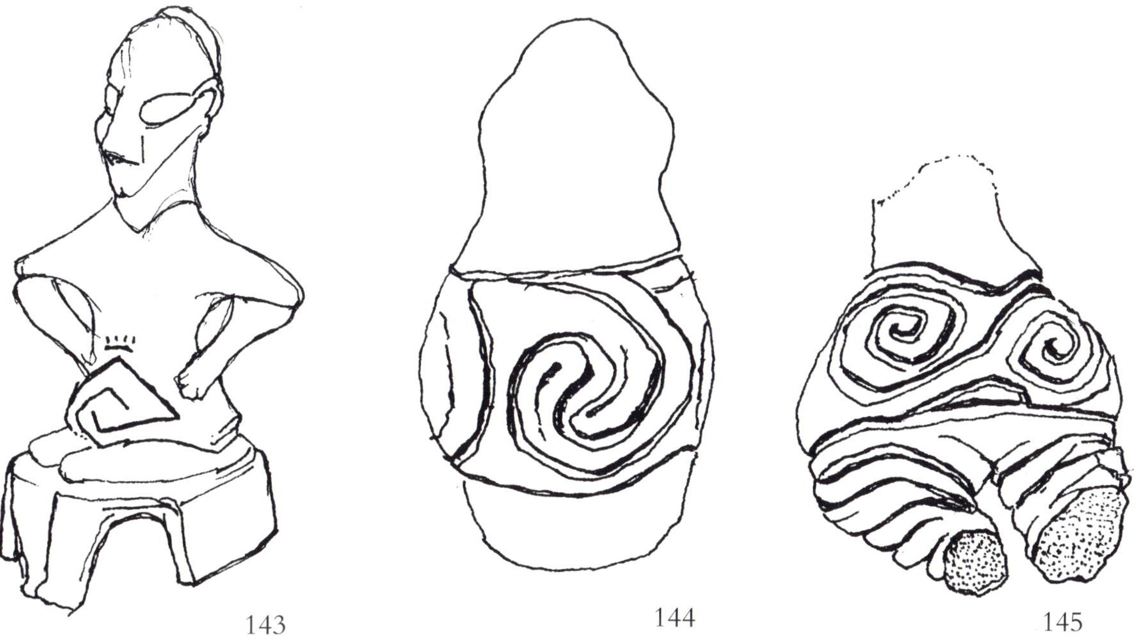

143   144   145

Note especially the spiral on the womb of the great Mother in a still and tranquil meditation that is found in **143** and **146**.

Her womb is like a vessel or a cauldron containing things. It is this womb that gives birth. In the upper part of the sculptures is the head, which has a phallic, masculine aspect

The very essence of the framework depicting the great Mother includes a lower part suggesting feminine pregnancy

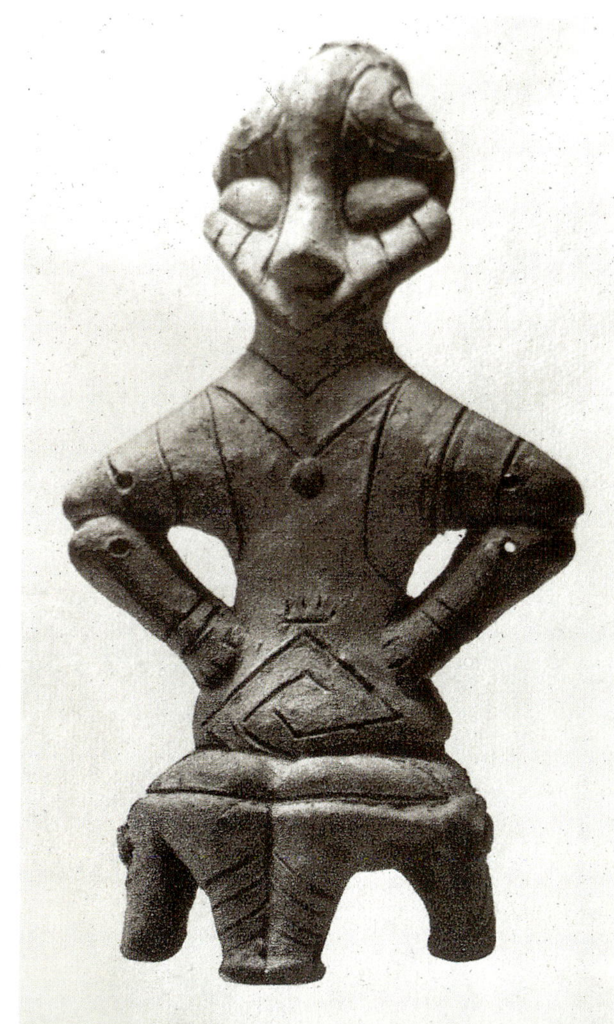

146

This spiral line is not a decoration: it suggests agitation in the womb as a part of the basic framework. It suggests primitive magic, the wonder of primitive man at the power of fertility. We have a splendid example in **147**, which is a sacred sanctuary. The spiralling lines entice our eyes into the sacred place. Above all of this we have the still and majestic presence of the two heads, which, in this instance, are the heads of animals.

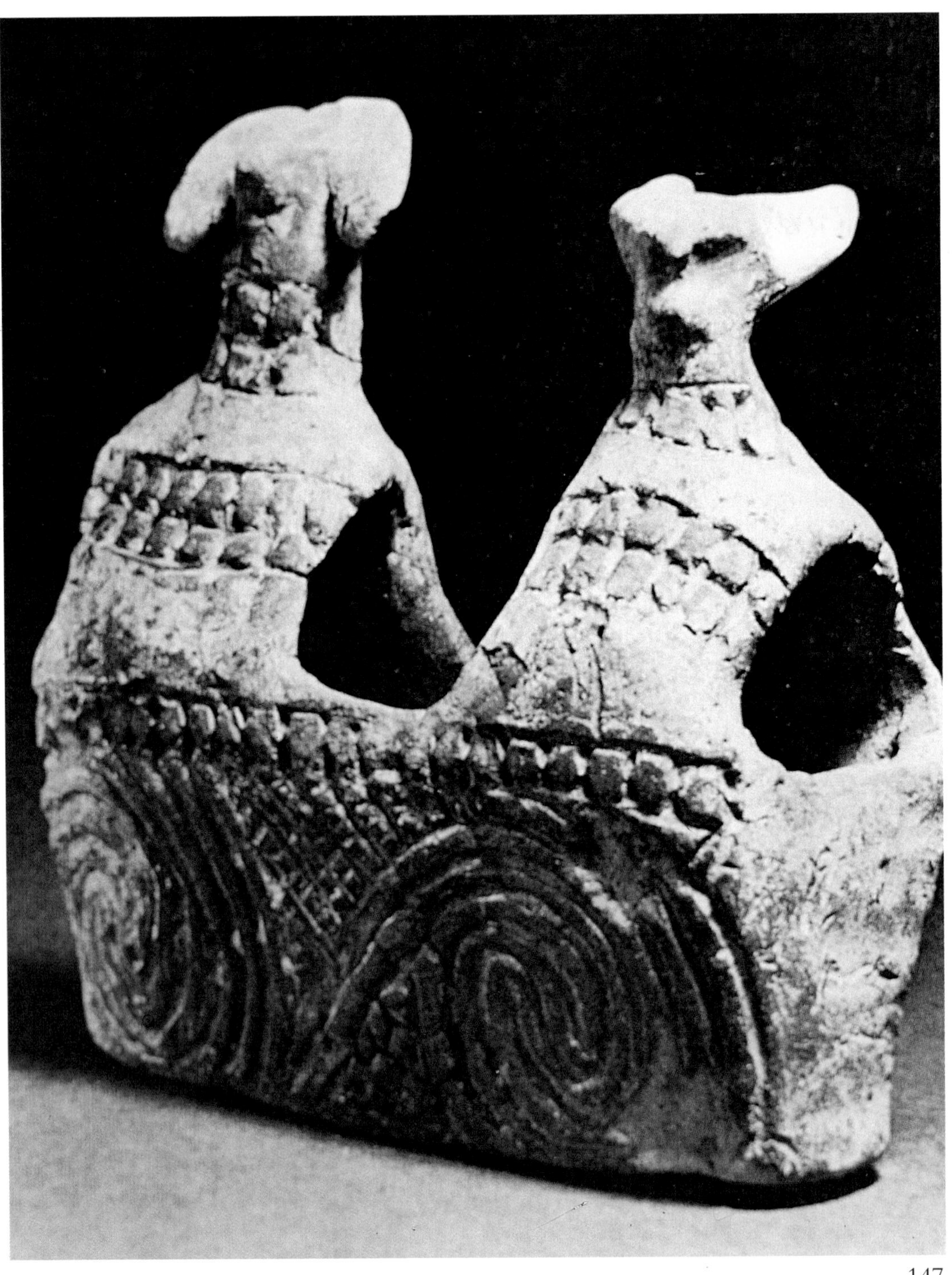

147

Let us examine other examples of this spiralling line and its connection with the womb of the great Mother. Figures **148** and **149** show the spiralling line on a sculpture and a piece of pottery in female form. In **150** the spiral on the pottery forms the symbol of a serpent.

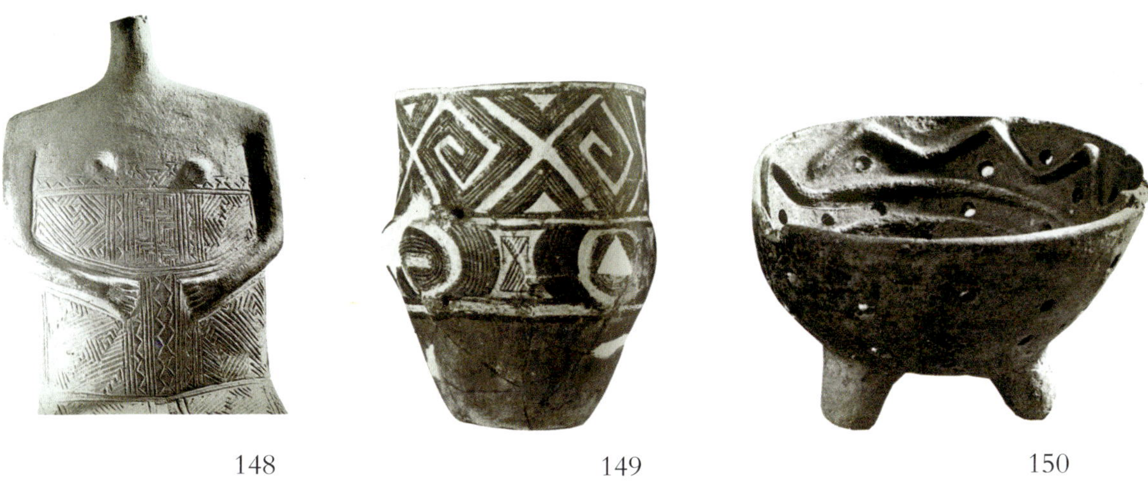

148   149   150

The spiral is also found on stones. There is an example on the entrance stone of New Grange, in Ireland, **151**:

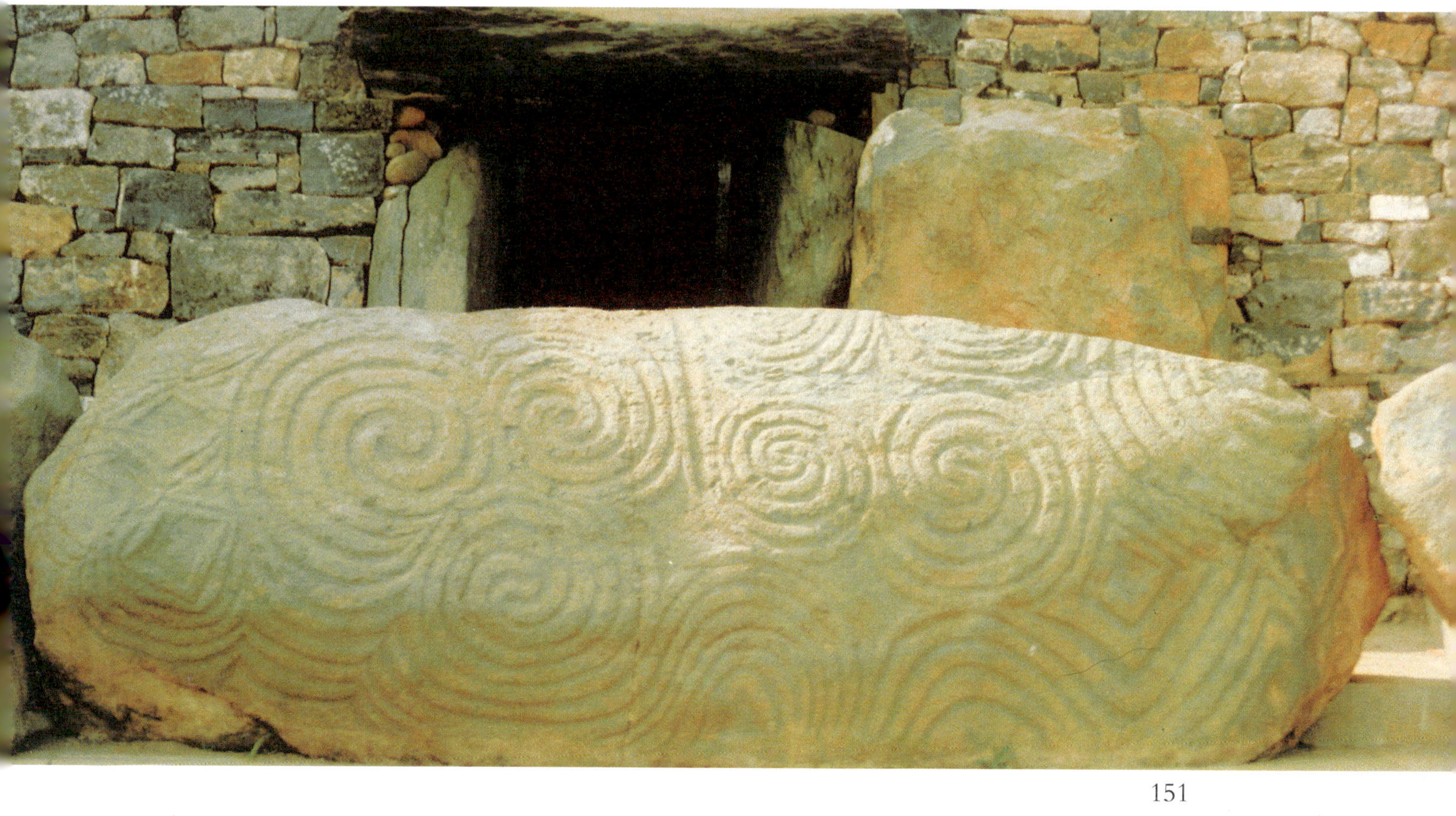

151

New Grange is a burial mound, but the spiral suggests that it is also a womb, the womb of the Earth-mother, a place from which life will come again. The main difference between the spirals of New Grange and the examples of spiral lines on the old Mothers is that those found in New Grange are bigger and more numerous and, because of this, they are more potent in evoking a magical power.

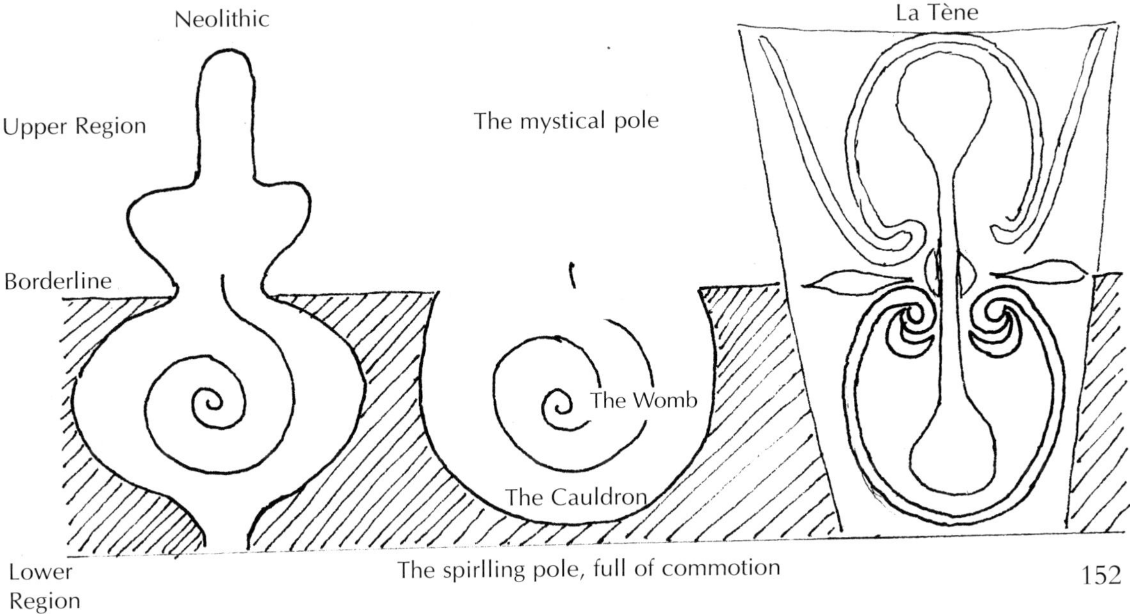

Now let us compare the basic framework of works from the Neolithic period, that we have been discussing here, with the basic framework of works which belong to the art of La Tène, see **152**.

In both works there is a phallic head, a womb (the Deep in the art of La Tène), a spiralling line that suggests agitation – mostly in the Lower Part of the works. The symbols and the craft of the works of art of La Tène are more sophisticated and more magical than those of the Neolithic period, but both types of art convey the same awareness. Life comes into being, it dies, and it comes back again. The realization that existence is eternal raises people to a spiritual dimension that is expressed as a quiet meditation that transcends all the accidents that happen to individual things. The tranquillity of the highest spiritual meditation forms one part of a cycle together with the agitation of the earthly death and birth of the Lower Region. What is put into a grave in the earth is also being put into a fruitful womb. The Borderline between the two regions or the two states, the Upper and the Lower, is one that can be crossed, and crossed constantly.

In the art of La Tène we have seen a particularly adept expression of this basic concept of the cycle of life and of spiritual quietude. We have seen that there are different levels to the relationship between the spiritual quietude of some heads in the Upper Region and the cycle of birth, death, and rebirth that is found in the Lower Region. We have seen that the Celts used many ways to stimulate different levels of experiences of the forces of descent, like the narrative way, fairly easy to follow, as on the Gundestrup Cauldron. We have also mentioned the more sophisticated heads of the art, where the expression is far more evocative and withheld (including the use of triads) to convey a magical and spiritual consciousness that is above and beyond the cycle of birth and death and rebirth, the kind of expression that produces a unique mystical vision.

It is fitting to conclude this chapter and this book by reminding ourselves of the magic, beauty and the majesty of the ancient art of the Celts, an art that is an extension and a development of Neolithic art, an art that encompasses life and death and elevates us to a quiet, eternal meditation above the activities and accidents of our individual lives. The single notable sculpture that I have chosen to convey the beauty and the majesty of the art of the Celts is that seen in **153**, from Waldalgesheim in Germany. In it, the Upper Region and the Deep, and the Borderline between them, produced the quiet, majestic, still centre and a transcendent meditation that is above the duality of life.

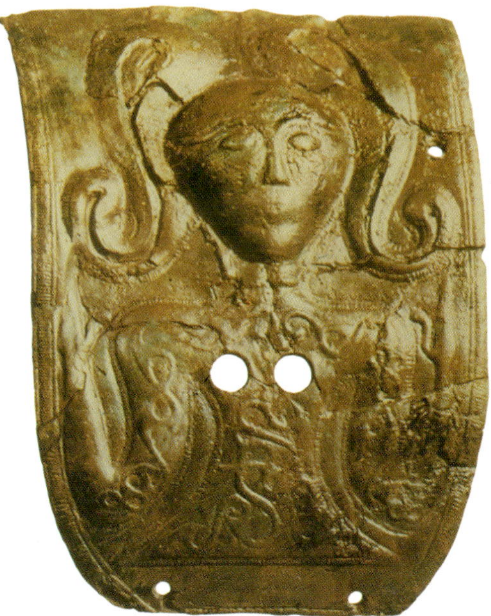

153

Notes

Foreword

[1] Green, Miranda, *Symbols and Images in Celtic Religious Art* (London, 1989), p. 1.
[2] Ibid. p. 1.
[3] Ibid. p. 1.
[4] Ibid. p. 1.
[5] Ibid. p. 1.
[6] Ibid. p. 1.
[7] Piggott, Stuart, *Ancient Europe* (Edinburgh, 1965), p. 7.

1 The Inner Vision: The Spiritual Vision

[1] Bain, George, *Celtic Art* (London, 1951), p. 17

4 The Narrative, Ritual Aspect of the Art

[1] Cunliffe, Barry, *The Celtic World* (England, 1979), p. 93.
[2] Ibid. p. 92.
[3] Ibid. p. 92.
[4] Ross, Anne, *Pagan Celtic Britain* (London, 1967), p. 24.
[5] Rees, Alwyn and Brinley, *Celtic Heritage* (London, 1961), p. 14.
[6] Campbell, Joseph, *Occidental Mythology* (London, 1976), p. 3.
[7] Eliade, Mircea, *Rites and Symbols of Initiation* (New York, 1965), x.
[8] Ibid. x.
[9] Ibid. xiv.

5 Ritual Implements, Ritual Art, Ritual Tales

[1] Eliade, Mircea, *Shamanism* (Great Britain, 1964), p. 4
[2] Ibid. p. 5
[3] Ibid. p. 64
[4] Ibid. p. 375
[5] Rees, A and B, *Celtic Heritage*, p. 14
[6] See Williams, Ifor, *Chwedl Taliesin* (Cardiff, 1961), p. 3–7
[7] Rees, A and B, *Celtic Heritage*, p. 127

7 Dualities

[1] Peate, Iorwerth C., *Diwylliant Gwerin Cymru* (Liverpool, 1943), p. 22.
[2] Wilhelm, Richard, *I Ching* (London, 1951), lv.
[3] Ibid. lvi.
[4] Ross, Anne, *The Religion of the Pagan Celts* (London, 1970), p. 135.
[5] Ibid. p. 35–6.

8 The Third Force – Triads

[1] Ifans, Dafydd and Rhiannon, *Y Mabinogion* (Llandysul, 1980), p. 33.
[2] Williams, Ifor, *Chwedl Taliesin* (Cardiff, 1957), p. 5.
[3] Ibid., p. 7.
[4] Bromwich, Rachel, *Trioedd Ynys Prydain* (Cardiff, 1961), Ixx.

9 Celtic Art: The Visual Code

[1] Eliade, Mircea, *Shamanism* (USA, 1960), p. 84: 'Seeing' a spirit, either in dream or awake, is a certain sign that one has attained a 'spiritual condition', that is, that one has transcended the profane condition of humanity.
[2] Ibid., p. 43
[3] Julius Caesar a Hirtius, *Y Rhyfeloedd yng Ngâl*, VI. p. 16
[4] Cunliffe, Barry, *The Ancient Celts* (New York, 1997), p. 192
[5] Hutton, Ronald, *The Pagan Religions of the Ancient British Isles* (Oxford, 1991), p. 146
[6] Ibid. p. 145–6
[7] Ifans, Dafydd and Rhiannon, *Y Mabinogion*, p. 6
[8] Thomas, Gwyn, *Duwiau'r Celtiaid* (Llanrwst, 1992), p. 66
[9] Ibid. p. 67
[10] Ifans, Dafydd and Rhiannon, *Y Mabinogion*, p. 1
[11] Brunaux, Jean Louis, *The Celtic Gauls* (London, 1988), p. 27–8
[12] See Tierney, J J, 'The Celtic Ethnography of Posidonius' in *Proceedings of the Royal Irish Academy* (Dublin, 1960), p. 272
[13] Ibid. p. 250
[14] Ifans, Dafydd and Rhiannon, *Y Mabinogion*, p. 29

10 The Art of War

[1] Tierney, J J, 'The Celtic Ethnography of Posidonius' yn *Proceedings of the Royal Irish Academy* (Dublin, 1960), p. 250
[2] Ibid., p. 250
[3] Megaw, J V S, *Art of the European Iron Age* (Bath, 1970), p. 150

11 The Old and Original Art

[1] Cunliffe, Barry, *The Celtic World* (London, 1979), p. 8–9
[2] Gimbutas, Marija, *The Language of the Goddess* (London, 1989), p. 316
[3] Ibid. p. 316
[4] Ibid. p. 317
[5] Ibid. p. 318

Index – Text

Index – Images

53	Detail from horned figure panel, Gundestrup Cauldron; Denmark. 150 BC
54	Diagram of torque; Saint Germain, Marne, France. 300 BC
55	14 ibid.
56	Gold torque; Norfolk, England. 100 BC
57	18 ibid. and 24 ibid.
58	Torque and braclets, Waldalgesheim, Germany. 470 BC
59	Diagram of a decorated magical pole, Waldelgesheim torque
60	Diagram of back of bracelet, Waldalgesheim
61	Diagram on head of torque, Reinheim, Germany. 450 BC
62	Torque and bracelets, Reinheim, Germany. 450 BC
63	Diagram of head of torque, Reinheim, Germany. 450 BC
64	Bronze torque; Dumfries, Germany. 100 AD
65	Gold torques; Ipswich, England. 100 BC
66	Gold torque; Ipswich, England 100 BC
67	Torques; Ertfeld, Uri, Switzerland. 450 BC
68	Torque; Ertfeld, Uri, Switzerland. 450 BC
69	Panel, Gundestrup Cauldron; Denmark. 150 BC
70	Aylesford Bucket, England. 100 BC
71	Diagrams of dualities
72	Detail from Aylesford bucket, England. 100 BC
73	Pottery; Marne, France. 350 BC
74	Bronze harness mount decorated with enamel; Norfolk, England. 50 BC
75	Bronze harness mount decorated with enamel; Norfolk, England. 50 BC

76	Diagram of decoration on bowl Schwarsenbach
77	18 ibid.
78	Diagram of neck of wine flagon, Basse-Yutz
79	Bowl with gold and bronze decoration; Schwarsenbach, Germany. 450 BC
80	Enamel broach; England. 100 AD
81	Mount on bronze pitcher; Czechoslovakia. 300 BC
82	Belt buckle; Weiskirchen, Germany. 450 BC
83	Diagram representing forces in the pattern of a belt buckle from Weiskirchen
84	Wooden cup with bronze mounts; Trawsfynydd, Wales. 50 BC
85	Two chalk stone heads; Roquepertuse, France. 330 BC
86	Iron hearth; Capel Garmon, Wales. 100 BC
87	Bronze broach; Pasberg, Germany. 450 BC
88	Iron pin with bronze head; Austria. 450 BC
89	Bracelet head; Reinheim, Germany. 450 BC
90	82 ibid.
91	Detail from bucket; Aylesford, England. 100 BC.
92	Pin; Weiskirchen, Germany. 300 BC
93	Gold bracelet; Rodenbach, Germany. 400 BC
94	Diagram of bracelet, Rodenbach
95	Bronze torque; Benvray, Marne, France. 450 BC
96	Bronze torque; Barbuise, France. 350 BC
97	Top of iron sword scabbard; La Tène, Switzerland. 200 BC
98	Top of iron sword scabbard; Obermenzing, Germany. 200 BC
99	Triad on clay pot; Bavay, France. 200 BC

Photograph Credits

Every attempt has been made to contact copyright holders; we apologise if anyone has been overlooked.